Argumentation Mining

Synthesis Lectures on Human Language Technologies

Editor
Graeme Hirst, *University of Toronto*

Synthesis Lectures on Human Language Technologies is edited by Graeme Hirst of the University of Toronto. The series consists of 50- to 150-page monographs on topics relating to natural language processing, computational linguistics, information retrieval, and spoken language understanding. Emphasis is on important new techniques, on new applications, and on topics that combine two or more HLT subfields.

Linguistic Fundamentals for Natural Language Processing: 100 Essentials from
Morphology and Syntax
Emily M. Bender
2013

Semi-Supervised Learning and Domain Adaptation in Natural Language Processing
Anders Søgaard
2013

Semantic Relations Between Nominals
Vivi Nastase, Preslav Nakov, Diarmuid Ó Séaghdha, and Stan Szpakowicz
2013

Computational Modeling of Narrative
Inderjeet Mani
2012

Natural Language Processing for Historical Texts
Michael Piotrowski
2012

Sentiment Analysis and Opinion Mining
Bing Liu
2012

Discourse Processing
Manfred Stede
2011

Bitext Alignment
Jörg Tiedemann
2011

Linguistic Structure Prediction
Noah A. Smith
2011

Learning to Rank for Information Retrieval and Natural Language Processing
Hang Li
2011

Computational Modeling of Human Language Acquisition
Afra Alishahi
2010

Introduction to Arabic Natural Language Processing
Nizar Y. Habash
2010

Argumentation Mining

Manfred Stede and Jodi Schneider

ISBN: 978-3-031-01041-5 paperback
ISBN: 978-3-031-02169-5 ebook
ISBN: 978-3-031-00180-2 hardcover

DOI 10.1007/978-3-031-02169-5

A Publication in the Springer series
SYNTHESIS LECTURES ON ADVANCES IN AUTOMOTIVE TECHNOLOGY

Lecture #40
Series Editor: Graeme Hirst, *University of Toronto*
Series ISSN
Print 1947-4040   Electronic 1947-4059

Argumentation Mining

Manfred Stede
University of Potsdam

Jodi Schneider
University of Illinois at Urbana-Champaign

SYNTHESIS LECTURES ON HUMAN LANGUAGE TECHNOLOGIES #40

ABSTRACT

Argumentation mining is an application of natural language processing (NLP) that emerged a few years ago and has recently enjoyed considerable popularity, as demonstrated by a series of international workshops and by a rising number of publications at the major conferences and journals of the field. Its goals are to identify argumentation in text or dialogue; to construct representations of the constellation of claims, supporting and attacking moves (in different levels of detail); and to characterize the patterns of reasoning that appear to license the argumentation. Furthermore, recent work also addresses the difficult tasks of evaluating the persuasiveness and quality of arguments. Some of the linguistic genres that are being studied include legal text, student essays, political discourse and debate, newspaper editorials, scientific writing, and others.

The book starts with a discussion of the linguistic perspective, characteristics of argumentative language, and their relationship to certain other notions such as subjectivity.

Besides the connection to linguistics, argumentation has for a long time been a topic in Artificial Intelligence, where the focus is on devising adequate representations and reasoning formalisms that capture the properties of argumentative exchange. It is generally very difficult to connect the two realms of reasoning and text analysis, but we are convinced that it should be attempted in the long term, and therefore we also touch upon some fundamentals of reasoning approaches.

Then the book turns to its focus, the computational side of mining argumentation in text. We first introduce a number of annotated corpora that have been used in the research. From the NLP perspective, argumentation mining shares subtasks with research fields such as subjectivity and sentiment analysis, semantic relation extraction, and discourse parsing. Therefore, many technical approaches are being borrowed from those (and other) fields. We break argumentation mining into a series of subtasks, starting with the preparatory steps of classifying text as argumentative (or not) and segmenting it into elementary units. Then, central steps are the automatic identification of claims, and finding statements that support or oppose the claim. For certain applications, it is also of interest to compute a full structure of an argumentative constellation of statements.

Next, we discuss a few steps that try to 'dig deeper': to infer the underlying reasoning pattern for a textual argument, to reconstruct unstated premises (so-called 'enthymemes'), and to evaluate the quality of the argumentation. We also take a brief look at 'the other side' of mining, i.e., the generation or synthesis of argumentative text.

The book finishes with a summary of the argumentation mining tasks, a sketch of potential applications, and a—necessarily subjective—outlook for the field.

KEYWORDS

argumentation mining, natural language processing, claim detection, evidence detection, argumentative language, argument models, enthymemes

Contents

Preface

This book is aimed at graduate students and researchers interested in contributing to the field of argumentation mining, a fast-growing field at the intersection of human language technologies and computational argumentation. The book's purpose is to spread existing concepts and methods about argumentation mining widely, providing background about argumentation and a snapshot of the current state of this burgeoning field. As part of the Synthesis Lectures on HLT series, this book is directed primarily at the natural language processing and computational linguistics community. A secondary audience is the broader computational argumentation community. Growing the common ground between these complementary realms will, we believe, drive further progress in the field.

The book focuses on key background, current approaches, and possible future directions. It describes existing models, corpora, and annotation schemes that researchers everywhere can reuse in building their own systems. It structures the overall problem of argumentation mining into a number of subtasks used to mine arguments from written documents. Given the primary target audience stated above, we assume a basic knowledge of natural language processing (NLP), as it can be obtained for example from Jurafsky and Martin [2009] and Clark et al. [2013]. Conversely, for readers coming from an NLP background who would like to study some argumentation literature, good starting points include van Eemeren et al. [2014] and Baroni et al. [2018].

Our aim is to give a representative review of progress and challenges in the field, as of late 2017 and early 2018. We have focused on capturing work presented on the one hand in the international Computational Linguistics literature—conferences such as ACL, COLING, EMNLP, and LREC; workshops such as SemDial and the Argument(ation) Mining series; journals such as *Computational Linguistics* and *Transactions of the Association for Computational Linguistics*—and on the other hand (to a somewhat smaller extent) at computational argumentation venues such as the COMMA conference, the CMNA workshop, or the *Argumentation & Computation* journal. Argumentation is also studied in the wider artificial intelligence community, which is however beyond our scope, as are a number of specific tasks such as political ideology detection. On the whole, unsurprisingly, our choice of literature is influenced by our own past work and the community with which we have interacted.

We hope that parts of this book quickly become obsolete due to new results, new knowledge, new approaches, and more synthesis. At the same time, it would be nice if the role of a gentle introduction to the nature of the field and its manifold aspects worked for a number of years. In any case, we look forward to the future advances you, our readers, will make!

Manfred Stede and Jodi Schneider
November 2018

Acknowledgments

Thank you to Ming Jiang, Maria Skeppstedt, and Henning Wachsmuth for extensive feedback on early versions. Thanks to Patricia M. Jones for information on NASA mishap investigation boards. We also thank Fabien Gandon, Andreas Peldszus, and Adam Wyner for helpful discussions, and Kiel Gilleade and Neil Smalheiser for their supportive feedback.

The book also benefitted greatly from the constructive comments of our anonymous reviewers.

Manfred Stede and Jodi Schneider
November 2018

CHAPTER 1

Introduction

In this first chapter, we begin (Section 1.1) by studying one of the common definitions of *argument* and explaining it point by point. This is supplemented by outlining further central aspects of argumentation, viz. the dimensions of logos, ethos, and pathos, and the concept of the 'critical discussion' as a fundamental idealized context for activities of arguing. We then move to the applied side of computational linguistics, and provide a definition of argumentation mining in Section 1.2, followed by an outline of reasons for studying automatic argumentation mining in Section 1.3. We finish the chapter by explaining the structure of the book in Section 1.4.

1.1 ARGUMENTS AND ARGUING

1.1.1 A DEFINITION

Argumentation (as an activity of human beings seeking to sort out their conflicting views) has been of interest to philosophers for a long time, with the best-known of the traditional work being that of Aristotle. In his *Rhetorics*, he sought to develop a general theory of persuasion and applied it to three types of speeches: the deliberative speech, which advises on a course of future action; the judicial speech, which accuses or defends someone whose past activities are to be judged; and the epideictic speech, which praises or blames a person of public interest. As the concrete starting point for our introduction, however, we selected a definition proposed in much more recent work by van Eemeren and Grootendorst [2004, p. 1]:

> "Argumentation is a verbal, social, and rational activity aimed at convincing a reasonable critic of the acceptability of a standpoint by putting forward a constellation of propositions justifying or refuting the proposition expressed in the standpoint."

The main elegance of this definition is in its bringing together the range of crucial aspects in a rather compact form (a single sentence). Let us consider each aspect in a little more detail.

A verbal activity. People can and do gesture and frown at each other, and occasionally this might be a way of resolving some disagreement. In our conception here, however, argumentation is an inherently linguistic activity—either in spoken or written mode. This is to be distinguished from, for instance, a fistfight, which can be a different means of sorting out a conflict.

A social activity. *Social* emphasizes that argumentation is a matter of interaction among a number of people, with a minimum of two. Granted, many of us munch on a difficult decision for some time by mentally walking through the consequences of the alternatives, but genuine arguing requires a person to argue *with*.

A rational activity.   Obviously, we can perform verbal and social activities in very many ways. Among these, argumentation targets specifically the dimension of reason. When one person reminds the other "Be reasonable!", the point is to call for a style of dialogue that is not driven by emotional outbreak, power struggle, personal offense, etc., but by the sober exchange of— reasonable arguments.

A standpoint.   In argumentation, the heart of the matter is some issue on which people may have divergent views. Thus, the argument does not target an undisputed 'fact' but a 'standpoint' (or a 'stance'). Where there is no potential disagreement, there is no need to argue.

Convincing of acceptability.   At the end of an argument, the parties involved may not necessarily be completely 'on the same page' about the standpoint. An argument (usually) does not prove beyond any doubt that one particular viewpoint is the single correct one. Instead, the party who initially was skeptical may now be somewhat more inclined to accept the view of the other party (if the argument was successful).

A constellation of propositions.   The shape of a justification might be quite simple, for instance a single convincing sentence. But quite often it will be more complex and involve a web of interrelated points that the speaker carefully assembles in a non-arbitrary way; an example of such a constellation will be shown at the end of this section.

Justifying the proposition of the standpoint.   If the reader is more inclined to accept the particular standpoint after the argument is finished, that result is not just due to the speaker having pointed out that he is the boss, or some such; it is due to the speaker having successfully justified their view.[1]

A reasonable critic.   This phrase in fact combines two distinct aspects. *Reasonable* reinforces the point made earlier by the 'rational activity': the argument is subject to scrutiny on the level of rational thought. But in addition, the presence of the external *critic* points to a social context in which the argumentation takes place. This can be common political discourse for which most people have the background, or it can be a much more specialized realm such as the scientific, medical, or legal. Whatever the context, it includes particular rules of conduct that have become convention, which the implicit judge of the argument watches over.

As an illustration for the theoretical considerations given so far, here is an example from the corpus of 'argumentative microtexts' [Peldszus and Stede, 2016b]:

---

[1]The proviso (given in the quotation from van Eemeren and Grootendorst) that the goal can also be to *refute* the proposition refers merely to the situation where said standpoint is about *not* believing something or doing something.

(1.1) Some may find the idea of a school uniform anachronistic, or regard it as too much of an intervention into the leeway of students and parents to make decisions. Indeed, however, it's already the case today that students of apparently 'uniform-free' schools are essentially wearing a uniform consisting of certain brand-name garments. A simply designed practical outfit would even out the overall visual image of a school, and direct attention toward the character and achievements of the students—and not their buying power. (micro-b012.txt)

This text was written in response to the trigger question "Should students wear school uniforms?", and thus the controversial standpoint defended here is "Students should wear school uniforms at school". Incidentally, this standpoint is not spelled out completely explicitly in the text, but it can—and needs to—be inferred by the hearer. For argumentation mining, this situation of implicit standpoints can be difficult to handle, as we will see later on.

One question to ask at this point concerns the range of possible standpoints, or the range of 'things that we can argue for'. That range is naturally very wide, but broad classifications have been suggested, in addition to that by Aristotle mentioned above. For Eggs [2000], the three basic categories are:

- the *epistemic* argument: some proposition is true or false;

- the *ethical* (or *esthetical*) argument: something is good or bad (or: beautiful or ugly); and

- the *deontic* argument: some action should be done or not done.

Sometimes, the vocabulary used in an argument provides hints as to which category the standpoint belongs to—at least as long as the argument is not too indirect. For illustration, here is an example of an esthetical argument, taken from a film review.[2] We marked some words indicating the realm of esthetics in boldface.

(1.2) Of all Greenaway's works (...), this is probably the British filmmaker's least effective. As with all of his films, the **choreography** of people and objects before the camera (...) is elaborate and **splendid**. The film also marks some of Greenaway's favorite thematic obsessions, including (in no particular order) **spiritual** and corporeal **rotting**, Sir Isaac Newton and arcane mullings on things historic, classical and numerical.
But Greenaway's **narrative** and his direction of actors—two elements which only recently has he concerned himself with—are without foundation. After the effects of the **visual** presentation have **worn off**, the film becomes rather **tiresome** to follow.

---

[2]Desson Howe, *The Washington Post*. Review of 'The Belly of an Architect', June 29, 1990. http://www.washingtonpost.com/wp-srv/style/longterm/movies/videos/thebellyofanarchitectnrhowe_a0b289.htm (accessed May 28, 2018).

1.1.2 HOW DO WE ARGUE?

Having described the static view of *what* constitutes argumentation, we now move to a more process-oriented perspective that is interested in *how* argumentation unfolds. We already emphasized that we are dealing with a social activity that involves a speaker[3] and a hearer, where the latter can be a specific person, or alternatively a broader and possibly quite unspecific audience (as with the film review in *The Washington Post*).

Let us start with the case where two (or more) people seek to resolve a disagreement. They engage in a debate and aim for reaching a conclusion that—at best—leaves everybody happy, or—at least—makes none of the participants too unhappy. This is a process that constitutes the heart of, for instance, political deliberation: making decisions after a careful and thorough weighing of the options and their potential consequences. Greek philosophy had a lot to say about the rules of conduct that enable successful deliberation; in more recent times, the German philosopher Habermas [1981] (among others) studied the role of rational activity in modern society and especially in communication. Within the field of argumentation theory, the pragma-dialectical school [van Eemeren and Grootendorst, 2004] put forward a theory of what constitutes a 'critical discussion': what kind of behavior is expected of the participants, what protocol to use, and so on. Their work exemplifies foremost a *normative* approach to argumentation theory: It seeks to specify how things should be done, ideally. For the practical goals of argumentation mining, this may seem of a lesser relevance, but in fact, work in the pragma-dialectical school has also studied the linguistic aspects of the enterprise. For instance, van Eemeren et al. [2007] identified patterns of formulation that can typically occur at different stages of a critical discussion.

The normative perspective emphasizes the central role of rational thought in argumentation, as does the definition we quoted in the beginning. Indeed, most arguments should ultimately reflect a pattern of sound reasoning, but still, in most real-world instances of argumentation, there are additional influences at work. For one thing, beyond claiming to demonstrate a sound inference, speakers may very well stress their own personal authority on the subject, in order to reinforce the acceptability of their standpoint. They may point out that they have studied the matter for a long time, remind the hearer that they are formally in a teacher-student relation, cite an external source that enjoys high public esteem, etc. Obviously, such moves are independent of the underlying reasoning, but they can add 'weight' to the standpoint the speaker puts forward.

Furthermore, as we so far only hinted at, argumentation in most cases is a *process* that can stretch across multiple dialogue turns, or across a sequence of sentences. It brings together the "constellation of propositions", as the definition calls them, and importantly, speakers face the task of *organizing* that constellation in a linear linguistic contribution. Some portions of a complex argument may be closely related, others may be more distinct. Some points may be rated as more important or 'weighty' (by the speaker) than others. Therefore, the linearization

---

[3]Throughout the book, we use 'speaker' and 'hearer' as cover terms that should be taken to also subsume writers and readers; in other words, we generally do not distinguish between the different linguistic modes.

of the argument's portions in a text should not be left to coincidence. On the contrary: being able to arrange one's argumentative speech in such a manner that it promises to be effective has for a long time been considered an art. The discipline in charge of this is *Rhetoric*, and it studies the relative merits of different strategies for communicating a standpoint. The psychological side of this task is *persuasion*: techniques for trying to make sure that the audience will respond to the speaker's message in the desired way. Persuasion is closely related to argumentation, but it clearly has other ingredients in addition.

In the terminology of Aristotle, the three central factors determining the success of an argumentative exchange are labeled as follows.

- *Logos:* Speakers employ rules of sound reasoning:

  (1.3) That building needs to be demolished, because it is full of asbestos, which is known to be hazardous, and there is no way to stop its diffusion from the different parts of the building.

- *Ethos:* Speakers signal their authority or credibility (or that of their source):

  (1.4) That building needs to be demolished, because it is full of asbestos, as the report by the university engineers has shown.

- *Pathos:* Speakers seek to communicate their standpoint in a manner that seeks to evoke an emotional response:

  (1.5) That building needs to be demolished, because it is an irresponsible source of danger to the health and indeed the life of our children who spend so many hours in those poisonous rooms every day!

Of course, the three dimensions do not usually occur in isolation; most arguments will mix them with each other, to different degrees. But the logos dimension is arguably the most important one, and for argumentation mining the most relevant. Notice that the definition we worked through at the beginning of the chapter also centered on logos ("a rational activity").

Both in dialogue and in monologue text, argumentation can become quite complex and give rise to intricate relationships among different linguistic units. As argumentation mining has so far focused mainly on written text (monologue, or social media interactions), we will in the following emphasize this perspective. In many argumentative texts, such as newspaper editorials or blog posts, the audience is not a clearly identified hearer but an unspecific set of readers. Still, the task for the speakers remains the same: they seek to influence the standpoint of the audience, and for doing that they need to anticipate the positions that the audience likely takes on the issue. In response to this *hearer model*, the speaker selects material to present in support of their view, and furthermore has the option to explicitly consider possible objections by the audience. Such counter-considerations, as we will call them, represent the viewpoint not of the speaker but of the anticipated hearer—the 'opposing view'—and the speaker is advised to not only cite them but also refute them, as in this example, which has already been divided into its 'minimal units' as a first step of analysis:

(1.6) [We really need to turn down that building.]$_0$ [Granted, it will be expensive,]$_1$ [but the degree of asbestos contamination is not tolerable anymore.]$_2$ [Also, it is one of the most ugly buildings in town!]$_3$

Argumentation structure is the term we will use for what was called a 'constellation of propositions' in the definition given at the beginning of this chapter. Looking at Example 1.6, this structure consists of claims made by the speaker (here: unit 0), material they present in support of their claims (here: 3), as well as possible counter-considerations (here: 1) and their refutations (here: 2). In a similar (yet less explicit) way, the author of Example 1.2 above first states his verdict (the director's least effective film), then presents a positive evaluation (nice choreography; an observation that is in opposition to the general verdict) before closing with an argument that supports the negative verdict, suitably initiated with the conjunction *but*.

Finally, to complicate matters, an argumentative text may of course also contain *non-argumentative* portions such as background information, whose identification is part of the overall task of argumentation mining.

1.2 MINING ARGUMENTS: A DEFINITION

For illustration, Figure 1.1 gives a possible graph representation of the structure found in Example 1.6. It follows the notation proposed by Peldszus and Stede [2013] (which is in turn based on that of Freeman [1991]). Circle nodes denote statements representing the proponent's view, while the boxed node (1) indicates the voice of the opposing viewpoint. Unit (0) is the central claim of the text, on which (1) places an 'attack' of type 'rebut': It gives a reason why (0) should not hold. The author proceeds with a counterargument (2), which is an 'undercut' type of attack on the 'rebut' relation, thus indicating that (1) is not regarded as a good or sufficient argument against (0). Finally, (3) provides an argument directly in favor of (0); this is commonly called the 'support' relation.

We will look into such argument diagrams in depth in Section 3.6, and the distinction between undercutting and rebutting is taken up in Sections 4.1 and 6.2. At this point, however, we regard a graph of this kind as one possible outcome of argumentation mining and will now briefly summarize the overall problem. In its full-fledged form, it involves the following subtasks (possibly, but not necessarily, in this order).

1. Identify argumentative text (or a portion of a text) (see Chapter 5).

2. Segment the text into *argumentative discourse units* (ADUs) (see Chapter 5).

3. Identify the central claim (see Chapter 5).

4. Identify the role/function of ADUs (see Chapters 5 and 6).

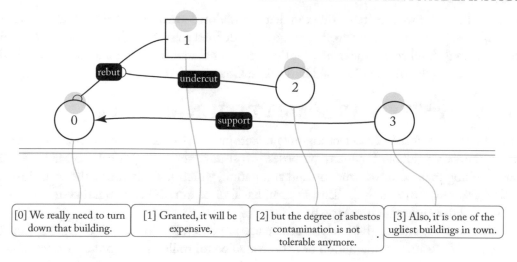

Figure 1.1: Graph representation of argumentation structure for Example 1.6.

5. Identify relations between ADUs (see Chapter 6).

6. Build the overall structural representation (see Chapter 7).

7. Identify the type and the quality of the argumentation (see Chapter 8).

Step 1 is of course unnecessary if the text genre under consideration is by definition argumentative. Otherwise, in a scenario where the type of text is not clearly known, an argumentativity classification is needed, which can be applied either to complete texts or to portions of text, if documents can contain both argumentative and non-argumentative parts. Step 2 can either be combined with some of the other tasks, or carried out as a separate procedure, which designates clauses, sentences, or sequences of them as ADUs of the argumentative structure. An essential task for any argumentation mining scenario is step 3, which tries to isolate the central claim that is being argued for. Similarly, step 4 classifies the role that ADUs play for the argumentation, such as whether it is a piece of evidence, or a possible objection. Step 5 establishes relations (like 'Support' and 'Attack') between the ADUs.

For some purposes, simpler versions will do: Often, argument is defined as merely 'a set of premises and a conclusion', which reduces step 4 to identifying premises, and eliminates step 5 (as the Support relation then is implicitly given).

On the other hand, an application that aims at building a full structure like the one given in Figure 1.1 needs step 6.

Finally, if desired, in step 7 one can detect additional attributes of the argument, such as the particular type of argument from a range of predefined classes, or the underlying reasoning pattern; or in general assess the quality of the argument made: is it coherent and convincing?

All these tasks will be discussed in detail in Chapters 5–8.

1.3 WHY STUDY ARGUMENTATION MINING?

The ability to automatically detect arguments and particularly the support in an argumentation can be very valuable for many purposes. Most analyses of arguments so far have relied on painstaking manual reconstruction and annotation, which severely limits the scalability and speed of argumentative analysis. This, in turn, has limited our ability to build systems that depend on and use argumentative structure.

(Manual) argumentative analysis can be used to check the soundness of a given (line of) argument. *Fallacies* in argumentation have been studied for millennia, in order to determine the conditions under which an argument that is typically a fallacy may be reasonable after all. Thus, manual analysis allows arguments to be examined and either validated or discarded. In particular, when an argument is fully formalized and represented in logic, it can be treated as blobs that are not evaluated internally, where only the overall structure is evaluated. For example, Figure 1.1 can be viewed without attention to the meaning of each numbered text fragment, focusing just on the structure, wherein statement 1 is supported by statement 4; statement 2 attacks statement 1 and is in turn attacked by statement 3. This can be interpreted as a bipolar argumentation framework [Cayrol and Lagasquie-Schiex, 2005], which we will introduce in Section 3.4.1.

In such a context, automatic reasoners can be used to determine whether an argument is sound. Given conflicting information, reasoners can also determine maximally consistent subsets. However, the application of such systems is naturally limited by the input available to them. Argumentation mining could fill this gap by finding instances of 'real-life' arguments in texts. We will discuss the connection between argumentation and reasoning in Chapter 3.

Natural language processing (NLP) has already contributed to mining both social media and open knowledge. Global communication technologies, including social media, have raised interest in large-scale analysis of written conversations. Meanwhile, large corpora of open access scientific documents in some fields have enabled large-scale mining of knowledge. Argumentation mining can deepen and enrich these current mining efforts, to truly support web-scale discourse and debate.

Given the importance of arguments in human sensemaking and decision making, the ability to detect and extract arguments in written texts can enable computer support using argumentative structure. Thereby, an online discussion board could visually summarize the current state of a discussion, without constraining individual replies or needing a human analyst, showing each person's perspective and its relation to the overall discussion. Currently, human sensemaking and decision making is easily overwhelmed because the work in making sense of a debate grows with each new contribution, limiting the potential of massive groups to have debates.

Further, argument identification can be used to identify arguments in a written essay, to aid in essay scoring or to provide instantaneous feedback to support writing instruction. The Educational Testing Service in the U.S. is investigating how argumentation mining can contribute to automated scoring of argumentative essays that students write as part of college admissions testing; we will come back to these topics throughout Chapters 5–7.

Also, argument summarization in near-real-time could be facilitated with argumentation mining, by enabling detailed arguments to be viewed at multiple levels of granularity: zooming out of the structure would show the main points in the argument, while zooming in would show the detail in each point. This would enable small groups to carefully check the validity of arguments. For example, researchers in an Alzheimer's research consortium are investigating how to automatically interlink scholarly arguments to source materials, and how to capture the research lab data supporting these arguments.

Automatic argument retrieval could help lawyers find relevant case law. Similarly, retrieving arguments for or against a position can also be relevant for e-government and gaining feedback on public policy.

Finally, we mention the current activity of IBM Research, who are working on *Debating Technology* with the ultimate goal of a software agent that is able to understand and produce arguments, and do so in a dialogue with human beings. Various contributions made by this research group so far will be covered in Chapters 5 and 6.

1.4   OVERVIEW OF THE BOOK

In Chapter 2 we approach the notion of argumentation from a linguistic perspective and discuss a range of phenomena that motivate distinctions between argumentative text and non-argumentative text. We also touch on a number of concepts that are closely related to argumentation, such as subjectivity, opinion, and rhetoric. Chapter 3, in contrast, takes the viewpoint of argumentation theory and introduces several key aspects of argumentative reasoning and the formal representation of arguments. Afterward, in Chapter 4 we turn to natural language processing and begin with a brief overview of schemata that have been proposed to annotate arguments in text, and we introduce a number of relevant corpora that can be used in argumentation mining research. Chapter 5 explains our approach to dividing argumentation mining into a number of relatively isolated subtasks, which reflects the practice of most current research. The chapter begins with the goals of identifying text as argumentative, and finding claims, i.e., the most important part of an argument. The second most important parts are the statements being made in support of a claim, and this is the topic of Chapter 6, which also looks at finding possible objections to claims. For some purposes, it is important to derive the complete constellation of claims and supporting and objecting statements, which is covered in Chapter 7. Then, Chapter 8 addresses several tasks that seek more detailed information about the arguments found, e.g., their quality and consistency. That concludes the perspective of *mining*, and we continue in

Chapter 9 with a brief discussion of the problem of producing argumentative text automatically. Finally, Chapter 10 provides a summary and suggests an outlook for the field.

CHAPTER 2

Argumentative Language

In this chapter, we consider the linguistic side of argumentation: What does the language of arguing look like, and how does it differ from other ways of speaking or writing? The chapter thus is intended to serve primarily as background for readers who approach argumentation mining from a technical perspective and are interested in the underlying linguistic phenomena and their terminology.

For a start, we consider the notion of *subjectivity* (Section 2.1), which quite clearly subsumes the phenomenon of argumentation. As a vast amount of NLP work on subjectivity centers specifically on *opinion*, we briefly explore its relationship to argumentation (Section 2.2). Then, we approach our topic from the perspective of *speech act theory*: some scholars hold the view that an argument should be regarded as a complex speech act (Section 2.3). The linguistic realization of arguments is often very similar to that of *explanations* and *justifications*, which can be seen as related speech acts, and we will draw comparisons (Section 2.4). Thereafter, we turn to the idea of analyzing argumentation as one of five basic linguistic *modes*, which supposedly correlate (albeit not in a simple way) with particular surface features of utterances or text (Section 2.5). The chapter closes with a look at *rhetoric*, i.e., the art of crafting a text in such a way that it is most likely to have the intended effects on the readers (Section 2.6).

2.1 SUBJECTIVITY

For defining subjectivity, we follow Wiebe et al. [2005] in adopting the notion of *private state* from the English grammar of Quirk et al. [1985]. The idea is: while a person's actions can be observed by the outside world, her current mental state (what does she think, how does she feel, etc.) is not open to that observation. This distinction can be projected to that person's linguistic utterances: some of them describe a state of affairs in the world, and listeners can in principle judge them as true or false—these 'objective' statements are a matter of intersubjective agreement or disagreement.

(2.1) There is a cat on the mat.

(2.2) Winston Churchill came to office in 1940.

On the other hand, when the speaker decides to reveal a private state, there is no point in replying *Not true!* We may very well like or dislike that particular revelation, but objecting to its truth is usually not an option. Here are some kinds of private state verbalization that we can distinguish.

(2.3) Reveal an emotion: *Hooray!*

(2.4) Give an opinion: *That's a really bad wine.*

(2.5) Make a judgment: *You don't deserve the prize.*

(2.6) Make a prognosis: *There will be snow tomorrow.*

(2.7) Give an estimate or speculation: *I guess that's a llama over there.*

Granted, a listener may legitimately react to these statements with some objection, but then the objection applies to the expressed *content* of the private state, not to its revelation. For example, a listener responding with *Wrong!* to 2.7 objects to the notion of the creature over there being a llama—and not to the fact that the speaker *thinks* otherwise (more technically: *wrong* does not scope over *I guess*). Very often, these cases are ambiguous (and can sometimes produce misunderstanding) when those verbs of cognition are not explicitly stated but left implicit by the speaker, as is the case in Examples 2.4–2.6.

Opinion and emotion   In NLP, some of these subjectivity categories have received more attention than others. The most-researched one is that of 'opinion', which we will consider in more detail in the next section. The task of 'opinion mining' is sometimes interchangeably called 'sentiment analysis', but it seems appropriate to differentiate between these terms. We will use 'sentiment' for the subclass of subjective utterances that comprises opinion, judgment, and emotion, where 'opinion' is reserved for evaluations that are directed toward some entity—an object, institution, abstract idea, etc. This list should not include human beings, though, as we follow *appraisal theory* [Martin and White, 2005] in distinguishing 'judgment' (the evaluation of a person's behavior, character, appearance, ex. 2.5) from opinions about non-human entities (ex. 2.4).

Emotion detection (ex. 2.3) is a popular NLP task, too, and it can obviously overlap with opinion mining, when, for example, a customer review contains an expression of enthusiasm in response to the product in question. But in general the two have to be kept distinct: We can find both non-opinionated emotions (ex. 2.3) and non-emotional opinions (ex. 2.4).

Prognoses and speculations   While a large portion of opinion, judgment, and emotion essentially centers on *valence*, i.e., whether a positive or negative polarity is expressed, prognoses (ex. 2.6) and speculations (ex. 2.7) focus instead on truth vs. falsity, or more specifically the degree of belief in the truth of a proposition. We view prognoses as always referring to the future, whereas speculations may pertain to the past, present, or future.

In NLP, detecting speculation or 'hedging' is a prominent task (e.g., Farkas et al. [2010]). It can be applied for instance to the analysis of scientific writing, medical reports, or political discourse. Hedging can be intentionally employed by a speaker to remain vague so that she can't be held accountable for having committed to the truth of a statement. The following example carefully avoids taking a definite stance on the question of the patient having diabetes or not.

(2.8) There is no clear symptom of diabetes.

Detecting subjectivity For many computational tasks it is important to automatically distinguish subjective from non-subjective language. The term *subjectivity classification*, however, today is most frequently used in conjunction with the more narrow goal of opinion mining, where it is employed as an initial step of identifying documents or parts of documents in which opinions should be looked for (or not). The classical work on subjectivity classification by Wiebe et al. [2004], however, started out from a broader goal, viewing subjective language as "expressing opinions, evaluations, and speculations" in the spirit of the range we sketched above (cf. ex. 2.3–2.7). Their features were purely lexical (n-grams), and the main evaluation task was to separate opinionated from non-opinionated Wall Street Journal texts (as derived from the category labels given in the corpus). This makes the work quite similar to that of *genre classification*, when it is applied to genres that are partly defined by subjectivity. The works by Petrenz and Webber [2011] or Krüger et al. [2017], for example, address separating newspaper text into opinionated vs. non-opinionated sub-genres (essentially: editorials and letters to the editor vs. news); here, the emphasis is less on lexical n-grams but on linguistically motivated features such as the presence of modal verbs or the tense of verbs: For news reports, there is a tendency to favor past tense, while editorials more often use present tense.

An ambitious version of subjectivity classification would aim not merely at making a binary distinction of whether or not a passage is subjective (or opinionated, or hedged), but rather at differentiating the different kinds of subjectivity we have illustrated above (and possibly more). The current work in the field, however, tends to focus on specific subproblems, which are obviously easier to tackle.

Regarding argumentative language, we conclude that it is by definition subjective, but that subjectivity classification (as currently operationalized) is too coarse-grained to solve the task of finding text passages containing arguments in particular. Since argumentation involves more than a single statement and thus is inherently relational, it is important to consider the subjectivity status of individual statements as well as the constraints on their potential combination.

Verifiability A move into this direction was made by Park and Cardie [2014], who were specifically interested in the argumentative relation of support. They proposed to distinguish between the following categories of statements.

- Verifiable: objective assertions (not about personal feelings or interpretations), which comprise two subcategories:

  - Verifiable-private: statements that concern the speaker's personal state or experience.
  - Verifiable-public: no personal state or experience is involved; public information is sufficient to verify the statement.

- Unverifiable: statements that cannot be proven with objective evidence.

The distinction we made at the beginning of this section already separated Verifiable-public from the other categories; hence, we need to consider Park and Cardie's suggestion to also separate the categories Verifiable-Private and Unverifiable. They reserve the former for statements that report on a speaker's experiences, which are 'in principle' verifiable, but for practical purposes the necessary information is just not publicly available. Here are three of their examples.[1]

(2.9) My son has hypoglycemia.

(2.10) They flew me to NY in February.

(2.11) The flight attendant yelled at the passengers.

So, in such verifiable-private statements, the speaker often talks explicitly about herself, but the third example shows that this is not obligatory: speakers can recall past perceptions, where their audience usually has no means of verifying the statement.

When making categorizations of this kind, it is important to be clear about how certain modalizers and verbs of perception or cognition are handled (as we pointed out earlier when discussing ex. 2.7). For Park and Cardie, both "Peanuts do not kill people" and "I believe that peanuts do not kill people" are verifiable-public, so in the second example, *I believe* is merely a way of weakening the assertion. Along these lines, our Example 2.7 ("I guess that's a llama over there") is also verifiable-public: the verification pertains to the question of the presence of a llama, and not to the speaker's guessing activity. (Note, however, that in other contexts, expressions like *I believe that X* may need a more elaborate analysis than that of weakening the statement of X.)

As their next step, Park and Cardie propose some constraints on how the different types of statements are to be supported in argumentation: for unverifiable statements, speakers may give a *reason* ("I don't like this wine, because it has so much tannin"), while for verifiable-public statements they can provide *evidence*: "I tell you Winston Churchill came to office in 1940. I saw it on Wikipedia!" For verifiable-private statements, providing evidence is an optional move; although hearers are not really in a position to question a statement like ("I have a headache"), still the speaker may go on to explain it ("Maybe I had too much wine last night").

Similar classifications have been proposed elsewhere in the literature, and we will return to this matter later on in Chapter 6. For now, relating the ideas to the initial definition of 'argument' that we quoted from van Eemeren and Grootendorst (see page 1), notice that classifications of statements along the lines of Park and Cardie try to add more fine-grained distinctions to the move of 'justifying a standpoint'. One question that has to be dealt with here is: what kind of statement qualifies as a *standpoint* and thus as something that can or should be argued for?

2.2   OPINION, STANCE, AND ARGUMENT

With opinion mining being such a prominent subtask of subjectivity analysis, we briefly take a specific look at the relationship that arguments have to opinions, and to the related notion of stance.

[1]For more examples from a different corpus study, see Habernal and Gurevych [2017, p. 154].

Following Liu [2012, p. 11], we define an *opinion* as a tuple consisting (maximally) of a target (the entity being evaluated), the expressed sentiment toward that target, the holder of the opinion, and the time at which it is known to hold. A program performing opinion mining thus tries to locate the presence of an opinion in a document, and then to instantiate the tuple, as far as possible (some elements of the tuple may be regarded as optional).

The obvious connection to argumentation mining is given when authors provide one or more *reasons* for their opinion. An opinionated statement is an instance of a standpoint, as we defined it in Section 1.1, because clearly, different people may evaluate the target in different and potentially conflicting ways. Then, when a reason is provided, as in Example 2.12 below, we have a constellation of a claim and a supporting statement. This easily extends to multiple reasons, and also to more complex structures where a reason can in turn be supported. In 2.12, for instance, the speaker might continue with a statement providing evidence for the overloaded nature of a Wagner opera.

(2.12) I never enjoyed Wagner's operas, as they are so enormously overloaded.

Finding the constellation of reasons for an opinion can thus be regarded as an instance of argumentation mining.

A more elaborate relationship between the two realms is proposed by Rajendran et al. [2016], who are interested in so-called 'implicit opinions'. In these opinions, the sentiment arises not from words that generally convey polarity (and thus are to be listed in general sentiment lexicons) but from factual statements that only imply an evaluation. These so-called 'polar facts' are domain-specific and rather difficult to detect automatically; two examples are given below.

(2.13) [camera review] The viewfinder is somewhat dark.

(2.14) [hotel review] The rooms turned out to be small.

The two attributes (dark, small) are not in general negative, but when applied to the specific objects here, they invite us to infer a disappointed attitude on the writer's side. Rajendran et al. now see a parallel to the task of reconstructing enthymemes[2] in argumentation analysis: Given our two examples above, when the conclusion is a negative verdict by the reviewer, then an unstated major premise provides the link between the explicated minor premise (as above) and the conclusion.

(2.15) The viewfinder is somewhat dark (+ A dark viewfinder is considered bad).
    → I am not in favor of the camera.

(2.16) The rooms turned out to be small (+ A small room is considered bad).
    → I am not in favor of the hotel.

Enthymeme reconstruction is a very difficult problem, but it has been addressed in argumentation mining to some extent in recent years, as we will discuss in Section 8.1.

---

[2]Enthymemes are arguments in which a premise or the conclusion are left unstated, for the hearer to supply.

Stance   Finally, the similarity between opinion classification and *stance* classification is in the common goal of determining a polarity, i.e., a for-or-against attitude on the side of the speaker. In stance classification, however, the 'target' is pre-defined, and it is often not a specific entity (such as a product) but an issue or a topic under debate. It is often performed for tweets, and also for online forums, where users exchange their views on questions like "behavior X (is/is not) acceptable" or "legislation X (should/should not) be dropped".

Another popular genre for stance classification is student essays, whose authors have been instructed to explain their position on a certain topic. Here, as well as in online forums, the topic or issue is clearly a 'critical standpoint', and the texts that are being analyzed are by definition argumentative.

Therefore, stance classification can be considered as a subproblem of argumentation mining, when the pairing of topic and stance—such as (mandatory vaccination of children/against)—corresponds to what we called the 'central claim' of the text, i.e., the statement that the speaker is arguing for. We will take a closer look at the task of stance classification in Section 6.3.

2.3   ARGUMENT AND SPEECH ACTS

As pointed out in Chapter 1, the goal of argumentation usually is to influence the state of mind of the addressees, or to change their behavior. This is, generally speaking, a matter of inflicting change on 'the world', and this in turn is conspicuously close to the slogan underlying the notion of *speech act theory*[3]: Using language is a form of carrying out *actions*—comparable to switching on the light, cooking dinner, and so on—and therefore it has consequences. A linguistic utterance made by a speaker, once completed, does not simply vanish but leaves its marks on the world (or at least on a very small portion of it): The listener may have new information, or be doubtful of a previously assumed 'fact', or feel offended, etc. Thus, there is a close connection between the realms of speech acts and argumentation, and hence we provide a brief overview here.

The most profound changes to 'the world' are triggered by utterances that occur in situations such as the judge sentencing the defendant in court, an authority christening a ship, or the priest marrying a couple. Contexts like these were a central motivation for the work of Austin [1975], who is nowadays widely credited for the first systematic exposition of a theory of speech acts. Beyond the relatively dramatic examples just mentioned, Austin entertained—at least for some time—the hypothesis that a certain class of 'performative' verbs plays such a fundamental role that they can be used to paraphrase essentially any sentence in such a way that its function becomes transparent.

(2.17) You shouldn't read that book. → I advise you not to read that book.

(2.18) What is your name? → I ask you to tell me your name.

---

[3]For a slightly more elaborate, chapter-long introduction to the topic and a discussion of its contentious points, see Saddock [2005].

(2.19) Yesterday I met a philosopher. → I assert that I met a philosopher yesterday.

(2.20) Max is the smartest kid in the world. → I claim that Max is the smartest kid in the world.

(2.21) It's about 15 degrees out there.→ I estimate that it is about 15 degrees out there.

The fact that people in daily life typically do *not* constantly use those extended versions contributes to ambiguity and sometimes to misunderstanding (but, arguably, makes communication much more interesting); recall our discussion of Examples 2.3–2.7 at the beginning of the chapter. This ambiguity in the roles that utterances can play also makes the task of argumentation mining difficult, because in some way or another, the status of individual statements that take part in argumentation needs to be determined (and that would be much easier if those performative verbs were present).

Classifying speech acts   Austin's idea of collecting all the relevant verbs in a language in order to define the 'landscape' of speech acts is today generally regarded as a dead end for the advancement of speech act theory. Instead, a prominent task has been to come up with a classification (and definition) of generalized types of speech acts. A number of such typologies have been proposed, and a popular one is that by Searle [1976].

- **Representatives:** Speaker commits to the truth of an assertion.

- **Directives:** Speaker tries to make addressee perform some action.

- **Expressives:** Speaker expresses an emotional state.

- **Declaratives:** Speaker changes the state of the world by means of performing the utterance.

- **Commissives:** Speaker comits to doing some action in the future.

Within these broad classes, sub-taxonomies may be postulated, and ultimately, specific speech acts can be defined. Searle [1969] proposed to construct systematic definitions by means of different kinds of rules that characterize the propositional content of the utterance, the situational conditions that need to hold for the speech act to be performed successfully ('preparatory rules'), a 'sincerity' rule committing the speaker to be sincere in expressing her psychological states, and an 'essential' rule that describes the central pragmatic impact of the speech act in question. It is important to note that these rules (as opposed to, say, rules of grammar) are not about well-formedness—this is a notion that does not apply to speech acts. Instead, the key concept is that of a speech act to be 'felicitous', to successfully serve its purpose. Infelicitous speech act attempts occur, for example, when somebody pronounces somebody else to be married but is in no legal position to do so; or when somebody promises an addressee to do him a favor yet does not really intend to do so (insincerity).

Components of a speech act   The five class labels mentioned above are often said to describe the 'illocutionary force' of an utterance. This derives from another important sub-classification made by Austin and (in a slightly different way) by Searle. The idea is that the performance of a speech act involves the following three sub-acts that occur (more or less) simultaneously.

- **Locutionary act:** producing the linguistic utterance, by speaking or writing (or gesturing).

- **Illocutionary act:** the intention or goal the speaker has in mind when performing the act.

- **Perlocutionary act:** the effect that the performance of the act has on the addressee.

One reason to distinguish illocution from perlocution is that an utterance may well have—from the speaker's perspective—unintended or even undesired effects. A speaker could comment on the addressee's new hairstyle in a neutral way, and the addressee might derive the literal meaning (as intended by the speaker) but in addition surmise a secondary meaning and feel offended (as not intended by the speaker).

For argumentation, the perlocution is of obvious relevance, as it characterizes precisely that 'change of mind' on the addressee's side, which is the purpose of the speaker devising their argument. Research on *persuasion* seeks to detect or even measure the strength of such effects. For speech act theory, however, the perlocution is a private state that is of limited interest; the heart of the matter is the perspective of the speaker and thus the illocutionary force of her utterance.

Linguistic signals   Languages provide a variety of means to explicitly signal the presence of a speech act, or to constrain the class of possible speech acts, so that listeners may reconstruct the speaker's intention. Above, we mentioned performative verbs (e.g., ask, advise, ...), which in fact are the clearest indicators of illocutionary force. In general, however, the surface of an utterance contains only hints about the underlying illocution, and there is no simple 1:1 mapping. The term 'illocutionary force indicating device', or IFID for short, was coined by Searle [1969] and is nowadays often used for referring to those hints. A prominent syntactic IFID is sentence mode (declarative, interrogative, imperative), which often enables straightforward identification of a directive or a question.[4] But of course, both of these illocutions can also be produced with declarative mode (e.g., "I would like to inquire about the price of that car over there."), which therefore is quite ambiguous with respect to the speech act. The class of lexical IFIDs contains, besides the performative verbs mentioned above, modal verbs and many different kinds of adverbials from which the illocutionary force can be inferred. On the side of linguistic pragmatics, IFIDs for *apologies* have been studied intensively for many languages (e.g., Ogiermann [2009]). Some examples (more or less explicit) for English are as follows.

(2.22) I apologize for being late.

(2.23) Sorry I'm late.

---

[4]Many speech act researchers consider (different kinds of) questions as another basic speech act type in addition to the list of Searle [1976].

(2.24) I'm a bit late, unfortunately.

(2.25) I'm afraid I didn't quite make it on time.

Indirect speech acts   The observation that illocutions can be marked more or less explicitly points to another central notion in speech act theory: the 'indirect' speech act. The much-cited example "Can you pass the salt?" on the surface is a yes-no question but is interpreted by the hearer as a polite form of a directive (or a subcategory 'request'). The ambiguity also occurs very frequently with declarative sentences that *prima facie* merely assert some information, yet are intended to convey additional illocutionary force. Our Examples 2.22 and 2.23 above are direct (explicit) apologies, with one being more formal than the other, whereas in Examples 2.24 and 2.25 it is up to the hearer to read an apology into the utterances—this depends on the situational context, how close the interlocutors are, etc.

Speech act theorists have tried to explain how these interpretations actually originate in communication. The two main approaches emphasize either a process of conventionalization, or the role of active inferencing on the hearer's side; see Saddock [2005].

Argumentation and complex speech acts   In Section 2.1, we described the ideas of Park and Cardie [2014] on associating statements with different 'verifiability' statuses, and deriving consequences for their possible roles in an argument. The realm of speech acts provides an alternative perspective on the same goal: when the inventory of illocutionary force labels makes distinctions relevant to argument components, a process of speech act labeling could be a preparatory step that constrains the identification of those components. Specifically, this can help with finding *claims*, which can be opinions, speculations, prognoses, etc.—but not factual statements such as "I bought a new coffee maker yesterday". For practical purposes, a crucial empirical question is to what extent IFIDs can be exploited for recognizing the relevant distinctions.

But the connection between speech act theory and argumentation can go a step further. While the traditional work on speech acts used the (idealized) notion of 'sentence' as the unit to be labeled, it is not impossible to extend it to pairs or even more complex constellations of linguistic clauses. A systematic study on the possibilities of combining clauses into complex speech acts of 'concluding' was presented (in German) by Klein [1987].

2.4   ARGUMENTATION, EXPLANATION, AND JUSTIFICATION

Several times in this chapter we mentioned the problems of ambiguity for identifying the components of arguments and the relations between them. In this section, we provide a concrete example, looking at the straightforward English construction "A, because B" (or equivalently: "Because B, A"). Of course, this can be the template for an argument, as Example 2.26 demonstrates: a is the claim (or standpoint), and B is the supporting statement.

(2.26) Using airplanes is really a bad idea because they are among the worst air polluters we have ever created. (Argumentation/Persuasion)

(2.27) An airplane is able to take off because the shape of the wings produces an upward force when the air flows across them. (Explanation)

(2.28) I need to use airplanes a lot because my job requires me to be in different parts of the country every week. (Justification)

Examples 2.27 and 2.28 make use of the same construction, but they have different communicative effects. Example 2.27 is easily used in a context where the listener already believes that airplanes can take off—the speaker thus does not aim to convince the hearer of that fact. Instead, the new information for the hearer is (supposedly) in the second clause. This is the constellation of an *explanation*, where A is not a claim but an undisputed fact and B does not 'support' A but provides the reason why A holds. Example 2.28 can be regarded as a special case, where the explanation pertains to a personal decision. Hence, A does not necessarily have the status of an undisputed fact; the speaker has to consider that some hearers might not approve. This is the situation of *justification*: giving a reason for an attitude or an action that might be controversial—and if it is, then justification becomes a special case of argumentation. Various theories of text structure model differences like those in Examples 2.26–2.28 by using a specific *coherence relation* for each case; we will discuss this below in Section 2.6.2 .

While we used one linguistic construction for illustration here, English of course provides many more ways to express the three constellations: other connectives are available, such as *therefore* or *due to*, and often the sentences can be adjoined without any connective at all. But notice that our three examples do not behave the same way in this respect: replacing the conjunction with a full stop in 2.27 produces a somewhat odd result, while it is perfectly possible for the other two.

In English, the conjunction *because* is highly versatile and can fulfill a wide range of pragmatic functions. Other languages have tendencies to associate different preferences with similar connectives. In German, for example, the conjunctions *weil* and *denn* for many speakers appear to be interchangeable (save for their syntactic differences: one is subordinating, one is coordinating); but research has shown that *weil* tends to mark objective causal relations (descriptions of causes in the world), whereas *denn* is more often used for subjective relations such as claim—support [Pasch, 1982]. In Dutch, an even more pronounced effect along these lines has been shown for the conjunctions *want* and *omdat* by Sanders and Spooren [2009].

2.5　TEXT TYPES AND DISCOURSE MODES

In Section 1.3, we mentioned a variety of genres that are particularly relevant for argumentation mining. The idea of the 'genre' (a set of texts that fulfill a common purpose and have commonalities in terms of functional components and/or linguistic conventions)[5] is generally well-known, and the importance of genre for many tasks in language technology is undisputed. In this section, however, we take a look at a lesser known notion, which has been alternatively called 'text type' or 'discourse mode'. It is related to genre, but should not be confused with it.

Text type = Discourse Mode   In particular, while the genre is a property of a complete text, we here focus on the unit of a stretch of sentences, often, but not necessarily, forming a paragraph. Hence, the term 'text type' (as used, e.g., by Werlich [1975]) is a bit confusing, and we prefer 'discourse mode', which Smith [2003] introduced for pretty much the same idea. It posits that there is only a small set of basic functions that a series of sentences, or text passage, can fulfill. These functions are to a good extent determined by the types of 'discourse entities' (events, states, generalizations, abstractions) that are mentioned in the passage, which in turn tend to correlate with certain surface-linguistic features. One main theoretical goal for Smith (and earlier for Werlich) therefore was to establish the discourse passage as a unit of analysis for linguistics proper (rather than for the shady area of pragmatics). In Smith's approach, there are five classes.

- **Narrative:** Events and states are introduced, with events being temporally related. The semantic types of events (un-/boundedness) indicate the progression of narrative time. Temporal connectives and adverbials are frequent instruments of clause linkage.

    (2.29) The passengers landed in New York in the middle of the night and then moved on to Hoboken immediately.

- **Description:** Passages include states and ongoing or atelic[6] events. Text progression is driven by spatial rather than by temporal patterns; time is static. Locative phrases often appear in topic position.

    (2.30) Hundreds of people occupied the square. In front of them, the speaker was standing on a small podium.

- **Report:** Events, states, and sometimes general statives are introduced; they are not related relative to each other (as in narrative). Tensed verbs, modals, and temporal adverbs are frequent.

    (2.31) My sister visited the new exhibition yesterday.

- **Information:** Facts, propositions, and generalizing states are introduced, which need not be anchored in time and space. The text progresses through a 'metaphorical' space.

    (2.32) Krypton is one of the noble gases. It is one of the rarest elements on earth.

---

[5]A more thorough introduction to the concept of genre and its role in computational linguistics is given in Stede [2011, Sct. 2.1].

[6]A *telic* event is one that comprises both a preparation and a culmination phase, e.g., 'traveling to London', 'climbing the mountain'. An atelic event is homogeneous in time: 'being ill', 'reading'.

- **Argument:** Like 'information', this is an atemporal mode. States of affairs, facts, and propositions are introduced and related to each other, often contrastively.

(2.33) The award was given to Paul, but he did not deserve it. His work is very shallow.

Even though these correlations between text types and linguistic features are obviously tendencies rather than strict rules, they can serve as useful indicators, and Smith's book (as well as the work of Werlich and others) discusses them in much more detail. Also, a computational approach to recognizing modes automatically was presented by Song et al. [2017]. Unfortunately, for our purposes here, the mode 'argument' is the most vague in the sense that it is less tightly connected to characteristic patterns than the others are. Still, as demonstrated by Becker et al. [2016], it is possible to operationalize it for the purposes of recognizing argumentation. Following up on the huge body of linguistic research on aspectual verb classes, the authors focus on one crucial feature for separating discourse modes, viz. the 'situation entity (SE) types'. The following types are distinguished.

- **State:** *Armin has brown eyes.*

- **Event:** *Bonnie ate three tacos.*

- **Report:** *The agency said applications had increased.*

- **Generic sentence:** *Scientific papers make arguments.*

- **Generalizing sentence:** *Fei travels to India every year.*

- **Fact:** *Georg knows that Reza won the competition.*

- **Proposition:** *Georg thinks that Reza won the competition.*

- **Resemblance:** *Reza looks like he won the competition.*

- **Question:** *Why do you torment me so?*

- **Imperative:** *Listen to this.*

Becker et al. [2016] annotated these SE types in the texts of the 'argumentative microtext' corpus of Peldszus and Stede [2016b] and showed that the SE distribution can help distinguishing argumentative text passages from non-argumentative ones. Furthermore, Becker et al. demonstrated that the distribution of SE types correlates with the different types of argument component (premise/conclusion) and argumentative relations (support, attack).

2.6   RHETORIC

According to the *New Dictionary of the History of Ideas* [Carron, 2005, p. 2122], "Rhetoric governs the effective use of verbal and nonverbal communication designed to influence an audience. …in its original and historical form, rhetoric is associated with the use of human discourse to persuade and can be defined as the art of speaking, of speaking well, or of speaking effectively with the aim of persuading." This clearly suggests a connection to argumentation, and indeed this relationship was studied intensively by Aristotle, whom we mentioned in the first chapter as the proponent of the three 'means of persuasion', logos, ethos, and pathos. For our purposes here, the question is which aspects of language use can contribute to a text being argumentatively *effective*, and we look briefly at the two levels of linguistic description where rhetoric can unfold its power: the choices in building a sentence, and the organization of the text.

2.6.1   BUILDING SENTENCES: RHETORICAL CHOICES

When person A wants person B to close the window, there are many possibilities to formulate the request; consider just two of them.

(2.34) Close the window! It's cold.

(2.35) It is rather cold in here and I'm already not feeling so well. Would you be so kind to close the window for me?

In both cases, we have a directive speech act and a justification, but stated very differently. Which one is more appropriate, and correspondingly, more *effective*, of course depends very much on context: Who is talking to whom under what circumstances. This may seem trivial, but the point is that a similar array of linguistic options for articulating a sentence is essentially always at the writer's disposal. We can choose rare and difficult words, or common and simple ones; we can speak or write in a long sequence of short sentences, or in a short sequence of complex, deeply structured sentences; and so forth. This borders on the notion of *stylistics*, where many textbooks are available and some are probably known to the reader. More unusual are approaches that explicitly make the connection between rhetoric and grammar. Jeanne Fahnestock's introductory textbook [Fahnestock, 2011] gives vivid examples of how small changes in word choice, sentence construction, and passage construction can produce different rhetorical effects. The introduction by Kolln [2003], centered around the notion of *choice*, also points to the different rhetorical effects of each choice, and explains the alternatives by referring to grammatical concepts (rather than to intuition). To mention just one example, the author looks at the correlation between lexical and grammatical decisions and the resulting *intonation pattern* or *rhythm* of a sentence, which influences the perception by the hearer and the reader alike, and can contribute to rhetorical effects—or not, if bad choices have been made.

Rhetorical figures   One phenomenon that is sometimes mentioned in connection with argumentation is that of *figures of speech*, also called *rhetorical figures*, which have been studied extensively in classical rhetoric. This, too, is a vast area, and we can only scratch the surface here. Two such examples are as follows.

- **Hyperbole:** *Phew, the distance from Newark to Manhattan is a hundred miles!*
  The statement is literally false, but the exaggeration is consciously used (and probably understood) to emphasize the speaker's point.

- **Tautology:** *That nice restaurant was really great.*
  The two predications on the restaurant are barely distinguishable; yet the repetition can contribute to overall effect.

In connection to argumentation, we point to the research efforts of Harris and Di Marco [2017], who have extensively analyzed rhetorical figures and studied many of them as devices for producing effective arguments. Following up on their work, Lawrence et al. [2017b] tried to detect the presence of rhetorical figures in text automatically. They used the Moral Maze radio debate corpus (see Section 3.6) for their experiments. For actually computing correlations with argumentative moves, the number of instances of rhetorical figures found was too small, however. Most recently, with an eye toward automation, Harris et al. [2018] proposed a new annotation scheme for Rhetorical Figures, using standoff XML. They suggest focusing on computationally tractable figures such as antimetabole (reverse repetition of at least two words), which they map to several different rhetorical functions.

2.6.2 TEXT ORGANIZATION: RHETORICAL EFFECTS

As with sentences, the structure of a text is not arbitrary, either. There are many factors influencing the choices of how to order sentences and link them together, with an important one being the genre of the text, which often suggests conventional linearizations. But usually, an author has considerable room left for making choices, which in turn can contribute to rhetorical effect. We look at two alternative ways of capturing this: a flat segmentation and labeling of a sequence of text spans, and the postulation of a hierarchical text structure.

Functional labels on text spans The idea that a text can be analyzed as a sequence of genre-specific 'moves' goes back to Swales [1990], who suggested that a number of adjacent sentences constitute such a move, and that the text then be a contiguous sequence of moves. Among the genres studied was scientific writing, which (depending on the type of science) usually follows conventionalized patterns of 'when to say what' in a research paper (or in a grant proposal, a book, etc.). A computational implementation was later proposed by Teufel and Moens [2002], who coined the term 'argumentative zoning' for this approach. Teufel and colleagues annotated passages of scientific papers for the roles they play as a part of the paper's overall contribution, and hence, zone labels include 'aim' (research goal), 'own' (description of author's work), 'background' (generally accepted scientific background), 'conclusion', and several others. Having shown that substantial human annotator agreement can be achieved, the authors then trained automatic classifiers and demonstrated that the recognition of zone labels can be automated with quite impressive quality.

In a similar vein, Yamada et al. [2017] studied legal arguments in Japanese court judgments, and ran a human agreement study on labeling units as 'identifying' (setting a topic), 'fact', 'background', 'conclusion', and 'framing' (argumentative material in support of the conclusion unit), and they obtained good annotator agreement (κ=0.7).

Hierarchical text structure A complementary perspective on text structure suggests that a text can be seen as a hierarchy of text spans that are (recursively) connected via so-called *coherence relations*. These relations state that a span can, for example, be followed by another one that *elaborates* on the former, as in this example, where the spans are marked with square brackets.

(2.36) **Elaboration:** [The new Smart Watch was introduced today.] [It costs $50 more than the old model.]

Recursion arises when these two segments in turn enter into a coherence relation, for example *Motivation*, which links a recommendation for the reader to the reason:

(2.37) **Motivation:** [[The new Smart Watch was introduced today.] [It costs $50 more than the old model.]] [You should really buy it.]

A widely used corpus annotated with such coherence relations is the *Penn Discourse Treebank* or PDTB [Prasad et al., 2008]. Annotators inspected all the 'boundaries' in a text (roughly, clause and sentence boundaries) and decided whether some relation can be discerned between the adjacent spans. The accompanying computational task of recognizing those relations is called *Shallow Discourse Parsing* (for an introduction to the problem, see Stede [2011, Sct. 4.3]).

In the PDTB, the relations are being annotated independently of one another. Accordingly, there are no assumptions on any overall structure that may arise. In contrast, *Rhetorical Structure Theory* or RST [Mann and Thompson, 1988] postulates that a well-formed tree structure can be built, which spans the text completely.[7] The authors postulate that some 25 different coherence relations are sufficient for analyzing most texts. A sample RST tree (for an excerpt of a text) is shown in Figure 2.1. The best-known English RST corpus is the RST Discourse Treebank or RST-DT [Carlson et al., 2003], and it has led to numerous proposals of automatic parsers that try to build the tree structures automatically. Stede [2011, Sct. 4.4] gives an overview.

Evidently, the analysis of argumentation is not entirely different from the analyses in the PDTB and in the RST-DT. For RST, in particular, parallels between the tree structures and similar analyses of argumentation structure (recall the example shown in Figure 1.1) are easy to notice. However, there is no consensus yet as to how the relationship is to be construed exactly. A summary of the discussion was provided by Peldszus and Stede [2013], and later on,

---

[7]RST is a theory of linguistic pragmatics; notice that for rhetoricians, the use of 'rhetorical' in the name of RST is not uncontroversial, as there is certainly more to text-level rhetoric than what is captured by RST.

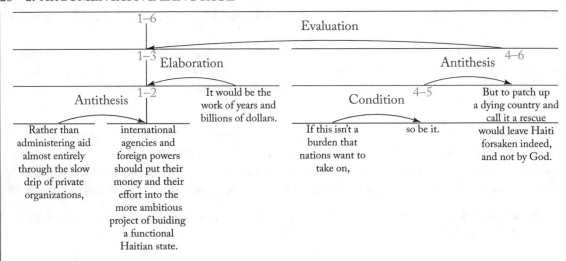

Figure 2.1: Sample analysis of a text fragment according to Rhetorical Structure Theory from [Stede, 2011, p. 115].

Peldszus and Stede [2016a] gave a first empirical analysis based on a corpus that was annotated both for argumentation and for rhetorical structure (the 'argumentative microtext corpus'; cf. Section 4.2.2).

CHAPTER 3

Modeling Arguments

In this chapter we discuss structural models for arguments, as they have been proposed in the field of argumentation theory. Models describe the components of an argument, such as the 'standpoint' in our definition from Section 1.1.1. Models differ in how many components they distinguish, and how they connect these components. Various names are used; we will generally refer to the *standpoint* as a *claim*. There is no single best model: Approaches to argumentation depend on the type of text and the task. Argumentation theory itself is interdisciplinary, and argumentation mining has been influenced by rhetoric, informal logic, and formal logic.

In the following, we first discuss argument components and structure (Section 3.1) and then take a look at the way in which argumentation extends classical inference with defeasible reasoning (Section 3.2). Next we introduce the notion of *argumentation scheme* (Section 3.3) and take a look at important types of argument models (Section 3.4). The chapter closes with a short discussion of early artificial intelligence approaches to representing arguments (Section 3.5), and an overview of argument *mapping* (Section 3.6) techniques.

3.1 ARGUMENT COMPONENTS AND STRUCTURE

Main components of arguments   Earlier we said that that an argument consists of claims made by the speaker, along with material they present in support of their claim, as well as possible counter-considerations, and their refutations. We can further define certain terminology used for argumentation structures. An argument structure is comprised of a constellation of propositions related to a *claim* (also called *standpoint* or *conclusion*), which is the proposition that the argument seeks to establish. Other propositions are used as *premises*, which are brought to bear, in *support* of the conclusion, and sometimes also to *attack* it. Any claim may play the role of final conclusion of some argument, and any conclusion can be made into a premise supporting further reasoning.

Diagramming arguments   Diagramming can represent an argument's structure. We saw one argument map in Figure 1.1 on page 7. We will give further examples of argument maps in Section 3.6 below.

Typically, an argument map represents propositions with some geometric shape such as circles and rectangles. Often there is no visual distinction between the proposition's role in the argument, whether it serves as a top-level claim and final conclusion or an intermediate one. Text representing the proposition may appear directly in the diagram (as we will see in Figure 3.7 below) or may be referenced to a key (for instance Figure 1.1 refers back to the text in Example 1.6). Support and attack relationships between the propositions are distinguished (with different line types, as in Figure 1.1, or using colors, as in Figure 3.7); sometimes only support or attack relationships are given.

Linked, convergent, serial, divergent   The structure of arguments, including the relation of argument components to one another can also be considered, as shown in Figure 3.1. Various proposals have been made. The essential distinction is whether there are multiple distinct premises that each stand alone to support a claim (convergent), whether two reasons together strengthen each other (linked), or whether a chain of reasoning is required where one premise supports an interim conclusion, which is the premise of the next argument (e.g., if p, then q, if q then r; serial), or one premise that supports two or more conclusions (divergent). Some graphs and examples are shown compactly in Wei and Prakken [2012]. Also, Henkemans [2000] surveys historical approaches and enduring philosophical questions about distinguishing these structure types. Subtleties do arise; for instance, Grennan [1997, pp. 71-72], "[S]ome arguments contain assertions that have a bearing on conclusion support but are not direct evidence for the conclusion." This is an issue of relevance of conclusions, related to the knowledge of the hearer.

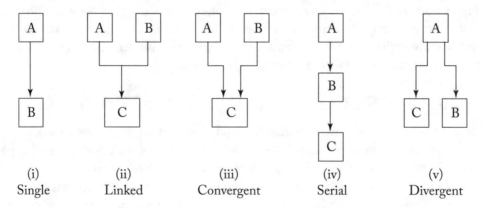

| (i) | (ii) | (iii) | (iv) | (v) |
| Single | Linked | Convergent | Serial | Divergent |

Figure 3.1: Common basic argument structures based on Rahwan [2008].

Granularity   Arguments are recursive, zippered structures. The conclusion of one argument may be the premise of the next argument, building a more complex tree. Wyner et al. distinguish between three different kinds of argument based on the features of this tree: an Argument (capital A) that cannot be subdivided into any other parts that are still arguments ("a one-step reason for a claim"); a Case, with only supporting evidence for a claim ("a chain of reasoning leading toward a claim"); and a Debate which has both supporting and conflicting evidence ("reasons for and against a claim (Debate)") [Wyner et al., 2015, p. 51].

When we want to think about the internal structure of the argument, this distinction is helpful. The internal structure of an Argument of this sort is just made up of the components we discussed above. By contrast, a Case must have multiple inference steps, but without any attacks on the central claim. And the Debate can be broken into two Cases: one for the claim and one against it.

3.2 ARGUMENTATION EXTENDS CLASSICAL INFERENCE WITH DEFEASIBLE REASONING

Argumentation extends classical inference, enabling tentative conclusions. By contrast, in classical logic, the conclusion is guaranteed to hold whenever the premises hold, using *classical inference rules*.

Defeasibility   Argumentation is defeasible: it considers tentative conclusions, which can be revised when new information comes to light. That is, argumentation admits belief revision, is *defeasible*, and follows a *non-monotonic* logic. See Koons [2017] for more on defeasible reasoning.

Classical inference rules   In classical logic, however, the conclusion is guaranteed to hold whenever the premises hold, using *classical inference rules*, such as syllogism, modus ponens, and modus tollens.

A *syllogism* derives a conclusion via inference from two premises which share a related term. For example:

(3.1)   Socrates is a man; (*Minor premise*)
Every man is mortal; (*Major premise*)
Therefore, Socrates is mortal. (*Conclusion*)

A syllogism's premises are called minor and major. This distinction is based on which term they contain; the minor term is identified by the subject ('Socrates') of the conclusion while the major term is identified by the predicate ('mortal') of the conclusion.

The rule *modus ponens* enables deriving the consequent, or right-hand side of a conditional:

(3.2)   Given if p, then q.
Given p.
Therefore, q.

The rule *modus tollens* enables ruling out the antecedent, or left-hand side of a conditional:

(3.3)   Given if p, then q.
Given not q.
Therefore, not p.

See Prior [2006] for further examples. Argumentation theory has collected its own schemes, which can be considered as defeasible rules of inference. We discuss those next.

3.3   ARGUMENTATION SCHEMES

Argumentation schemes are patterns of everyday reasoning made up of propositions, a defeasible inference rule with the propositions as premises, and a conclusion (a proposition) inferred from the rule using the propositions.

An argumentation scheme expresses a defeasible inference rule for showing the acceptability of a standpoint. Various treatments of argumentation schemes, highlighting different aspects, have been given, with wide variation in the number of schemes. A recent and authoritative overview of influential approaches can be found in Walton et al. [2018].

Walton's argumentation schemes   Walton, Reed, and Macagno's Compendium of Schemes collects 60 schemes, along with critical questions that identify the potential points of weakness in an argument [Walton et al., 2008]. One such scheme is *Position to Know*.

Major Premise: Source *a* is in a position to know about things in a certain subject domain *S* containing proposition *A*.

Minor Premise: *a* asserts that *A* (in Domain *S*) is true (false).

Conclusion: *A* is true (false).

They list three critical questions.

1. Is *a* in a position to know whether *A* is true (false)?

2. Is *a* an honest (trustworthy, reliable) source?

3. Did *a* assert that *A* is true (false)?

Note here that the structure of different premises may need to be distinguished, e.g., the minor premise "serves as independent evidence or support for the conclusion" whereas the major premise does not [Grennan, 1997, p. 75].

Pragma-dialectic argumentation schemes   The classical pragma-dialectic approach classifies schemes into three types: sign, comparison, and cause [Hitchcock and Wagemans, 2011]. As a prototypical example, the "argument from comparison" scheme compares two situations and uses their similarity as a justification. Analyzing "It's not at all necessary to give James 10 dollars allowance, because his brother always got just 5 dollars a week." Hitchcock and Wagemans [2011, p. 187] write:

1 James (X) does not need 10 dollars a week (Y).

1.1 James' brother (Z) did not need 10 dollars a week (Y).

1.1′ James (X) is similar to James' brother with respect to the sum needed for their weekly

allowance
along with three critical questions for the comparison scheme:

1. Are the things that are compared actually comparable?

2. Are there enough relevant similarities between the things that are compared?

3. Are there any relevant differences between the things that are compared?

The other two main pragma-dialectic schemes, sign and cause, have similar considerations; variants and subtypes of each of the three types are recognized.

Argumentum model of topics Rigotti and Morasso's Argumentum Model of Topics (AMT) [Rigotti and Greco Morasso, 2010] draws on the study of *topoi* and *loci*, from ancient and medieval rhetoric. (See also Rapp [2010, Section 7].) The name of a scheme, such as cause-effect or analogy, is only the first level: the procedural starting point. At the second level, certain inference patterns that Rigotti and Morasso call 'maxims' are needed. In the third level, each of these maxims activates a rule, such as modus ponens or modus tollens. An example maxim is the following [Rigotti and Greco Morasso, 2010, p. 495].

1. If a certain goal is to be achieved, it is reasonable to activate a cause chain allowing to reach it.

2. If no causal chain is available, the goal cannot be achieved.

3. If a certain behavior is not oriented toward a goal (as it cannot be considered a proper human action), it cannot be endowed with any property typically congruous with human action (responsibility, merit, guilt, and so on).

Semantic analysis is used to fill the gap between the scheme type and the maxim. For instance, in the AMT analysis shown in Figure 3.2, an assumption in the audience's common ground ('endoxon', following Aristotle) is made explicit, namely that the national holiday and New Year's Eve are comparable ("belong to the same functional genus"). Their approach is more fine-grained than others, since a particular maxim must be specified and its applicability justified.

3.4 TYPES OF ARGUMENT MODELS

Bentahar, Moulin, and Bélanger classify argumentation models into rhetorical models, dialogical models, and monological models [Bentahar et al., 2010]. These types of models are complementary, each coming from different perspectives, as shown in Table 3.1. Monological models view arguments as tentative proofs, and link premises and claims to describe the microstructure: the internal inference structure of each argument. Rhetorical models view arguments based on an audience's perception, and link whole arguments in a rhetorical structure emphasizing the

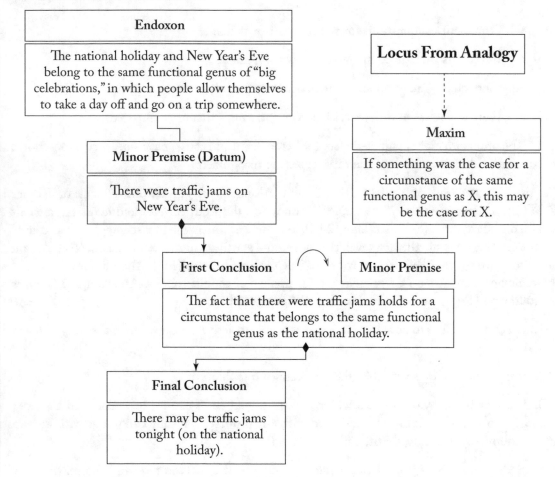

Figure 3.2: An example argument using the Argumentum Model of Topics based on Rigotti and Greco Morasso [2010, p. 499].

persuasion structure of arguments. Finally, dialogical models view arguments through the lens of defeasible reasoning and link whole arguments in a macrostructure: the dialogical structure.

Next, we will cover some prototypical models exemplifying the monological, rhetorical, and dialogical perspectives.

Table 3.1: Bentahar, Moulin, and Bélanger's taxonomy of argumentation models, modified from Bentahar et al. [2010, p. 215]

Model Type	Argument Evaluation Based On	What is Linked	How They Are Linked	Structure
Monological	Tentative proofs	Premises, claims	Internal inference structure	Microstructure
Rhetorical	Audience's perception	Whole arguments	Persuasion structure	Rhetorical structure
Dialogical	Defeasible reasoning	Whole arguments	Dialogical structure	Macrostructure

3.4.1 EXAMPLES OF THE THREE TYPES

We now discuss the Toulmin model, the New Rhetoric, and the Dung model, which, respectively, exemplify monological, rhetorical, and dialogical models as described by Bentahar et al. [2010, pp. 213–5]. We also discuss the IBIS model, which does not fit neatly into these three types.

Toulmin model   One of the most influential models of argumentation, the Toulmin model, was first proposed by British philosopher Stephen Toulmin in 1958. This model takes a monological view of argumentation, focusing on the internal structure of an argument, which is viewed as a tentative proof. The Toulmin model has a detailed internal structure, as shown in Figure 3.3. In the model, a claim is defeasibly supported by its grounds (also called the data), according to some warrant. If necessary, the warrant may be further supported by a backing. Qualifiers or rebuttals can also be diagrammed, but are not required.

In Figure 3.3, the claim is "Anne now has red hair". Its grounds is "Anne is one of Jack's sisters". Its warrant is "any sister of Jack's may be taken to have red hair", which has the backing, "All his sisters have previously been observed to have red hair." Its qualifier is "presumably". Its rebuttal is "unless Anne has dyed/ gone white/ lost her hair...".

Argument mapping and education have been among the areas influenced by the Toulmin model. Furthermore, it has been taken up in Computational Linguistics and—with modifications—used for annotating texts by Habernal and Gurevych [2017]; we will introduce that work in the next chapters.

The New Rhetoric   Perelman and Olbrechts-Tyteca's 1969 book *The New Rhetoric: A Treatise on Argumentation* has been very influential. It takes persuasion and audience as central concerns:

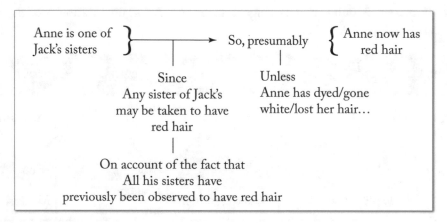

Figure 3.3: Sample Toulmin diagram based on Toulmin [2008].

argumentation, in their view, cannot be reduced to formal defeasible logic. Rather, arguments seek to persuade a given audience, or to convince the universal audience. Argumentation is thus a persuasive act involving two or more interlocutors, and it is "relative to the audience to be influenced" [Perelman and Olbrechts-Tyteca, 1969, p. 19]. From this perspective, "The goal of all argumentation...is to create or increase the adherence of minds to the theses presented for their assent." [Perelman and Olbrechts-Tyteca, 1969, p. 45]. We can describe this as a rhetorical approach to argumentation.

Dung's argumentation frameworks   Dung's influential 1995 paper [Dung, 1995] models the attack structure between arguments. Dung is not concerned with the internal structure of the argument or with support relationships: this is a macroscopic, dialogical view of argumentation in which constellations of arguments are evaluated based on defeasible reasoning.

An argumentation framework is a directed graph whose nodes represent arguments and whose edges represent relationships between arguments. More formally, Dung defines an argument framework as a pair $\langle S, attacks \rangle$ where S is a set of arguments and *attacks* is a binary relationship on the arguments contained in $S \times S$.

All arguments are considered to have the same strength and each attack is considered to be successful, unless it is in turn attacked. For instance, in Figure 3.4, A attacks B and B attacks C. In this situation, it is not coherent to accept both B and either its attacker (A) or what it attacks (B). More formally, acceptability involves means finding a subset which is conflict-free and collectively defends itself. A set S *defends* an argument a if for any argument b that attacks a, S contains an argument that attacks b. An argument a is *acceptable* with respect to the set that defends it.

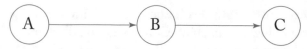

Figure 3.4: In this sample Dungian argumentation framework, A attacks B and B attacks C. The acceptable sets are: $\emptyset, \{A\}, \{B\}, \{C\}, \{A, C\}$.

Solvers for Dungian argumentation frameworks can compute the subsets (*extensions*) satisfying some property. In general, semantics (e.g., *credulous*, *skeptical*) are used to determine which coherent sets of arguments are jointly *acceptable*.

A number of formal argumentation approaches are modified from Dung's framework. Modifications may involve using probabilities or values to evaluate argument strength, or additional node types, or additional edge types. Several of these are being used to evaluate the acceptability of manually and automatically mined arguments, including *bipolar argumentation frameworks*, which allow support as well as attack; *abstract dialectical frameworks*, where each node gets its own acceptance condition; and the aforementioned Quantitative Argumentation Debate (QuAD) framework. These will be discussed when we present examples applying solvers in Section 8.3.1.

IBIS model   Not all models fit neatly into Bentahar's taxonomy. For instance, the IBIS model—Issue-Based Information Systems—was proposed in 1970 as a coordination and documentation system for political decision-making such as in urban planning [Kunz and Rittel, 1970]. It is a process for turning an unstructured problem (a controversial topic in a particular context) into a decision. Parts of the controversial topic are framed as *issues*—questions that can be debated with *arguments* either pro or con. *Questions of fact* can reference external information.

IBIS has inspired numerous systems, including a recent computational argumentation formalism called the *Quantitative Argumentation Debate (QuAD) framework* [Baroni et al., 2015] which connects issues with questions, answers, pros, and cons. QuAD frameworks can be evaluated with the Arg&Dec tool[1] [Aurisicchio et al., 2015], which we will return to in Section 8.3.1.

3.5   EARLY ARTIFICIAL INTELLIGENCE APPROACHES TO REPRESENTING ARGUMENTS

We now discuss two examples of classical artificial intelligence approaches to representing arguments from the 1980's and 1990's.

Robin Cohen   One of the earliest approaches to argumentation and natural language was Robin Cohen's 1983 dissertation [Cohen, 1983], which focuses on understanding argumen-

---

[1]http://www.arganddec.com (accessed May 28, 2018).

tative monologues by reconstructing their structure, as claim and evidence relations between propositions supporting a single main point. Cohen relies on discourse coherence and proposes cue words and metadiscourse used in arguing. The system focuses on "everyday arguments" [Cohen, 1983, p. 12], leaving aside quality and credibility judgments of logical validity.

Viewing an argument as a tree in which each claim is the parent of its evidence, Cohen [1987] presents a design for an argument understanding system. To determine where a proposition fits, Cohen uses three main considerations: coherence, cue words, and intended support relationships (that the hearer might not believe) in order to restrict the search space. Examples of Cohen's cue words ("linguistic clues") are shown in Figure 3.5.

P is prior proposition; **S** is the proposition with the clue

Category	Relation: P to S	Example
parallel	brother	First, Second
inference	son	As a result
detail	father	In particular
summary	multiple sons	In sum
reformulation	son (& father)	In other words
contrast	brother or father	On the other hand

Figure 3.5: Cohen's semantic classes for clue interpretation based on Cohen [1987].

Argument units   OpEd—an early question-answering system—used what were called 'Argument Units' such as the one shown in Figure 3.6. These "represent patterns of support and attack relationships among beliefs" [Alvarado, 1990, p. 9]. The clearest treatment is found in Chapter 4 of Alvarado [1990]. "AUs encode language-free and domain-free knowledge which can be instantiated to argue about plans in any domain" (p. 119).

3.6   ARGUMENT MAPPING

Argument maps are diagrams used to help make sense of complex arguments. An argument map separates arguments into the various components. Such maps have been manually constructed for 150 years, particularly in philosophy, and came into legal argumentation in the early 20th century [Walton, 2005]. Argument maps can show the big picture—which is sometimes quite big, such as Robert Horns' large-scale map of the artificial intelligence debate. Titled "Can Computers Think?", and exploring 50 years of philosophical argument, the map spreads over 7 poster-size pages and covers over 800 arguments presented by more than 300 people[2] [Horn, 2003].

[2]http://debategraph.org/Details.aspx?nid=75 (accessed May 28, 2018).

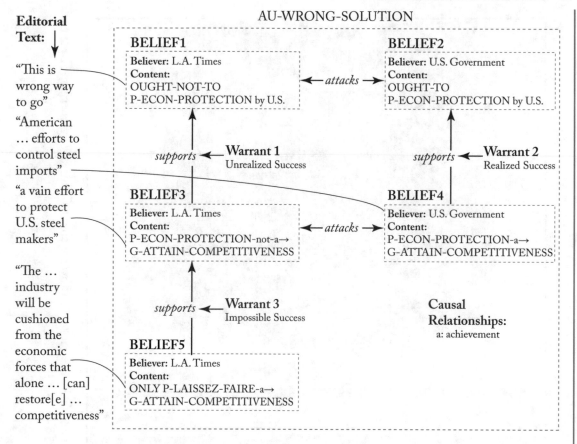

AU-WRONG-SOLUTION

Editorial Text:

"This is wrong way to go"

"American … efforts to control steel imports"

"a vain effort to protect U.S. steel makers"

"The … industry will be cushioned from the economic forces that alone … [can] restore[e] … competitiveness"

BELIEF1
Believer: L.A. Times
Content:
OUGHT-NOT-TO
P-ECON-PROTECTION by U.S.

← *attacks* →

BELIEF2
Believer: U.S. Government
Content:
OUGHT-TO
P-ECON-PROTECTION by U.S.

supports ← **Warrant 1** Unrealized Success

supports ← **Warrant 2** Realized Success

BELIEF3
Believer: L.A. Times
Content:
P-ECON-PROTECTION-not-a→
G-ATTAIN-COMPETITIVENESS

← *attacks* →

BELIEF4
Believer: U.S. Government
Content:
P-ECON-PROTECTION-a→
G-ATTAIN-COMPETITIVENESS

supports ← **Warrant 3** Impossible Success

Causal Relationships:
a: achievement

BELIEF5
Believer: L.A. Times
Content:
ONLY P-LAISSEZ-FAIRE-a→
G-ATTAIN-COMPETITIVENESS

Figure 3.6: An Instance of the "Wrong Solution" Argument Unit based on Alvarado [1990, p. 90].

Determining the argument made by a given text, however, is typically a complex matter. Interpretation decisions need to be made when mapping a typical text, based in part on how explicit and coherent the text is. Argument maps may also be constructed in the process of writing a document. For example, the argument map shown in Figure 3.7 was created by Sebastian Cacean and Gregor Betz [Betz and Cacean, 2012a][3] while writing a report for the German Ministry of Education and Research about ethical aspects of climate engineering [Betz and Cacean, 2012a]. Boxes in the figure indicate theses/central claims (white background), and

[3] http://www.argunet.org/2013/05/13/mapping-the-climate-engineering-controversy-a-case-of-argument-analysis-driven-policy-advice/#more-179 (accessed May 28, 2018).

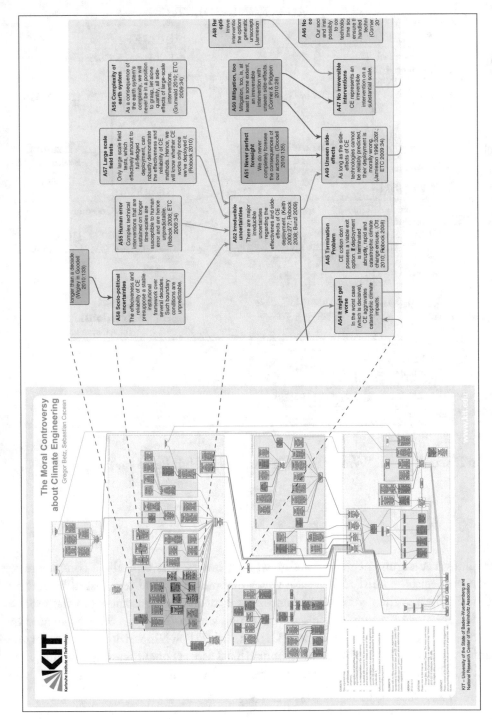

Figure 3.7: An excerpt from the argument map entitled "The moral controversy about Climate Engineering" [Betz and Cacean, 2012b], used with permission.

arguments both for (blue) and against (yellow) climate engineering. Their theses and arguments are given short titles and labels (starting with T or A respectively). Arrows in the figure indicate support (green) and attack (red) relationships between theses and arguments or pairs of arguments. Subarguments are collected together in dashed boxes. The inset in Figure 3.7 shows part of the "ethics of risk" subargument.

3.6.1   APPLICATIONS OF ARGUMENT MAPPING

Argument maps have been used in a variety of applications. Dialogue mapping is an approach to group deliberation that iteratively develops argument maps during a meeting [Conklin, 2006]. Tim Van Gelder reports that argument maps both encode knowledge and make it "readily recoverable for anyone in the future" [Van Gelder, 2003, p. 114]. These maps make the arguments and their counterarguments visible all at once, which can help with decision-making and can help retain and revisit the rationale for a previously taken decision. Such maps also make it possible to see more of an argument than the average person can hold in their head at one time, making it possible to think more critically and with more detachment from a particular way of expressing a claim or rationale or a particular speaker who put it forward [Van Gelder, 2003]. In particular, with external maps "it is safer to make a case against an idea because it isn't an attack on the person who suggested it" [Conklin, 2006, p. 175].

Structured arguments are used to construct safety cases or assurance cases for critical industries such as nuclear plants, airplanes, trains, automobiles, and medical devices; for examples, see Rinehart et al. [2015, pp. 23-62]. Several different argument mapping structures are used [Rinehart et al., 2015], including the Goal Structuring Notation [Spriggs, 2012] (specified in a 2011 standard [Attwood et al., 2011]), the Claims-Argument-Evidence graphical format, which links evidence to claims based on some sort of inference structure, which CAE refers to as the 'argument', or sometimes 'argument approach' [Bishop and Bloomfield, 1998].[4]

Recently, live radio debates have been mapped in real-time by a team at the University of Dundee. On the British Broadcasting Corporation radio program Moral Maze, panelists debate ethical issues related to a recent news story. Using a touch screen they call the Argument AnalysisWall [Bex et al., 2013], a team of argumentation analysts have collaborated to map radio debates as shown in Figure 3.8. The process starts with real-time transcripts, which are chunked into components by segmentation analysts, and then a team of 8 analysts have connected these components into supporting and conflicting arguments [Bex et al., 2013].[5]

Argument maps were used to express stakeholders' opinions, based on interviews and surveys in the EcoBioCap project [Tamani et al., 2014]. A map of the relationship between 11 arguments around food packaging was developed using data from interviews and surveys of stakeholders. Besides conflicts and attacks, the system considers preferences, which it resolves

---

[4]https://www.adelard.com/asce/choosing-asce/cae.html (accessed May 28, 2018).
[5]For a video of the process, see https://www.youtube.com/watch?v=8iELLjHAjEc (accessed May 28, 2018). Annotated Moral Maze data is available from http://corpora.aifdb.org/index.php (accessed May 28, 2018).

Figure 3.8: Analysts mapping a BBC radio debate in real time on the AnalysisWall at the Center for Argument Technology, Dundee, Scotland. Photo from http://www.arg-tech.org/index .php/projects/argument-analysis-wall/ (accessed May 28, 2018); online representation of the ultimate argument map is available at http://aifdb.org/argview/789 (accessed May 28, 2018), used with permission.

into 'justified preferences' using computational reasoning with Argumentation Service Platform with Integrated Components (ASPIC) and DLR-Lite. We will return to computational reasoning systems in Section 8.3.1.

Argument maps also have a potential use in medical decision-making. Typically, argument maps have been made from text. Data tables that have come from text can also be seen as a starting point. Hunter and Williams have modeled medical evidence from published clinical guidelines for treatments for 3 conditions—glaucoma, hypertension, and hypertension during pregnancy [Hunter and Williams, 2012]. They use argument maps to connect pairs of possible treatment options: arrows in the graph go from the preferred treatment to the disprefered treatment, functioning as attack relations. They define a formal semantics over the graph and calculate overall preferred treatments (a 'superiority graph') given up to 25 treatment pairs. A tutorial [Hunter and Williams, 2015] further explains their approach. Noor et al. [2017] take an analogous approach for reasoning about side effects and experiences, using argument graphs developed from patients' reviews on medical forums.

3.6.2   ARGUMENT MAPPING TOOLS

Numerous tools for argument mapping are available. While even explicitly mapping an argument on paper can enable a clearer understanding of a topic, many computational tools offer additional computational support such as calculating the consistent results as we will discuss in Section 8.3.1.

Next, we briefly review seven representative argument mapping tools; this is just a small selection of a diverse and crowded field of tools. For more comprehensive reviews of tools, see Scheuer et al. [2010], which covers computer-supported learning, and Schneider et al. [2013a] which focuses on web-based tools.

- AGORA-net[6] [Hoffmann, 2011] is free, collaborative web-based argument visualization software that aims to help people recognize good reasoning. The system provides four argument schemes: modus ponens, modus tollens, disjunctive syllogism, and not-all syllogism. Sample maps can be viewed online with Adobe Flash. Its creator characterizes the underlying method as "requir[ing] logical validity as a normative standard for the construction of arguments" [Hoffmann, 2011, p. 151]. Curriculum development has been a focus of the project; for instance AGORA-net has been used to teach engineering ethics in Russian Universities and the software is available in five common world languages.

- The Adelard Safety Case Editor (ASCE)[7] [Emmet and Cleland, 2002] is primarily used in safety assurance, and can use the common formats of Goal Structuring Notation and Claims-Argument-Evidence.

- Argunet[8] [Schneider et al., 2007] is an open source (GNU General Public License v2) cross-platform editor that can be used as standalone system or with a shared server. In Argunet, sentences are the basic elements, which are connected together into arguments. Support and conflict relationships are visually distinguished, and the user can add descriptions for any inference patterns they wish. Individual arguments appear in argument maps which may be part of larger debates. The debating system can be used by multiple users and maps made in Argunet can be displayed online with a JavaScript widget.

---

[6]http://agora.gatech.edu (accessed May 28, 2018).
[7]https://www.adelard.com/asce/choosing-asce/index/ (accessed May 28, 2018).
[8]http://www.argunet.org/editor/ (accessed May 28, 2018).

- Compendium[9] [Shum et al., 2006] is a widely adopted tool designed for dialogue mapping. It follows Issue-Based Information Systems [Kunz and Rittel, 1970] in distinguishing issues and position nodes, and adds additional types such as questions, references, and notes to create a rich hypertext network. Its online sibling Cohere[10] [Buckingham Shum, 2008] focuses on marking connections between pairs of ideas, which can then be visualized in a larger graph. Cohere has a rich selection of connections, including both negative ('challenges', 'is inconsistent with', 'refutes') and positive ('causes', 'improves on', 'is a value of', 'is an example of', 'is analogous to', 'is consistent with', 'predicts', and 'proves'), and can function as a bookmarking tool using the Cohere Firefox plugin. Both use the lesser GNU public license.

- DebateGraph[11] is an online mapping tool that has been used by media organizations to help users browse complex ideas, integrated with rich media. Maps can be viewed graphically or in outline format. Its main types are issues, positions, supportive arguments, and opposing arguments.

- Online Visualization of Argument (OVA)[12] [Snaith et al., 2010] facilitates analysis of web pages. Various semantics can be automatically applied to compute winning/losing arguments. It has been adapted into OVA+ [Janier et al., 2014] to provide particular support for a dialogue-based argument annotation system called Inference Anchoring Theory (see Section 4.1, page 50).

- Rationale[13] [Van Gelder, 2007] and its cousin bCisive[14] are commercial argument mapping tools created by the Australian Austhink company and overseen by the Dutch parent company Critical Thinking Skills BV. Rationale is an online system focused on teaching critical thinking as well as essay writing while bCisive is designed for business decision making. Maps can be public or private. Different types of argument maps are supported; for instance, in writing-oriented maps concepts might connected with words such as *but*, *however*, and *because*.

3.6.3   FORMALIZING, SHARING, AND QUERYING ARGUMENT MAPS

With so many different argument mapping tools, approaches for sharing argument maps are needed. The best known format for sharing between computer tools is called the Argument Interchange Format (AIF). AIF is intended as a XML representation of key argumentation components. It is extensible, and has been used for formalizing, storing and sharing, and querying argument maps.

---

[9]https://github.com/CompendiumNG/CompendiumNG (accessed May 28, 2018).
[10]http://cohere.open.ac.uk/ (accessed May 28, 2018).
[11]http://debategraph.org/ (accessed May 28, 2018).
[12]http://ova.arg-tech.org (accessed May 28, 2018).
[13]https://www.rationaleonline.com (accessed May 28, 2018).
[14]https://www.bcisiveonline.com (accessed May 28, 2018).

Formalizing argument maps for interchange   Argument Interchange Format is a formal model—an ontology—introduced by an international group in 2006 [Chesñevar et al., 2006] to model the argument networks, communication locutions, and protocols for interchange between two participants or two software packages, and contexts such as agents and theories. AIF has provided a technological foundation for various experimental systems for supporting argumentation on the Web, such as ArgDF [Zablith, 2007] and argument blogging [Wells et al., 2009], as well as an interchange format for some of the argumentation mapping tools described above.

AIF core ontology includes information nodes (I-nodes) and scheme application nodes (S-nodes). Multiple extensions have been made to the original, core ontology. For instance, in 2007, Rahwan et al. [2007] added Form Nodes, which enables argumentation schemes (see Section 3.3) to be directly modeled within the graph. The AIF+ extension distinguishes between locutions and their propositional content, catering for dialogue and dialogue games [Reed et al., 2008b], and has been extensively used by the work of the Dundee group. Another recent extension, targeting social web discussions, adds Personal, Faction, Audience, Personal Support, Personal Conflict, and Implication nodes [Blount et al., 2016].

Storing and sharing   AIFdb provides a database implementation of AIF [Lawrence et al., 2012]. In practice, AIFdb is not just a database for storing but also a web interface providing worldwide-shared access to AIF-formatted data. Currently, a number of corpora, including the Araucaria database [Katzav et al., 2003] used for early argumentation mining work, have been translated into AIF and published online[15] [Lawrence et al., 2012]. Reed et al. [2017] reports that the current database stores 70 corpora containing 11,000 arguments (60,000 claims; 1.2 million words), with source materials in 14 different languages, with a variety of different scripts. We will discuss corpora further in Chapter 4.

Querying   Complex queries are possible from arguments expressed in AIF. A higher-level query language called ArgQL uses the Resource Description Framework representation of AIF to define queries using the SPARQL standard, for instance "Find arguments which 'defend' (attack their attackers) all arguments with conclusion 'cloning is immoral'." [Zografistou et al., 2017] or "Match pairs of arguments whose premise sets join each other." ArgQL enables users to directly query for Argument, Debate Graph, Path, Attack, Support, Rebut, Undercut, Endorse, and Back, or any combinations.

---

[15]http://corpora.aifdb.org/index.php (accessed May 28, 2018).

CHAPTER 4

Corpus Annotation

As in other branches of natural language processing, the majority of research on argumentation mining is based on corpora, and usually on annotated corpora. Creating them has therefore been a focus of interest in the years around 2015 when the field gained momentum. In this chapter, we first describe some relatively generic annotation schemes[1] that have been suggested and used for corpus annotation (Section 4.1), and then we provide brief descriptions of some corpora that have been made freely available to the research community (Section 4.2). There is some overlap, as several of these corpora use schemes we describe in Section 4.1, but for most corpora there are separate, purpose-specific schemes being used.

4.1 ANNOTATION SCHEMES

The general considerations on the structure of argumentation, such as those outlined in the previous chapter, have been translated in various ways into schemes for annotating instances of arguments found in text. In the following, we present some schemes that have been used for corpus annotation. As they were devised with different applications and purposes in mind, the reader should be prepared for some notable differences between the various approaches.

The microtext scheme   Following up on early pilot studies by Stede and Sauermann [2008], a tree-oriented annotation scheme was proposed by Peldszus and Stede [2013]. It is inspired by the work of Freeman [1991, 2011], whose perspective on argumentation is that of a hypothetical dialectical exchange between the *proponent*, who presents and defends his claims, and the *opponent*, who critically questions ('attacks') them in a regimented fashion. Every move in such an exchange corresponds to a structural element in the argumentation tree.

The argumentation structure annotation scheme then distinguishes between simple support (one ADU provides a justification of another) and *linked* support, where several ADUs collectively fulfill the role of justification; in other words, one of the ADUs in isolation would not be sufficient to perform the support. (This distinction was also made by Rahwan [2008] in the basic constellations shown earlier in Figure 3.1.) On the side of attacks, the annotation scheme separates rebutting (denying the validity of a statement) and undercutting (denying the relevance of a statement in supporting another).[2] The annotation scheme is designed in such a

---

[1]There is a slightly unfortunate parallel between the terms 'argumentation scheme', as used for instance in Chapter 3 and 'annotation scheme', but we see no way of avoiding one or the other term here.
[2]For illustration, see Examples 6.6 and 6.7 on page 86.

way that the fine-grained representations may also be reduced to coarser ones that, for example, only distinguish between support and attack, as it is customary in most other schemes.

In Figure 4.1, we show the representation for a short sample text. The nodes of this tree represent the propositions expressed in text segments (grey boxes), and their shape indicates the role in the dialectical exchange: round nodes are the proponent's nodes, square ones are the opponent's nodes. The arcs connecting the nodes represent different supporting (arrow-head links) and attacking moves (circle/square-head links): 3 undercuts the attack of 2 on 1; 4 and 5 perform a linked support on 1. By means of recursive application of relations, representations of relatively complex texts can be created, identifying the central claim of a text, supporting premises, possible objections, and their counter-objections, with potential sub-structures involved in various places. As one example, 'serial support' originates when one segment supports another one, which in turn supports a third segment (see also Figure 3.1).

This annotation scheme is described in detail in Peldszus and Stede [2013], where illustrative examples for the various relevant constellations are given. It was encoded in specific annotation guidelines, and has been applied to German texts from the 'Potsdam Commentary Corpus' [Stede and Neumann, 2014], and to the German/English 'microtext' corpus (see the next section). A dedicated, web-based annotation tool was developed for building tree structures over text spans.[3] As for inter-annotator agreement, Peldszus [2014] reports κ=0.83 for well-trained expert annotators that start from pre-segmented text.

The persuasive essay scheme   The annotation scheme underlying the persuasive essay corpus by Stab and Gurevych [2014a] (see the next section) shares the basic idea of building a claim-rooted tree with the microtext scheme. There are a few differences, though. The first results from the genre: Each persuasive essay, according to the scheme, has one segment called the *major claim*, which is the thesis that the essay argues for. It tends to be found in the first paragraph of the essay. Independently of that, claim/premise trees are annotated on the level of paragraphs, i.e., one tree is built for each paragraph of an essay.

While there are no explicit proponent/opponent labels, the relation between premise and claim has to be labeled as either support or attack, which therefore also implicitly captures the difference in the roles of segments. This annotation scheme does not distinguish any further subcategories of support or attack. The reported inter-annotator agreement in terms of Krippendorf's unitized α is 0.72 for argument components and 0.81 for relations.

The science scheme   Kirschner et al. [2015] addressed a genre that, somewhat surprisingly, so far has not received very much attention in the argumentation mining community: scientific papers, in particular journal papers from educational research. A pilot study was performed on 24 papers (in German), with an average length of about 10 pages.

The argumentative units are always sentences, and they are not labeled with roles. Four relations are used to link the units: Support and Attack on the one hand, and Sequence and

[3]http://angcl.ling.uni-potsdam.de/resources/grapat.html (accessed May 28, 2018).

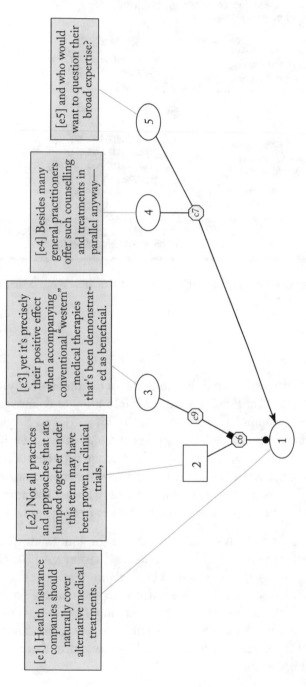

Figure 4.1: Sample representation of argumentation structure according to the microtext scheme [Peldszus and Stede, 2013].

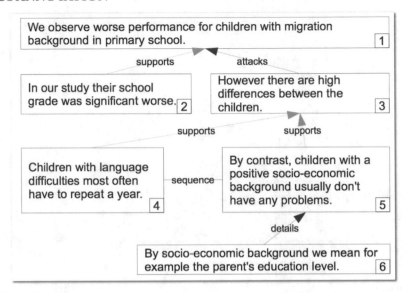

Figure 4.2: Sample representation of an argument in scientific literature based on Kirschner et al. [2015, p. 1]'s science scheme.

Detail on the other. The latter are inspired from theories of discourse structure (cf. Section 2.6): Detail is used when "A is a detail of B and gives more information or defines something stated in B without argumentative reasoning" [Kirschner et al., 2015, p. 5], and Sequence applies when "two (or more) argument components belong together and only make sense in combination" (p. 5). For illustration, Figure 4.2 shows a sample analysis of an argument along these lines. An interesting contribution of the work is a proposal for a new way of measuring inter-annotator agreement for graphs.—In general, however, it is not clear whether the authors indeed require the full power of graphs for their representations or whether trees are in fact sufficient.

The Modified Toulmin Scheme In selecting a scheme for annotating their corpus of user-generated web discourse (see next section), Habernal and Gurevych [2017] started from the Toulmin model (see Section 3.4.1). They kept its basic assumption that the argumentative role of a unit fully determines its position in the argument representation—and thus the scheme has no need to explicitly annotate any relations between units. In contrast to the microtext and persuasive essay schemes, it is hence not possible to build recursive structures (as needed for 'serial support' or complex counter-attack constellations). The annotation therefore is a flat labeling; an example is shown in Figure 4.3.

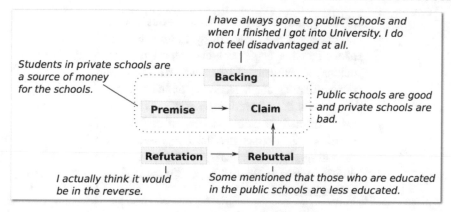

Figure 4.3: Diagrammatic representation of annotated argument in the Modified Toulmin Scheme based on Habernal and Gurevych [2017, p. 144].

However, Habernal and Gurevych did make a number of important modifications to the original Toulmin model. They removed the Qualifier and the Warrant, as these did not play a role in their corpus data. The notion of Backing was slightly redefined and now serves as 'additional evidence', which does not play the same role as a premise but still lends overall support to the argument. In order to account for counter-attacks, they introduce the unit type *Refutation*. And finally, to enable the annotation of texts where the claim is not explicit (which is often the case in their corpus), annotators were instructed to add an explicit statement of the author's stance, as they infer it from the text.

Since the annotation process consists of breaking the text into units and labeling them, annotator agreement was evaluated in terms of Krippendorff's unitized α; an overall value of 0.48 was achieved. Habernal and Gurevych [2017] provide an in-depth analysis of the various types of disagreement that they found.

The Cornell eRulemaking Scheme   While the majority of annotations on argumentative monologue text use trees, this is not entirely uncontroversial. Recently, Niculae et al. [2017] released a corpus of user comments on government rule making.[4] The authors argue that those texts are less 'well-formed' than those in, e.g., the microtext or the persuasive essay corpus, and that trees are not powerful enough to represent the structures adequately. Figure 4.4 shows a sample text and annotation, where unit c supports two other units, and furthermore there is no single root (claim).[5] The authors report that 20% of the comments in the corpus give rise to such

[4]The source website is http://regulationroom.org, and the corpus is available at http://joonsuk.org (accessed May 28, 2018).

[5]The support relation from c to a results from automatically adding the transitive closure over the links.

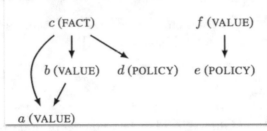

[Calling a debtor at work is counter-intuitive;]$_a$ [if collectors are continuously calling someone at work, other employees may report it to the debtor's supervisor.]$_b$ [Most companies have established rules about receiving or making personal calls during working hours.]$_c$ [If a collector or creditor calls a debtor on his/her cell phone and is informed that the debtor is at work, the call should be terminated.]$_d$ [No calls to employers should be allowed,]$_e$ [as this jeopardizes the debtor's job.]$_f$

Figure 4.4: Argumentation structure graph from the Cornell eRulemaking Corpus based on Niculae et al. [2017, p. 985].

non-tree representations, and that 28% of the comments have no links at all. Their annotation scheme uses specific argumentative role labels: *policy* and *value* for subjective judgments; *testimony* and *fact* for non-subjective personal experience and objective facts; and *reference* for URLs and citations. Relation types are *reason* and *evidence*.

Niculae et al. report annotator agreement in terms of Krippendorff's α: 0.65 for role assignment, and 0.44 for linking.

Inference Anchoring Theory   Inference Anchoring Theory (IAT) concerns what Asher and Lascarides [2003] called 'dialogue glue': the connections between utterances in dialogue, and the locutions put forward by these utterances. To describe the argumentative connections, IAT proposes illocutionary schemes that describe how speech acts are performed in dialogue. Example illocutionary schemes (see, e.g., Reed [2011]) are analogous to the argumentation schemes we discussed in Section 3.3, but they connect locutions to the logical arguments that they put forward. Their main elements are transitions between statements, indicating the illocutionary force (e.g., asserting, challenging, questioning, arguing).

IAT enables locutions in ordinary, everyday conversations to be translated into a dialogue game. Budzyńska and Reed [2011] gave the following example, which translates into the IAT model shown in Figure 4.5.

(4.1) (1.1) Bob says, The government will inevitably lower the tax rate.
       (1.2) Wilma says, Why?
       (1.3) Bob says, Because lower taxes stimulate the economy.

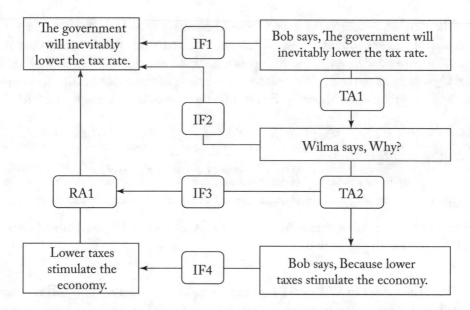

Figure 4.5: Sample annotation for Inference Anchoring Theory based on Budzyńska and Reed [2011]. IF=illocutionary force; RA=inference between propositions; TA=dialogue rule that relate communication acts.

Locutions may contain propositions, but properties of locution events (such as when or where they are spoken or by whom) may be important, so locution events themselves can also be used in arguments (e.g., about the speaker's communicative ability or motivation or to establish that someone really said something). Thus, Reed and Budzyńska [2011] describe pragmatics as the connection between the locutions and the logical arguments put forward.

4.2 CORPORA

In this section we list a number of annotated corpora that have been made available to the community, grouped in web-based and other text material. Notice that we do not strive for completeness here. In fact, a few other datasets are being briefly mentioned in other parts of the book.

4.2.1   ONLINE INTERACTIONS

IAC   The Internet Argument Corpus [Abbott et al., 2016] consists of posts from `4forums.com` discussions and has been annotated via Mechanical Turk. The goal of the annotation was to record the agreement or disagreement between posts. Annotators thus rated quote-response (Q-R) pairs with the level of dis/agreement using a scale from -5 (high disagreement) via 0 (no dis/agreement) to 5 (high agreement), reaching a Cohen κ of 0.47. This corpus is available for research.[6]

ABCD   The data of the Agreement by Create Debaters corpus [Rosenthal and McKeown, 2015] stems from `createdebate.com`. Posts were selected from the for-or-against portion, which contains two-sided debates, and each post is assigned to a side. Rosenthal and McKeown annotated Q-R pairs as to their dis/agreement on the basis of these side labels. An example for an instance of disagreement is shown in Figure 4.6. The corpus is available for research.[7]

Abortion is WRONG! God created that person for a reason. If your not ready to raise a kid then put it up for adoption so it can be with a good family. Dont murder it! Its wrong. It has a life. If you can have sex then you should be ready for the consequences tht come with it! **Side: *Against***
Those who were raped through the multiple varieties of means, are expected to birth this child although it was coerced rape. I don't think so. Taking a woman's right to choice is wrong regardless what a church or the government suggests. **Side: *For***

Figure 4.6: Sample data (disagreement) from the ABCD corpus [Rosenthal and McKeown, 2015, p. 169], used with permission.

AWTP   The Agreement in Wikipedia Talk Pages corpus [Andreas et al., 2012] is taken from 50 Wikipedia talk pages (used to discuss edits) and contains 822 posts, which were completely annotated with Q-R relations. The corpus is available for research.[8]

ComArg   373 user comments from `procon.org` and `idebate.org` have been collected by Boltužić and Šnajder [2014]. The comments address two different topics, for which 6 and 7 arguments, respectively, have been manually distilled. Comments are associated with a pro/con stance, and 2,249 comment-argument pairs are labeled with attack/support relations (recording whether it is explicit or implicit), or none (67%); see the examples in Figure 4.7. Fleiss κ for three annotators is 0.49. The corpus is available for research.[9]

Technical blogs   Ghosh et al. [2014] annotated blog comments on posts from `technorati.com`. Four technical topics were selected, represented by one original post and the first 100 responding comments. The annotation of 'callout' (a dis/agreeing reaction of a user) and 'target'

---

[6]`https://nlds.soe.ucsc.edu/iac` (accessed May 28, 2018).
[7]`http://www.cs.columbia.edu/~sara/data.php` (accessed May 28, 2018).
[8]`http://www.cs.columbia.edu/~sara/data.php` (accessed May 28, 2018).
[9]`http://takelab.fer.hr/data/comarg` (accessed May 28, 2018).

Comment	Argument	Label
All these arguments on my left are and have always been FALSE. Marriage is between a MAN and a WOMAN by divine definition. Sorry but, end of story.	*It is discriminatory to refuse gay couples the right to marry.*	s
Marriage isn't the joining of two people who have intentions of raising and nurturing children. It never has been. There have been many married couples whos have not had children. (...) If straight couples can attempt to work out a marriage, why can't homosexual couple have this same privilege? (...)	*It is discriminatory to refuse gay couples the right to marry*	s
(...) I truly believe that the powers behind the cause to re-define marriage stem from a stronger desire to attack a religious institution that does not support homosexuality, rather than a desire to achieve the same benefits as marriage for same sex couples. (...)"	*Gay couples should be able to take advantage of the fiscal and legal benefits of marriage.*	S

Figure 4.7: Sample comment/argument pairs from ComArg [Boltužić and Šnajder, 2014, p. 54], used with permission. s = implict support; S = explicit support.

(the specific phrase that the callout responds to) is based on Pragmatic Argumentation Theory [Van Eemeren et al., 1993]. An example is shown in Figure 4.8. The corpus is available for research.[10]

Web Discourse   Habernal and Gurevych [2017] built a corpus that is thematically restricted to six education-related topics and drawn from four sources: user comments on news articles and blog posts; forum posts; blog posts; and newswire articles. The texts are annotated using a variant of the Toulmin scheme (cf. Sections 3.4.1 and 4.1), and the corpus of 340 documents is available for research.[11]

4.2.2   OTHER CORPORA

Araucaria   An early corpus annotated with argumentation scheme information was AraucariaDB [Reed et al., 2008a]. It does not contain full texts, but arguments extracted from texts of a variety of different genres. The scheme annotation follows the approach of Walton, as described in Section 3.3. The corpus has since been incorporated into AIFdb.[12]

Argumentative Microtext Corpus   This corpus, described in Peldszus and Stede [2016b], consists of 112 short argumentative texts in German and English (translations), which are annotated

---

[10]https://salts.rutgers.edu/identifying-the-language-of-opposition-in-online-interactions/   (accessed May 28, 2018).
[11]https://www.ukp.tu-darmstadt.de/data/argumentation-mining/argument-annotated-user-generated-web-discourse/ (accessed May 28, 2018).
[12]http://corpora.aifdb.org/araucaria (accessed May 28, 2018).

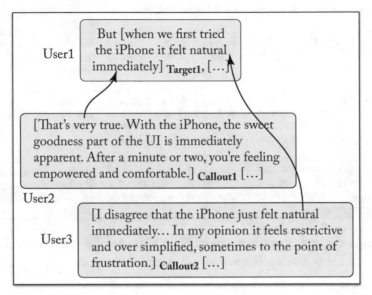

Figure 4.8: Sample callout/target annotation [Ghosh et al., 2014, p. 39], used with permission.

with complete argument structure trees involving support and several different attack relations, as described in Section 4.1. Later, additional annotation layers have been added: discourse structure and argumentation schemes. The corpus is available for research.[13] It has also been integrated into AIFdb.[14]

News Editorials   The Webis Editorial corpus [Al-Khatib et al., 2016b] contains 300 editorials from various English online news sites, which are annotated with argumentative discourse units and their role for the text function (such as Common Ground, Assumption, Anecdote). The corpus is available for research.[15]

Persuasive Essay Corpus   A corpus of annotated English argumentative essays was made publicly available by Stab and Gurevych [2014a]. The set consists of 90 texts (1,673 sentences) taken from the essayforum website.[16] The annotation comprises claims, premises, and support/attack relations, as outlined in Section 4.1. The authors computed inter-annotator agreement in terms

---

[13]http://angcl.ling.uni-potsdam.de/resources/argmicro.html (accessed May 28, 2018).
[14]http://corpora.aifdb.org/Microtext (accessed May 28, 2018).
[15]https://www.uni-weimar.de/en/media/chairs/computer-science-department/webis/data/corpus-webis-editorials-16/ (accessed May 28, 2018).
[16]http://www.essayforum.com (accessed May 28, 2018).

of Krippendorf's unitized α, which amounts to 0.72 for argument components and 0.81 for relations. The corpus is available for research.[17]

---

[17]https://www.ukp.tu-darmstadt.de/data/argumentation-mining/argument-annotated-essays/ (accessed May 28, 2018).

CHAPTER 5

Finding Claims

Unlike many of the standard tasks in NLP, argumentation mining is not a single unified process, but a constellation of subtasks, which are of different prominence depending on the goals of the underlying target application. For a (hypothetical) example, in order to obtain the gist of a Twitter conversation, it can be sufficient to extract claims and purported evidence material. By contrast, in order to run a deep analysis of argumentation strategies in left-wing vs. right-wing newspapers, the editorials ideally need to be mapped to a complete constellation of statements, their argumentative relationships, and the reasoning patterns underlying those relationships.

Therefore, similar to the surveys of Peldszus and Stede [2013] and Lippi and Torroni [2016a], we break the overall problem into a set of individual subtasks. In this chapter, we address the core task of finding the claim statements made by the writer, i.e., the central component of an argument. The next chapters will be concerned with finding additional components (viz., supporting and objecting statements), organizing them in a structured representation, and assessing some 'deeper' aspects of the argumentation.

Depending on the application scenario, before finding argument components it can be necessary to first filter a set of input texts as to whether they might contain an argument at all or not. Thus, in Section 5.1, we consider the task of classifying a text as argumentative or non-argumentative. This step applies both to full documents and to portions of text: many texts contain both argumentative and other material, which then can be separated.

Another potential preparatory step concerns the delimitation of potential minimal units of argument analysis, i.e., those units that may become argument components. In practice, this is not often operationalized as a separate task, but nonetheless we briefly address it in Section 5.2.

Then, in Section 5.3, we turn to the central task of identifying *claims* in a text: what does the writer argue *for*? Many implemented approaches combine this step with also finding the other core component of an argument—the supportive statements—but since for some purposes, just finding claims can be the most relevant problem, we discuss the two steps separately.

Throughout this and the following chapters, we mention both work involving human annotation (albeit to a smaller extent), and automatic processing, including relevant datasets, methods that have been applied, and the performance results that were achieved. Along the way we will see that there are several parallels to well-known NLP problems, such as opinion mining, semantic relation extraction, stance classification, and discourse parsing. Accordingly, many computational techniques can be borrowed from those areas.

5.1   CLASSIFYING TEXT AS ARGUMENTATIVE VS. NON-ARGUMENTATIVE

The question "Argumentative or not?" can be asked for a complete text document or for particular parts of a text. As a special case of the latter, portions of dialogic interaction can be deemed argumentatively-relevant. We discuss these three situations in turn.

5.1.1   DOCUMENT LEVEL

When dealing with 'traditional' kinds of documents, the task can be couched as one of *genre classification*. In linguistics, a genre is conceived as a class of texts that

- serve the same purpose,

- often have a typical structure in terms of 'zones' playing specific roles for the common purpose (cf. Section 2.6.2), and

- can have characteristic distributions of linguistic features.

Examples of fairly 'prototypical' genres are recipes, weather reports, and persuasive essays. In each case, we expect certain pieces of information, linearized in a suitable or conventionalized way.

Newspaper (and other print) text   In NLP, automatic genre classification has been applied, for instance, to newspapers, where opinionated text (editorials, letters to the editor) is to be distinguished from non-opinionated news. Even though not every opinionated text is necessarily argumentative, the ability to distinguish categories like these is of relevance to argumentation mining, too.

The early work of Karlgren and Cutting [1994] and Kessler et al. [1997] on the Brown Corpus aimed at distinguishing various categories from each other, with one setting being 'editorial' vs. 'reportage'. These researchers experimented with part-of-speech (PoS) tags, document and sentence length, type/token ratio, punctuation symbols, and frequencies of specific words that the authors considered relevant: 'therefore', 'I', 'me', 'it', 'that', and 'which'. Kessler et al. reported classification accuracies of 83% and 61% for reports and editorials, respectively.

Later work replaced linguistic analysis by bag-of-words [Freund et al., 2006] or bag-of-character-n-grams [Sharoff et al., 2010] models. Such knowledge-free approaches yielded very good results in the domains of the training data, but, as shown by Petrenz and Webber [2011], this idea is extremely vulnerable to shifts in topics and domains. Working with the *New York Times Annotated Corpus (NYTAC)*,[1] Petrenz and Webber reimplemented earlier approaches, built subsets of articles covering different topics, and demonstrated that the early work using linguistic features is more robust when the topics of the articles change.

[1] https://catalog.ldc.upenn.edu/ldc2008t19 (accessed May 28, 2018)

In the same spirit, Krüger et al. [2017] used texts with different topics, and they also varied the newspaper and the time of origin of the texts, by working with the Brown, NYTAC, and Wall Street Journal corpora. For distinguishing editorials and letters to the editor from news texts, they experimented with a large linguistic feature set and showed that it generally outperforms PoS and bag-of-lemma approaches. Among the most predictive features were first- and second-person pronouns, negation suffixes, and certain word classes such as sentiment words and communication verbs. The results differ quite a bit among the various settings they considered. We mention here just one: When classifying 'opinion' vs. 'news', trained on the mixed-topic WSJ corpus and tested on NYTAC 'medicine' articles, the F-score for the best model was 0.87.

Web text   To assist a user who is interested in different viewpoints on a controversial topic, Roitman et al. [2016] devised a document retrieval method for Wikipedia articles. First, this system finds articles that address the desired topic, by means of current information retrieval techniques. In a follow-up step, the document set is reranked according to its argumentative potential. To this end, the authors employ a manually-built list of words that can point to controversy, including 'justify', 'deny', and others.

Although Wikipedia text is relatively orderly, the majority of web text to be exploited for argumentation mining is generated by users and thus can pose well-known challenges for automatic processing. Habernal and Gurevych [2017] compiled a corpus of such texts, designed to cover a set of predefined topics within the domain of education. Their work includes an annotation study where contributions to online forums and user comments had to be judged as either persuasive or non-persuasive.[2] For a document to be considered persuasive, it also has to be on-topic, so that in effect a second classification dimension is mixed into the task. Three annotators labeled 990 documents and achieved a Fleiss κ of 0.59. This step lead to a gold-standard set of 524 persuasive on-topic documents. As a common source of disagreement, the authors note the presence of implicit claims or stances, thus involving interpretation on the side of the annotators. Habernal and Gurevych then built an automatic SVM classifier using lexical n-gram baseline features and obtained a macro-F score of 0.69. In a follow-up experiment, they used a rich feature set, but the results turned out to be worse than the baseline.

5.1.2   SUB-DOCUMENT LEVEL

In principle, the attribute of being 'argumentative' can also be applied to paragraphs or other stretches of text, but to our knowledge this has not been explicitly addressed in the research yet. Instead, the task is commonly tackled on the level of sentences or clauses.

---

[2]While in general not every argument aims at persuasion, within the genre considered here, 'argumentative' and 'persuasive' can be considered as referring to the same class of texts.

Sentences The majority of research on fine-grained argumentativity classification is concerned with finding sentences in monologue text, but the task has been framed in a variety of slightly different ways.

We begin with some pioneering work in argumentation mining by Moens et al. [2007]. They worked with texts from AraucariaDB [Reed et al., 2008a] and with court decisions from the European Court of Human Rights (ECHR), and as their first analysis step classified sentences as argumentative or not. (Some examples of argumentative sentences from the ECHR corpus are shown later in Figure 5.1 on page 65.) As features they used lexical (token n-grams, adverbs, verbs, modals, argumentative markers) and syntactic (punctuation, depth of parse tree, number of subclauses) features as well as some text statistics, such as length of sentence and position of sentence in the text. With multinomial naive Bayes and maximum entropy models, they achieved accuracies of 73% and 80%, respectively, for the two data sets.

Florou et al. [2013] worked with Greek texts concerning public policy-making, to identify sentences expressing a position toward a proposal. The authors specifically proposed that "future and conditional tenses and moods often indicate conjectures and hypotheses which are commonly used in argumentation techniques such as illustration, justification, rebuttal", and they studied these features in tandem with a manually compiled list of connectives signaling justification, explanation, deduction, rebuttal, and conditionals. With a C4.5 decision tree classifier, their best result is an F-score of 0.76 for a subset of the morphosyntactic and lexical features.

Among the first researchers applying the task to social media, Goudas et al. [2014] classified Greek sentences from blogs and other web sites as "containing an argument or not". They used a rich feature set including certain PoS distributions, position, and length features, manually selected cue words, the number of entities mentioned in previous sentences, as well as token n-grams. With a logistic regression classifier, they obtained an accuracy of 77%. Turning to Twitter, Dusmanu et al. [2017] used a feature set including n-grams, Twitter-specific tokens like emoticons, dependency triples, and sentiment information for classifying tweets as argumentative or not, and they report an F1-score of 0.78, obtained by a linear regression classifier.[3]

Al-Khatib et al. [2016a] suggest a distant supervision approach to classifying argumentative units: they automatically labeled text from idebate.org as argumentative or not, depending on which of the pre-defined components in the forum the text belongs to.[4] On this data, they train a classifier that uses n-grams, constituency syntax production rules, as well as various morphosyntactic features. They evaluated the model on the same type of data (obtaining an accuracy of 0.92), as well as on two other corpora: the persuasive essay corpus of Stab and Gurevych [2014a] and the web text corpus of Habernal and Gurevych [2017] (both mentioned in our list in Section 4.2.2). On those corpora, the accuracy is 0.67 and 0.88, respectively. The authors then also report results on cross-domain train/test experiments.

---

[3]The DART data set [Bosc et al., 2016a] contains 4,000 Twitter posts that annotators identified as non-/argumentative (defined as "(not) containing an opinion"). In addition, around 1,900 argumentative tweets were grouped by semantic similarity (topics) and then, within groups, pairwise linked via the relations support (446 tweets), attack (122), and unknown (1,323).

[4]The resulting corpus is available for research: https://www.webis.de/data (accessed May 28, 2018).

Student essays are another very popular genre for argumentation mining, where the ultimate goal is to evaluate the quality of the essay and hence of the argumentation therein. Following this direction, Song et al. [2014] posed the non-/argumentative distinction in a more specific way: they aimed to classify whether a sentence addresses a critical question of an argumentation scheme (in the sense of Walton, see Section 3.3) and can thus be considered argumentatively relevant. Features were n-grams of the sentence and the two surrounding ones, sentence position and length, PoS tag presence, and lexical overlap between the sentence and the writing prompt underlying the essay. The performance of their logistic regression model was measured by Cohen κ and was in the range of up to 0.5 in various train/test settings involving the same or different prompts.

While the approaches discussed thus far performed binary classification (argumentative or not), it is also possible to solve the problem as a byproduct of running a multi-class classifier that detects the specific argumentative role of a sentence, and also allows for a 'none' value. An example for this technique is the system by Stab and Gurevych [2014b], which is also trained and tested on student essays. Using a very rich set of features (structural, lexical, syntactic, and specific lexical cues) they experimented with several classification techniques, leading to a best result of 77.3% accuracy (macro-F 0.73) obtained by an SVM. The F-score for the class 'none' was 0.88. It turned out that the text-statistics and structural features are most helpful, which points to the role of conventionalized writing patterns in the genre of student essays. More details on this classifier will be provided below on page 70.

Sub-sentences   Presupposing that sentences are the proper unit for making the non-/argumentative distinction is for many use cases a simplification. As, for example, Palau and Moens [2009] or Lawrence et al. [2014] pointed out, a complex sentence may very well contain more than one argument component (i.e., a premise and a conclusion), and furthermore it may contain both argumentative and non-argumentative material, which ought to be kept separate when a fine-grained analysis is being targeted. For automatic analysis this is a complication, though, and hence it is not uncommon (see, e.g., Song et al. [2014]) to let human annotators mark arbitrary text spans as argumentative, but then for the automatic approach to reduce the fine-grained annotation to sentence-level.

Lawrence et al. [2014] argue that the initial step of non/-argument classification should be to separate the text into a sequence of individual 'propositions', by which the authors mean a sequence of words that is not necessarily delimited by punctuation or on syntactic grounds.[5] They tokenize the text, compute a feature set for each token, and train two classifiers for identifying tokens starting and ending a proposition, respectively. Features are the word, its PoS tag and length, and the two words preceding and following the word in question. The results were not very encouraging, though: on a cleaned version of a book chapter, this approach leads to an accuracy of 20% of correctly identified propositions (with exact matching), and the figure even

---

[5]Hence, like in the other work reported here, the authors are *not* aiming at any semantic analysis when speaking of 'propositions'.

decreases (surprisingly) as further chapters are added as training data. Lawrence et al. do not make the decision on the argumentativeness of propositions directly; rather it occurs as a side effect of classifying argument components (to be discussed in the next chapters). Any 'leftover' material from that step is considered non-argumentative.

5.1.3 SUMMARY

The performance figures quoted above are generally not bad, but when considering the features that are being used for classification, we largely find 'the usual suspects', including bag-of-words, PoS tag distributions, and positional and length information. This indicates that most approaches are geared toward separating a domain-specific document set in two parts, rather than to specifically capturing the linguistic signals of argumentativeness. Among the exceptions is the idea of manually compiling lists of words indicating controversy [Roitman et al., 2016], and of employing larger sets of linguistically motivated features. The latter approach, however, led to mixed results: it served the purpose of separating editorials from news in Krüger et al. [2017] but did not perform well on web text in Habernal and Gurevych [2017]. At any rate, the standard features appear to capture more general aspects of subjectivity and opinion, while not necessarily those of argumentation in particular. Hence, it is not clear yet whether a relatively domain-independent separation of argumentative and non-argumentative text spans can in fact be achieved using standard surface-based features.

5.2 SEGMENTING TEXT INTO ARGUMENTATIVE UNITS

The task of segmentation amounts to partitioning an argumentative text (or portion of text) into units that can later on be identified as playing a certain role—or none—in the argumentation. This is difficult, though, and from the perspective of NLP practitioners, it is tempting to effectively circumvent this segmentation step by using sentences as the 'default' unit. This strategy has two obvious consequences.

- Argumentative units that are smaller than sentences cannot be processed:

    (5.1) [Although the candidate has a few good ideas,] [you should not vote for her!]

- Argumentative units that consist of more than a single sentence are difficult to process:

    (5.2) [We need to tear the building down.]$_1$ [It is contaminated with asbestos.]$_2$ [In every single corner.]$_3$ [From the first to the last floor!]$_4$

The first problem is illustrated above in Example 5.1. The second problem can be particularly acute when working with user-generated texts, where the 'sentence' can be hard to define, and material between punctuation marks can be very short. In Example 5.2 (taken from Peldszus and Stede [2013]), statement 1 is the claim made by the speaker, and the evidence is provided by the sequence 2–4; there is no point in assigning an argumentative role to each sentence individually. Hence, a sentence-oriented system needs a way to distinguish between a sequence of sentences that each provide different evidence (and which play the same role for the argument), and a sequence of sentences that collectively form a single argumentative unit, as in Example 5.2.

So, in principle, the minimal units of argumentation may span multiple full sentences, or be shorter than a sentence, and thus we can characterize an *argumentative discourse unit (ADU)* as

> a span of text that plays a single role for the argument being analyzed, and is demarcated by neighboring text spans that play a different role, or none at all.

Human annotation   Taking our definition seriously would mean to assign the question of demarcating units to human annotators, and then try to reproduce it by automatic means. A few researchers took the first step and produced datasets where annotators have been asked to delimit the ADUs, without setting any restrictions on pre-defined unit candidates. For example, Wacholder et al. [2014], in their annotation of 'callout' and 'target' in online interactions (see Section 4.2), evaluated cases where annotators disagreed only by few tokens, and devised a strategy for deriving a gold standard from their annotations. Also, in the web text corpus of Habernal and Gurevych [2017] (see Section 5.3.5), boundaries were decided freely by annotators (yet in their automatic approach, the authors re-simplified the task to working with sentences only).

Computation   Among the few approaches that actually tackle the segmentation problem (instead of working with sentences as default units), some employ a syntax parser to supply clauses, which then serve as candidates for minimal units. For instance, the early work of Palau and Moens [2009] on legal text used syntactic clauses as units to be classified as argumentative or not. More recently, Persing and Ng [2016] used manually-devised rules for filtering parse trees and obtaining argumentative units for analyzing student essays. They worked with the corpus compiled by Stab and Gurevych [2014a] (see Section 4.2.2), which has been annotated on the level of clauses. Persing and Ng extracted ADU candidates from a parse tree, and in their evaluation, they accounted for boundary mismatches with two separate measures: one for exact matching, and one for partial matching, where success is defined as 50% of the tokens being in agreement. Their overall F-score for argument component identification is 0.57 with partial match and 0.47 for exact match, where the difference indicates the difficulties with exact ADU boundary detection. However, on the same corpus, Eger et al. [2017] perform a comparative study of various approaches, where the best one (an LSTM-based dependency parser) achieves an F1-score of 0.91 for finding the exact boundaries of argument components. The authors also provide an informative error analysis, and they point out that their result even beats the human agreement that was determined by Habernal and Gurevych [2017] as 0.89.

A recent thorough study of the segmentation problem was done by Ajjour et al. [2017]. These authors experimented with different feature sets as well as different machine learning models, and were also interested in cross-domain performance. For this reason they worked with three different available datasets (student essays, news editorials, and web discourse). In terms of features, it turned out that for in-domain analysis, bag-of-words features are most helpful (whereas embeddings did generally not help), while structural features (whether the token is at beginning/middle/end of a sentence/clause/phrase) proved most robust when training on one domain and testing on the other. Regarding machine learning approaches, a bidirectional LSTM achieved the best results in most cases, regardless of the domain or the features.

An important observation, however, was that the cross-domain scenario suffered from generally bad performance. The authors take this as an indication that the notion of ADU is not quite the same across different corpora, and hence across different annotation guidelines. Evidence for this hypothesis is the high variance that Aijour et al. found in the size of ADUs, ranging from clause-like segments in the newspaper data to the frequent occurrence of multiple sentences in a Wikipedia data set by Aharoni et al. [2014] (see Section 5.3.4).

5.3   IDENTIFYING CLAIMS

Detecting claims is the first of two indispensable tasks for any argumentation mining system (the second one being the detection of evidence or premises), and accordingly, a lot of work has been undertaken here. However, the reader should also be reminded that in many instances of argumentation, there is no explicit claim being formulated at all; instead the reader needs to derive it from what is said. In fact, Habernal and Gurevych [2017] report that in their social media data, almost half of all claims are only implicit. The ensuing problem of actually *inferring* claims is obviously very difficult and has not received much attention. Instead, the research has focused on the simpler task of only identifying explicit claims.

We can broadly distinguish two families of methods that have so far been applied to claim detection.

Classification   Given a minimal unit of analysis (in practice this is almost always a sentence, as described in the previous section), it can be classified in different ways.

- Binary classification: claim or no claim.

- Binary classification: claim/premise. When the overall goal of the system is restricted to finding claims and premises, thus adopting a coarse-grained definition of argument, then the classifier can directly distinguish between these two types of unit.

- Multi-class classification: When more types of argument components are being considered, they may be identified by a single classifier. Also, as pointed out earlier, one class can be 'none', so that the decision whether the unit is argumentative at all is also included here.

Sequence labeling   Some approaches tackle the identification of argument components (claims and possibly more) as an IOB labeling problem.[6] Thus, words are tagged as B-premise, B-claim, I-premise, I-claim, or O. Again, this can subsume the detection of non-argumentative material. Also, when claim detection is the *only* task performed by a system, it is trivially identical to the task of non-/argumentative classification. We will discuss this type of work in the present section (rather than above in 5.1), because the definitions used for 'claim' in this work are more specific than those generally adopted for 'argumentative'.

We organize the following summary by the genres being addressed, as these imply certain differences as to what exactly a 'claim' is.

5.3.1   LEGAL DOCUMENTS

{ [**SUPPORT**: The Court recalls that the rule of exhaustion of domestic remedies referred to in Article x of the Convention art. x obliges those seeking to bring their case against the State before an international judicial or arbitral organ to use first the remedies provided by the national legal system.
CONCLUSION: Consequently, States are dispensed from answering before an international body for their acts before they have had an opportunity to put matters right through their own legal systems.]

[**SUPPORT**: The Court considers that, even if it were accepted that the applicant made no complaint to the public prosecutor of ill-treatment in police custody, the injuries he had sustained must have been clearly visible during their meeting.
AGAINST: However, the prosecutor chose to make no enquiry as to the nature, extent and cause of these injuries, despite the fact that in Turkish law he was under a duty to investigate see paragraph above.
SUPPORT: It must be recalled that this omission on the part of the prosecutor took place after Mr Aksoy had been detained in police custody for at least fourteen days without access to legal or medical assistance or support.
SUPPORT: During this time he had sustained severe injuries requiring hospital treatment see paragraph above.
CONCLUSION: These circumstances alone would have given him cause to feel vulnerable, powerless and apprehensive of the representatives of the State.]
CONCLUSION: The Court therefore concludes that there existed special circumstances which absolved the applicant from his obligation to exhaust domestic remedies. }

Figure 5.1: Annotated text from an ECHR decision based on Palau and Moens [2009].

A prominent example for argumentation in legal texts is a court justifying its ruling in the decision document. In Figure 5.1, we reproduce an annotated example from Palau and Moens [2009], who worked on decisions of the European Court of Human Rights (ECHR). The bracketing indicates the hierarchical structure (to some extent): the first two paragraphs represent sub-arguments that both are given in support of the overall conclusion in the third paragraph. Thus, 'conclusion' in their terminology corresponds to what we call a 'claim'. For the central conclusions, the surface form "The court concludes that X" or some paraphrase can be regarded as typical; but notice that the interim conclusions can be descriptions of various kinds, in fairly general form.

---

[6]IOB stands for inside-outside-beginning. This method represents labeled "target" text spans by tagging the tokens of a text with one of the three letters: B = token is the beginning of a span; I = token is within a span ('inside'); O = token is not part of a span ('out'). As an example, consider finding all named entities (NE) in a text. B indicates that NE begins, I indicates that an NE continues: *We-O met-O in-O the-O New-B York-I City-I subway-O.*

Before the task of 'argumentation mining' was identified and labeled as such, legal case documents were analyzed from an information extraction point of view, in an attempt to distinguish the different functions of sentences, very similar to the 'argumentative zoning' idea of Teufel and Moens [2002], which we mentioned in Section 2.6.2. For example, Hachey and Grover [2006] annotated 'rhetorical roles' in judgments of the UK House of Lords, the goal being that of automatic summarization. Seven roles were distinguished, among them 'fact' (recounting the events triggering the legal proceedings), 'background' (citation of source of law material), and 'framing', which represents parts of the judge's argumentation. Using features similar to those of Teufel and Moens (cue phrases, location, entities, sentence length, quotations, thematic words), the authors obtained a micro-averaged F-score of 0.6 with an SVM classifier using all features, but, interestingly, a decision tree classifier using only location features achieved a considerably better score of 0.65.

Palau and Moens [2009] went a step further and distinguished the argumentative roles shown in Figure 5.1. Their SVM model for premise/conclusion classification takes as input sentences that have already been predicted to be argumentative (see our description in Section 5.1). The resulting F-scores for premise and conclusion are 0.68 and 0.74, respectively. Among their features are syntactic ones (subject type, main verb tense), domain-specific cues, token counts, position of sentence, and a contextual feature with the prediction for the previous and the following segment.

More recently, Rooney et al. [2012] proposed an SVM sequence kernel classifier as an alternative to the type of feature engineering done by Palau and Moens. The kernel compares subsequences of sentences, where a word is tagged with its root form and PoS label. These authors worked with the Araucaria DB dataset [Reed et al., 2008a], which contains arguments not only from legal documents but also from newspapers, advertising, and several other genres. The task is to label sentences as containing a premise (1299 instances in the annotated corpus), containing a claim (304 instances), being part of both a premise and a claim (161), or none (1686). Using 10-fold cross-validation, Rooney et al. report an overall accuracy of 0.65, which those authors consider as promising on the grounds of dispensing with sophisticated features. For claims, the result is particularly low, though (around 0.3).

In general, mining legal texts is a very difficult task. For an overview of the limitations of current IR systems and a sketch of necessary steps for automated argument retrieval, see Ashley and Walker [2013a].

5.3.2   INSTRUCTIONAL TEXT

Instructions, as they can be found in user manuals, often include advice and warnings; sometimes, these are backed up by an explanation designed to increase the reader's motivation to actually obey them. Here are some examples from Saint-Dizier [2012].

(5.3) Never put this cloth into the sun; otherwise it will shrink dramatically.

(5.4) It is essential that you switch off electricity before starting any operation. Electricity shocks are a major source of injuries and death.

As such, the structure and function correspond exactly to that of an argument, where the claim is of the specific type 'instruction' to do or not do something. Based on a corpus study covering French and English text, Saint-Dizier concluded that such constructions have a highly regular linguistic form, making it relatively easy to identify them. In his approach, a set of manually-constructed rules serves to identify both the 'claim' and the supporting statements. The rules exploit the linear order of the statements, and a set of common lexical patterns. These patterns may contain expressions on different levels of abstraction such as word form, word set, or part of speech. The rule language is processed by a dedicated text processing platform developed by the author, called <*TextCoop*>. Saint-Dizier reports recognition accuracies of 88%/91% (claim/support) for warnings and 79%/84% for advice.

5.3.3   STUDENT ESSAYS

Essays written by students in response to a given prompt are a target of NLP primarily for the application of automatically scoring them, or for supporting the human grader or peer-reviewer by automatically adding helpful markup (and thereby encouraging the grader to provide qualitative feedback). A significant portion of essays in education are persuasive, which Burstein and Marcu [2003, p. 457] define as requiring "the writer to state an opinion on a particular topic, and to support the stated opinion to convince the reader that the perspective is valid and well-supported."

We can broadly distinguish two lines of work here, which use slightly different labeling schemes.

Thesis and conclusion   Especially the American tradition of essay writing encourages students to make sure that their texts contain a 'thesis' and a 'conclusion'. According to Falakmasir et al. [2014, p. 254], a thesis "communicates the author's position and opinion about the essay prompt; it anchors the framework of the essay, serving as a hook for tying the reasons and evidence presented and anticipates critiques and counterarguments", whereas the conclusion "reiterates the main idea and summarizes the entire argument in an essay. It may contain new information, such as self-reflections on the writer's position."

Finding these two elements is made difficult by two features of student essays: as opposed to other genres like the legal texts discussed above, or scientific articles, student essays have little internal structure in terms of headings and subheadings. Furthermore, topics vary widely, and the students' theses are often substantiated by personal experience rather than by cited sources or authorities. Thus, the role of genre-specific wording can also be expected to be less helpful than for other texts. However, we will see that positional features can play an important role for the task.

"You can't always do what you want to do!," my mother said. She scolded me for doing what I thought was best for me. It is very difficult to do something that I do not want to do. <**Thesis**>But now that I am mature enough to take responsibility for my actions, I understand that many times in our lives we have to do what we should do. However, making important decisions, like determining your goal for the future, should be something that you want to do and enjoy doing.<**Thesis**>

I've seen many successful people who are doctors, artists, teachers, designers, etc. In my opinion they were considered successful people because they were able to find what they enjoy doing and worked hard for it. It is easy to determine that he/she is successful, not becaue it's what others think, but because he/she have succeed in what he/she wanted to do.

In Korea, where I grew up, many parents seem to push their children into being doctors, lawyers, engineer, etc. Parents believe that their kids should become what they believe is right for them, but most kids have their own choice and often doesn't choose the same career as their parent's. I've seen a doctor who wasn't happy at all with her job because she thought that becoming doctor is what she should do. That person later had to switch her job to what she really wanted to do since she was a little girl, which was teaching.

<**Conclusion**> Parents might know what's best for their own children in daily base; but deciding a long term goal for them should be one's own decision of what he/she likes to do and want to do. <**Conclusion**>

Figure 5.2: **Annotated essay from** Burstein and Marcu [2003, p. 457], used with permission.

Figure 5.2 shows an essay annotated with thesis and conclusion, taken from the early work of Burstein and Marcu [2003]. Their annotation rules state that both components can be one or more sentences, but no sub-sentences. For their decision-tree classifier, the authors used various positional features of sentences and paragraphs, syntactic clause types, and a set of manually-defined cue words. One group contained connectives (e.g., *first, in summary, in conclusion,* etc.), the other included modals and other lexical elements such as *agree.* Furthermore, the output of an early, cue-based discourse parser [Marcu, 2000] was mapped to two sentence features: the nuclearity status and the coherence relation the sentence takes part in (according to Rhetorical Structure Theory [Mann and Thompson, 1988]). Feature utility tests were not reported. A crucial question for an approach as lexically-based as this one is how to transfer to a new content domain, i.e., a new essay prompt. When evaluating on a prompt that was not present in the training set, the approach reached an average F-score of 0.54 for thesis and 0.8 for conclusion segments.

Falakmasir et al. [2014] tackled the same problem and worked with 432 essays (responding to 8 different prompts) for training and test, with the prompts in the 2 sets being disjoint. Human annotators identified sentences that were candidate thesis or conclusion statements, and rated their quality on a scale (1: vague or incomplete; 2: simple but acceptable; 3: sophisticated). The central goal of this work was feature engineering, and the authors used an iterative process to find the most predictive features: starting with 42 basic features (position, syntax, cues, rhetorical status) inspired by the Burstein/Marcu work, they employed several feature selection algorithms and experimented with various combinations. Finally, they converged on the following.

- **Positional** features: sentence number in the paragraph, paragraph number in text, and type of paragraph (first, body, and last paragraph). A positional baseline predicts all sentences in the first paragraph as a thesis and all sentences within the last paragraph as a conclusion.

- Various features based on the **syntactic/semantic analysis and dependency parsing** of the sentence. Prepositional and gerund phrases turned out as highly predictive of thesis and conclusion sentences, as did the number of adjectives and adverbs within the sentence.

- A set of **frequent words** (e.g., *although, even though, because, due to, led to, caused*).

- **Essay-level** features: number of keywords among the most frequent words of the essay, number of words overlapping with the assignment prompt, and a sentence importance score based on RST (similar to the feature used by Burstein and Marcu [2003], mentioned above).

A three-way classification experiment (thesis, conclusion, other) was performed, where thesis/conclusion sentences whose quality had been rated 1 were shifted to the 'other' category. Among three tested methods a decision tree classifier produced the best F-measures (0.83 for thesis and 0.59 for conclusion on the test set).

In a follow-up study on the same dataset, Jabbari et al. [2016] focused on finding thesis statements, and noted that the central challenge in the previous work was the skewed distribution of non-/thesis sentences, which had been tackled by means of complex feature optimization. As an alternative, they now proposed to instead balance the training data distribution. With random under- and oversampling as baselines, their experiment centered on the SMOTE approach for generating additional 'synthetic' examples [Chawla et al., 2002]. The idea of that technique is to produce new instances not on the text but on the feature vector level, by interpolating between existing minority instance vectors. The classification problem was somewhat simplified by considering only sentences in the first paragraph of the text (where theses commonly show up). Using an SVM, for finding theses the authors achieved a micro-F-score of 0.9, which compares favorably to the earlier work as well as to the two baselines (0.84 with undersampling; 0.87 with oversampling).

Major claim, claim, and premise   A second line of research was started with the Persuasive Essay Corpus [Stab and Gurevych, 2014a], which we introduced in Section 4.2.2. According to the annotation scheme, an essay can have one *major claim*, which expresses the author's stance with respect to the topic, and which is usually found in the first paragraph. (It appears to correspond to the *thesis* statement in the scheme explained above.) Two examples [Stab and Gurevych, 2014a, p. 1503] are as follows.

(5.5) I believe that **we should attach more importance to cooperation during education.**

(5.6) From my viewpoint, **people should perceive the value of museums in enhancing their own knowledge.**

Then, the paragraphs between the introduction and the conclusion usually contain arguments related to the major claim. These consist of *claims* and *premises*, which (in contrast to the work discussed above) are annotated not as complete sentences but as continuous token sequences, cf. the bold-faced portion of the examples above. Altogether, the corpus has 90 major claims (one per text) and 429 claims.

The detection of argument components is implemented as a four-way classifier (major claim, claim, premise, non-argumentative) presented by Stab and Gurevych [2014b], which was mentioned in Section 5.1.2. Features can be grouped as follows.

- **Structural:** location/length/punctuation.

- **Lexical:** n-grams, verbs, adverbs, modals.

- **Syntactic:** parse tree depth, production rules, verb tense.

- **Cues:** connectives from the Penn Discourse Treebank (PDTB) corpus [Prasad et al., 2008], first-person references.

- **Attributes of preceding and following sentence:** number of tokens and of punctuation, number of sub-clauses, presence of modal verbs.

Among various classifiers, an SVM performed best. The F-scores are: major claim 0.63, claim 0.54, premise 0.83, non-argumentative 0.88. While premises can be identified quite reliably also when using just a single group of features (F between 0.65 for syntactic and 0.78 for structural features), the corresponding values for claims and major claims are much lower, the maximum being 0.48 (major claim) and 0.42 (claim) for structural features. In other words, claim detection profits more from feature combination than premise detection does.

In later work on the same corpus, Nguyen and Litman [2015] describe an alternative approach that centers on lexical/cue features. Their idea is to separate the argumentative vocabulary from that indicating the domain. To do this, they use LDA topic modeling [Blei et al., 2003] for learning domain and argumentation vocabulary from a separate corpus of 6794 essays (i.e., excluding those from the Stab/Gurevych evaluation corpus), starting with sets of seed words. For argumentation, the set consists of 10 words. In Figure 5.3, we reproduce three of the top-ranked argumentation (Topic 1) and domain (Topic 2, 3) word stems produced by their algorithm. Altogether, 263 argument words are generated.

For the new classification model, Nguyen and Litman reimplemented the features of Stab/Gurevych, excluding the n-grams and the production rules. Instead, they added the newly harvested argument word unigrams, dependency pairs (as a replacement for skipped bigrams),

> **Topic 1** *reason exampl support agre think becaus disagre statement opinion believe therefor idea conclus*
>
> **Topic 2** *citi live big hous place area small apart town build communiti factori urban*
>
> **Topic 3** *children parent school educ teach kid adult grow childhood behavior taught*

Figure 5.3: LDA-topics (word stems) generated for student essays [Nguyen and Litman, 2015, p. 25], used with permission. Topic 1 shows argument words; Topic 2 and 3 are domain words.

and numbers of argument and domain words. Due to the removal of n-grams, the model has only 1/5 of the size of the Stab/Gurevych reimplementation. The authors show that the new model outperforms the reimplementation (and the results that had been reported by Stab/Gurevych), especially when only top-performing features are used.

5.3.4 WIKIPEDIA

A different perspective on claim detection is taken by Aharoni et al. [2014] and Levy et al. [2014]. These researchers work on the IBM *Debater* project (cf. Sct. 1.3), whose overall goal is a system that searches web pages for pro and con arguments on a given controversial topic. Thus, the claim detection task is dependent on a predefined *topic*, which Levy et al. (p. 1489) define as "a short phrase that frames the discussion"; and a context-dependent claim is "a general, concise statement that directly supports or contests the given topic." The text source is Wikipedia pages, where (in contrast to other web text) a certain quality of language and argumentation can be presumed.

A dataset was constructed on the basis of 32 debate motions from *Debatabase*.[7] Then, 326 Wikipedia articles were identified as relevant to these topics, and therein, annotators labeled 976 topic-related claims, achieving a rather moderate agreement of κ=0.39. Figure 5.4 shows examples for annotation decisions. (Notice that, in other terminology, this 'topic' would itself qualify as a 'claim', as it represents a thesis or demand by the author.) A 'V' indicates that a sentence was regarded as a topic-dependent claim, while 'X'-marked sentences were not.

In general, claims need not be complete sentences but can be smaller units. The automatic claim detection system thus needs to find, given a Wikipedia page and a topic, sentences and sub-sentences that qualify as a relevant claim. To achieve this, Levy et al. built a pipeline of three modules.

---

[7]http://www.idebate.org/Debatabase (accessed May 28, 2018). Upon request, the authors are making this dataset available for research.

Topic: The sale of violent video games to minors should be banned		
S1	Violent video games can increase children's aggression	V
S2	Video game addiction is excessive or compulsive use of computer and video games that interferes with daily life	X
S3	Many TV programmers argue that their shows just mirror the violence that goes on in the real world	X
S4	Violent video games should not be sold to children	X
S5	Video game publishers unethically train children in the use of weapons	V

Figure 5.4: Topic and associated claim candidates from Levy et al. [2014, p. 1490], used with permission.

The first module is in charge of identifying sentences that contain a claim. A logistic regression classifier uses features exploiting topic relevance (cosine similarity between the topic phrase and subjects in the sentence; and between the topic and a WordNet-expanded version of the sentence) and various topic-independent features (including morphosyntax, subjectivity, sentiment). It passes the top scoring 200 sentences to the next component.[8]

For each sentence found, the second module generates the 10 best candidate sub-sentences using a maximum likelihood model that primarily considers the tokens at the beginning and the end of the sequence. Then a logistic regression classifier selects the most probable claim, again looking at boundary tokens, along with a few other features.

The third module ranks the identified claims found for all the sentences, using another logistic regression classifier. It considers the scores produced by the previous components and also re-computes some of the features that have been used in the preceding modules.

In subsequent work, Shnarch et al. [2017] added a pattern matching approach called GRASP, which integrates information from different layers of analysis to the previous system. GRASP identifies the most discriminative features for the classification task, and composes patterns out of these. The authors note that these patterns are open to human inspection, hence allowing for qualitative error analyses. After adding this approach, significant improvements in performance on claim identification are reported.

Working on a slightly bigger version of the IBM dataset, Lippi and Torroni [2015] addressed only the first step, i.e., sentence classification, and suggested a rather different approach. They started from the observation that argumentative sentences are often characterized by common 'rhetorical structures' and operationalized that intuition as the similarity between syntactic (constituency) parse trees. Their goal thus is to account for argumentative language irrespective of the domain, and to do so on the basis of syntactic patterns. They obtained the parses from

---

[8]In this dataset, the input to step 1 consists of 1,500 Wikipedia sentences on average.

the Stanford CoreNLP suite, and trained an SVM classifier that exploits a partial tree kernel to compute similarities. The authors conclude that they can obtain results that are competitive to those of Levy et al. [2014], even without considering topic similarity. When adding a single context feature (cosine similarity between the candidate sentence and the topic, both represented as bag of words), the F-measure increases by a further 1.2 points.

In addition, Lippi and Torroni tested their tree-similarity approach on the essay dataset by Stab and Gurevych [2014a] (mentioned in the previous subsection). Considering the union of their categories 'claim' and 'major claim' as the target class, Lippi and Torroni obtained an F-score of 0.71, which compares favorably to the results of Stab and Gurevych (whose problem was a more difficult multi-class task, though).

Finally, we mention that the IBM dataset was used by Laha and Raykar [2016] for experiments with RNNs and CNNs for detecting both claims and evidence (see next section). Their goal was to establish the first deep learning baselines for these tasks, and they report comparisons of various architecture variants. For finding claims, however, the results were not as good as those obtained by Levy et al. [2014].

5.3.5   SOCIAL MEDIA AND USER-GENERATED WEB TEXT

For many practical applications, the various kinds of social media (or other user-generated text) are a highly relevant source of opinions and arguments to be mined. Some early work addressed public comments on proposed government regulations. Specifically, Kwon et al. [2007] studied a corpus of user comments on proposed U.S. Environmental Protection Agency legislation. Here, the claim detection task benefits from all documents addressing the same domain (the legislation in question). The authors exploited this by computing a feature representing the lexical overlap between sentences and the text topic 'public policy', in addition to various standard features (n-grams, frequencies of positive and negative words, position in text, and head verb token sequence). In the experiments, a boosting algorithm beat an SVM and achieved an agreement with a human annotator of κ=0.55. In a follow-up step, the authors then computed the polarity (stance) of the claim by means of a seed word approach that identifies positive and negative words.

In later work, Rosenthal and McKeown [2012] sought to detect claims in LiveJournal weblogs and in Wikipedia discussion pages. They define claims as "assertions by a speaker who is attempting to convince others that his opinion is true" (p. 30), and more specifically attend to the class of claims expressing opinionated beliefs, which are defined as "personal view[s] that others can disagree with" (p. 30). Figure 5.5 shows examples, which demonstrate that especially the LiveJournal text can be very informal. Not surprisingly, it is not trivial to demarcate this class of claims precisely; when two annotators labeled 2,000 sentences as claims (without considering the context) in each corpus, they achieved a Cohen κ of 0.50 for 663 LiveJournal sentences, and 0.56 for 997 Wikipedia sentences.

LiveJournal	1	oh yeah, you mentioned the race … that is so un-thanksgivingish !
	2	A good photographer can do awesome work with a polaroid or ‘ phonecam .
	3	hugs I feel ike I have completely lost track of a lot of stuff lately .
Wikipedia	4	The goal is to make Wikipedia as good as possible and, more specifically , this article as good as possible .
	5	This was part of his childhood , and should be mentioned in the article .
	6	If the book is POV or the writer has only a slender grasp of relevant issues , material can be wrong .

Figure 5.5: Examples of claims from two online corpora based on [Rosenthal and McKeown, 2012, p. 31].

The focus of the work was on measuring the utility of sentiment and so-called *comitted belief* features. For the latter, the authors adopted the system by Prabhakaran et al. [2010], which tags individual words for the underlying type of belief: committed (*I know*), non-committed (*I may*), and not applicable (*I wish*). Rosenthal and McKeown report various experiments on in-domain and cross-domain classification, including feature impact measurements. In brief, they found that sentiment features are more useful in LiveJournal, while committed belief features are more predictive for Wikipedia discussions.

On a corpus of 204 different social media and news documents (16,000 sentences) in Greek, Goudas et al. [2014] employed IOB sequence labeling for combined claim and premise detection. The features were the words in the sentence, domain-specific named entities, manually compiled cue words, and verbs and adverbs found representative for claim and premise sentences by a TF-IDF computation. Their CRF model achieved a precision of 0.62 and recall of 0.32, resulting in an F-measure of 0.42. In follow-up work on news text, Sardianos et al. [2015] sought to reduce the role of domain-dependent gazetteer lists and report on experiments with word embeddings generated by word2vec [Mikolov et al., 2013].

Recently, Habernal and Gurevych [2017] extended the IOB tagging approach to a set of argument components that they derived from the Toulmin scheme (see Section 3.4.1): backing, claim, premise, rebuttal, refutation. They used the Web Discourse corpus (see Section 4.2.1), whose annotation covers the aforementioned components, plus 'appeal to emotion' (representing the pathos dimension of argumentation); see the example in Figure 5.6. We will come back to this work in subsequent sections, and here just focus on the claim identification. The trained human annotators achieved an agreement of 0.59 on claims, measured by Krippendorf's unitized α.

The 11-class IOB tagging is applied to complete sentences as instances to be classified; the authors argue that a token-level annotation is too fine-grained for a machine learner. Consequently, the problem is simplified to deciding whether a sentence hosts an argument component or not. For sequence labeling, Habernal and Gurevych used SVM^{hmm}. The rich feature set is split into five groups:

Doc#163 (comment, homeschooling) Thank you for bringing this tragedy to light.
[*backing:* I am a Christian, an educator, a student and a parent and I have seen too
many children like the Powells. As an admissions officer, we had applicants whose
"record keeping" consisted of sending boxes full of paper for our office to review as
part of the application.] [*premise:* If their students did get an interview, which was rare,
they didn't have the social skills to survive the first round.]¶
[*premise:* I personlly am acquainted with four families who are home schooling their
large families. All four have no intention of book-schooling their daughters past age 13
as they need to learn :homemaking skills". One of the girls, who has not been taught for
two years, could be Josh Powell's twin. She is intelligent and desperate to learn, but her
parents won't allow it.] [*app-to-emot:* It is heartbreaking.¶
That the Commonwealth of Virginia has such a rich tradition of the education of young
people and allows this travesty is shameful.] All of us, no matter our religious beliefs,
need to pray that the law changes before more smart children are left behind.

Figure 5.6: Sample annotation from the corpus of Habernal and Gurevych [2017, p. 169], used
with permission.

- **Lexical:** word n-grams;

- **Structure and syntax:** initial and final tokens, relative positions, POS n-grams, dependency tree depth, constituency tree production rules, number of subclauses;

- **Topic and sentiment:** LDA topics and five sentiment categories (-2, …, 2);

- **Semantics and discourse:** semantic role labels, various coreference chain attributes, type
  of discourse relation, presence of connectives, attributions; and

- **Embeddings:** sums of word embedding vectors.

All features are considered not only for the current sentence but also for the four preceding and
four subsequent sentences. The overall best results are achieved with the full feature set, yielding
a macro-F score of 0.25, in comparison to 0.6 obtained by human annotators. The classes Claim-
B and Claim-I are among the top-performing classes, reaching 0.27 when omitting the lexical
and structure/syntax features. As these numbers show, the problem tackled here is much harder
than those we discussed before.

5.3.6   SUMMARY: FINDING CLAIMS OF DIFFERENT KINDS

The claim, undoubtedly, is at the heart of the argument—it states what the author wants us to
believe. Beyond this fairly general characterization, however, different authors provide somewhat
different characterizations, and the corpus examples we have seen make it clear that there is a

relatively broad range of statements treated as claims in different text types and genres. Often, but not always, claims are indicated by linguistic surface features, which some approaches try to isolate as topic-independent 'claim shells' that signal the claim. Also, in some genres, there seem to be relatively strong position-in-document tendencies that can be exploited, as for example in student essays.

Recently, the variety in claim realizations prompted Daxenberger et al. [2017] to run a systematic claim identification experiment across six different datasets.[9] They mapped the existing annotations to the sentence level, thus making a simplifying assumption, which, however, is shared by most of the previous work, as we have pointed out above. Daxenberger et al. wanted to measure the influence of different groups of features (structure, lexical, syntax, discourse, embedding)[10] and learning approaches; they ran three deep learning schemes, and a regularized logistic regression classifier.

For in-domain classification, they obtained an average macro-F score of 0.67, ranging from 0.6 (Wikipedia TalkPages) to 0.8 (arg. microtexts). Lexical (unigram), embedding, and syntax features were most predictive, whereas structural features did not help in most cases. Discourse features were useful only on the microtext corpus. The average performance of the best neural network and the logistic regression classifier was virtually the same.

With cross-domain training and testing, performance drops were found throughout, most pronounced for the datasets that performed best in the in-domain setting. The best feature-based approach outperformed the deep learning approach in most scenarios. However, the neural networks benefit when trained on all datasets but one and testing on the remaining one, yielding the best results on average. Still, the best NN approach did not show benefits over training on good (single) source training datasets.

After studying the six corpora further, Daxenberger et al. concluded that it is difficult to predict cross-domain performance from lexical similarity of the datasets. Their overall conclusion is that "the essence of a claim is not much more than a few lexical clues." This points to the important role of context: depending on genre and topic, a claim may on the surface look like any other declarative sentence, and only in the particular context assume the role of an opinion that the speaker wants to convince the hearers of.

Finally, we have to point out that the notion of claim will be given an additional facet of complication later in Chapter 7 when we discuss structures of complex arguments: a statement in a text may be supported by another statement (which makes the first one a claim) and at the same time it may in turn support yet another statement and thus play multiple roles in the argumentation. But before turning to such recursive structures, we first look more closely at the 'support' relation.

---

[9]Most of them have been introduced in Section 4.2.2 or will be mentioned in the next chapter: AraucariaDB [Reed et al., 2008a], essays from Stab and Gurevych [2014b], web discourse from Habernal and Gurevych [2017], online comments and Wikipedia talk pages from Biran and Rambow [2011], and argumentative microtexts from Peldszus and Stede [2016b].

[10]They also experimented with sentiment dictionaries (as in, e.g., Rosenthal and McKeown [2012]) but found these to be of very little value.

CHAPTER 6

Finding Supporting and Objecting Statements

Detecting claims, the topic of the previous chapter, is obviously a core task of argumentation mining, but in order to find a complete argument, there is at least one more component to be identified: the statement(s) that the author introduced to support the claim. In the argumentation literature, this is often called the 'premises' of the argument; in other places it is 'evidence' or 'justification'. In this chapter, we use these terms interchangeably with 'support'.

Besides claims and evidence, it may be important to also look for counter-arguments, in case the text also mentions the 'opposing view', and the application seeks to identify it. Here is a simple example.

(6.1) You should buy that camera, because it has a brand-new excellent sensor. OK, it is quite expensive. But it's worth the money!

Our speaker, in giving her recommendation, imagines an 'opponent' pointing out the high price of the product. After quoting that potential counterargument, she refutes it by emphasizing the good value one gets for the money here. Thus, the argument components to be detected are as follows.

- **Claim:** You should buy that camera.

- **Support:** That camera has a brand-new excellent sensor.

- **Objection:** That camera is quite expensive.

- **Support:** That camera is worth the money.

Notice that when 'digging deeper', we might want to not just enumerate the components but also record in what way the speaker wants them to relate to each other (here especially the link between the objection and the second support)—but that is the topic of the next chapter. For now, in the following sections, we look at the tasks of finding support (Section 6.1) and objections (Section 6.2). Furthermore, a potentially helpful related NLP task is *stance detection*, which determines whether a text communicates a positive or negative attitude toward a given topic. We examine it briefly in Section 6.3.

6.1   FINDING SUPPORTING STATEMENTS

Support or evidence, by definition, is evidence *for something*, and therefore stands in relation to a claim. As long as there is only a single claim in our text, however, there is no need to explicitly establish and represent this relation. Instead, it can just be left implicit. In these cases, sentence classification or sequence labeling, as described in the previous chapter for claim detection, is also sufficient for identifying evidence.

But even when left implicit, the relatedness between claim and evidence can be exploited in argumentation mining. For a start, usually one item of evidence is textually adjacent to the claim. Then, the relation may be marked linguistically by a connective such as *because*. But of course there can be multiple evidence statements spread across the text. Consider the following example from the 'argumentative microtext' corpus [Peldszus and Stede, 2016b], which consists of only a claim (marked with a C subscript) and a set of supporting statements, marked with S.

(6.2)   *Should the death penalty be introduced in Germany?*
[No human being or human committee should again be given the permission to rule over 'life or death'.]$_S$ [Courts are also subject to human error.]$_S$ [That's why Germany should not introduce capital punishment!]$_C$ [Every human, even those who have committed a despicable crime, can bring themselves to regret and change their opinion.]$_S$ [A door must remain open for making amends.]$_S$
(micro_b023)

Here, the claim contains a phrasal connective (*that's why*) linking it to the previous supporting statement. The others, however, must be identified without recurring to such explicit markers.

In the rest of this section, we first explain an approach that exploits relation marking in an interesting indirect way. Then we describe work on evidence detection in Wikipedia pages, which follows up on the corpus and claim detection of Aharoni et al. [2014] (see Section 5.3.4). Finally, we briefly mention again some approaches that were already introduced in the previous chapter, as they tackle claim and evidence detection as a unified task.

6.1.1   EXPLOITING DISCOURSE RELATION INDICATORS

When the focus is not on classifying claim and evidence individually but on the relation between the two, the problem is analogous to that of discourse relation identification, as studied in frameworks like PDTB [Prasad et al., 2008] or RST [Mann and Thompson, 1988]—recall our brief introduction in Section 2.6. The work of Biran and Rambow [2011] focused on finding instances of the relation of argumentative support, and it targeted two types of web text: Live Journal blog threads (henceforth: LJ) and Wikipedia talk pages (WT). Concentrating on finding supporting statements, they assumed the claims as already marked in gold-standard annotated data. For adding the support to the given claims, annotators achieved a κ of 0.69.

Biran and Rambow also offer a classification of different types of support they found in the data[1]:

- Recommendation for action, and motivation for proposed action.
  Claim: "I'd post an update with the new date immediately."
  Justification: "In case anyone makes plans between now and when you post the reminder."

- Statement of like or dislike or of desires and longing, and subjective reason for this.

- Statement of like or dislike or of desires and longing, and claimed objective reason for this.

- Statement of subjectively perceived fact, with a proposed objective explanation.

- A claimed general objective statement and a more specific objective statement that justifies the more general one.

In WT, on average there are 2.2 support statements per claim, compared to 1.5 in LJ. As for the position in the threads, in LJ 97.3% are in the same entry as the claim, and 32.4% are in the sentence following the claim. In WT, the corresponding numbers are 87.7% and 22.9%. Hence, looking only at individual entries when mining for support, in WT quite a few will not be found.

Claim-support relations in text may be explicitly signaled by connectives, or they may be only implicit. For handling the explicit cases, Biran and Rambow compiled a list of connectives from the annotated RST Discourse Treebank [Carlson et al., 2003] (see Section 2.6) and selected 12 coherence relations that they considered as likely to correspond to a claim-support constellation; they are shown in Figure 6.1, together with example connectives (and other phrases) that the authors retrieved from the corpus using a a variant of TF/IDF and a manual filtering step.

The resulting set of 69 explicit indicators was then used to indirectly get a handle also on implicit relations. The intuition is that we may expect certain lexical regularities between claim and support: When I say something is *expensive*, I can typically support that with quoting a *price*; when I suggest that the reader should attend a *concert*, I might indicate that the music will be *lovely*; and so forth. To establish a dictionary of such word pairs, Biran and Rambow looked for instances of the 69 indicators in a large raw corpus, viz. the standard Wikipedia.[2] Given the breadth of topics covered in Wikipedia, a potential domain-dependency of extracted word pairs is likely to be minimized. For each indicator, word pairs with a frequency >20 are extracted from sentences in which the indicator occurs.

Finally, for the target task of finding claim/support sentences in the LJ and WT corpora, Biran/Rambow determined that just using the 69 indicator words does not beat a relatively simple baseline. But when using the word pairs learned in the previous step as additional features,

---

[1]For reasons of space, we reproduce only one of the examples that the authors used to illustrate the classes (p. 364).
[2]This is not to be confused with the small Wikipedia Talk pages (WT) corpus, which along with LJ is used for the ultimate task of automatically finding support statements.

the results of a Naive Bayes classifier demonstrate that for both corpora, the large feature set clearly beats various baselines, reaching F-measures of 0.47 (LJ) and 0.5 (WT). When training on one and testing on the other corpus, results are about 0.04–0.05 worse.

Biran and Rambow [2011] concluded that plain single-sentence classification for finding support is difficult, but the presence of a claim and its location relative to the support candidate are important features that can significantly boost performance.

In contrast to this decidedly data-driven approach, Eckle-Kohler et al. [2015] started from a pre-defined list of connectives (and a few other particles) and determined their potential utility. Working with a relatively small German corpus (88 documents, mostly news text), the aim was to determine which connectives correlate with claim, support (before or after the claim), and attack (before or after the claim). The before/after distinction is relevant because causal connectives signal directionality (e.g., 'claim *because* support' vs. 'support, *therefore* claim'). German connectives that in the data of Eckle-Kohler et al. frequently occur with claims are *also* ('therefore'), *doch* ('however'), *jedoch* ('though'), and *sondern* ('but'); in premises they found *denn* ('as'), *oder* ('or'), and *und* ('and'). A classifier using such groups of connectives can discriminate between claims and premises with accuracies around 0.7, even though a unigram baseline is slightly better—but obviously using a much larger feature space.

While the important role of connectives is well known, Villalba and Saint-Dizier [2012] directed attention to some different means of expressing coherence relations, and pointed out that even non-argumentative coherence relations (i.e., others than those listed in Figure 6.1) can acquire an argumentative role when involving *evaluative* expressions, as they can be found for example in product reviews. They illustrate this with the contrast between:

(6.3) Red fruit tart (strawberries, raspberries)

(6.4) Excellent location (3 mns from the Capitole, 5 mns from St Sernin Cathedral,...)

In 6.3, the coherence relation is Elaboration: The parenthesis provides details on the red fruit. In 6.4, we find the same surface pattern, also expressing Elaboration, but in addition there is a claim-support constellation, as we are given a positive evaluation (of a hotel), and the elaborating material provides good evidence for this.

In general, the relationship between discourse structure (as induced by coherence relations) on the one hand and argumentation on the other is so far not entirely clear. In addition to the work by Biran and Rambow [2011] and Villalba and Saint-Dizier [2012] mentioned above, the issue is also discussed by Saint-Dizier [2012], Cabrio et al. [2013a], and Peldszus and Stede [2016a].

6.1.2 CLASSIFYING SEGMENTS WITHOUT DISCOURSE CONTEXT

The alternative to considering the discourse context is to examine segments in isolation and decide whether they represent evidence for a claim. One approach in this vein is that of Hasan

Relation	Nb	Sample indicators
analogy	15	as a, just as, comes from the same
antithesis	18	although, even while, on the other hand
cause	14	because, as a result, which in turn
concession	19	despite, regardless of, even if
consequence	15	because, largely because of, as a result of
contrast	8	but the, on the other hand, but it is the
evidence	7	attests, this year, according to
example	9	including, for instance, among the
explanation-argumentative	7	because, in addition, to comment on the
purpose	30	trying to, in order to, so as to see
reason	13	because, because it is, to find a way
result	23	resulting, because of, as a result of

Figure 6.1: Coherence relations and extracted indicators from the RST-DT [Biran and Rambow, 2011, p. 371], used with permission.

and Ng [2014], who used data from the online debate platform createdebate.com. It covers two-sided debates, and each post is already labeled (by the user) with its pro/contra stance toward the issue. Hasan and Ng were interested in the reasons that debaters have provided for their stance. Taking posts from four different domains, annotators marked sentences for containing a reason or not.[3] Afterward, the reasons were grouped and a number of classes identified; these labels were also added to the data.[4] For illustration, Figure 6.2 shows the pro/con reason classes that were identified for the topic 'abortion'.

A MaxEnt classifier was trained to decide which of the reasons from the predetermined set (if any) is present in a sentence. Hasan and Ng used uni- and bigrams, dependency relations, frame-semantic features from the SEMAFOR parser,[5] presence of quotations, and the position of the sentence in the post. The results for this difficult multi-class problem varied between 19.5% and 32.7% accuracy, depending on the domain. The main point of the work, however, was to demonstrate that these figures can be improved by adding *stance classification*, which we will describe below in Section 6.3.

---

[3]Hasan and Ng found that 3% of the sentences contained more than one reason; in these cases the annotation was reduced to the most prominent one. Notice that the multiplicity of reasons in a sentence is one aspect of the ADU demarcation problem discussed in Section 5.2.

[4]The corpus is available for research: http://www.hlt.utdallas.edu/~saidul/stance/ (accessed September 26, 2017).

[5]http://www.cs.cmu.edu/~ark/SEMAFOR/ (accessed September 26, 2017).

Domain	Stance	Reason classes
ABO	*for*	[F1] Abortion is a woman's right (26%); [F2] Rape victims need it to be legal (7%); [F3] A fetus is not human (38%); [F4] Mother's life in danger (5%); [F5] Unwanted babies are ill-treated by parents (8%); [F6] Birth control fails at times (3%); [F7] Abortion is not murder (3%); [F8] Mother is not healthy/financially solvent (4%); [F9] Others (6%)
	against	[A1] Put baby up for adoption (9%); [A2] Abortion kills a life (29%); [A3] An unborn baby is a human and has the right to live (40%); [A4] Be willing to have the baby if you have sex (14%); [A5] Abortion is harmful for women (5%); [A6] Others (3%)

Figure 6.2: Reason classes annotated in debate posts on abortion [Hasan and Ng, 2014, p. 753], used with permission.

Rinott et al. [2015] present an approach to identifying support statements in Wikipedia text, following up on the work by Levy et al. [2014] on topic-dependent claim identification (see Section 5.3.4). Now, the assumption is that a topic and a topic-relevant claim are already given, as well as a set of potentially relevant documents; and the goal is to find evidence that can support the claim. The following example [Rinott et al., 2015, p. 441] lists three statements that would ideally be classified as suitable evidence.

- **Topic:** Use of performance enhancing drugs (PEDs) in professional sports.

- **Claim:** PEDs can be harmful to athletes' health.

- **Evidence statements:**

  - (S1) A 2006 study examined 320 athletes for psychiatric side effects induced by anabolic steroid use. The study found a higher incidence of mood disorders in these athletes compared to a control group. [Study]

  - (S2) The International Agency for Research on Cancer classifies androgenic steroids as "probably carcinogenic to humans." [Expert]

  - (S3) Rica Reinisch, a triple Olympic champion and world record-setter at the Moscow Games in 1980, has suffered numerous miscarriages and recurring ovarian cysts following drug abuse. [Anecdotal]

Similar to Biran and Rambow [2011], the authors also provide a classification of different types of evidence; the categories are quite different, however, due to the different domains.

- **Study:** Results of a quantitative analysis of data, given as numbers, or as conclusions. (e.g., S1 above).

- **Expert:** Testimony by a person/group/committee/organization with some known expertise/authority on the topic (e.g., S2 above).

- **Anecdotal:** A description of an episode(s), centered on individual(s) or clearly located in place and/or in time. (e.g., S3 above).

The task is to go through all the relevant documents and for each sentence to decide whether it constitutes evidence for the claim. (More precisely, sequences of one, two, and three sentences are considered as instances to be classified.) The data set for training and testing the system consists of 274 articles associated with 39 different topics. Here, 3,057 sentences with context-dependent evidence were annotated. In the setting here, not all claims are associated with evidence,[6] but for those that are, on average, a claim is connected to 2.17 evidence statements. 95% of the evidence statements are full sentences.

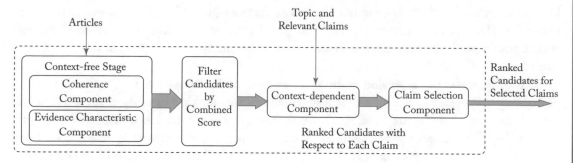

Figure 6.3: System architecture of evidence detection system based on Rinott et al. [2015, p. 443].

Rinott et al. devised a modular system architecture shown in Figure 6.3, responding to the observation that a target text segment should satisfy three criteria: it must be coherent; it must have characteristics of the relevant evidence type; and finally, of course, it must support the claim. Of these, the first two aspects are context-independent. In the following, we briefly describe the corresponding modules of the system.

The **coherence** component makes sure that, for example, there are no unresolved anaphors in a sentence and that the first sentence does not start with a connective.

The **evidence characteristics** component estimates how well the candidate corresponds to the desired type of evidence. Study evidence, for example, is strongly associated with quantitative analysis of data, i.e., the presence of numbers, among other features. Anecdotal evidence is expected to be less semantically related to the corresponding claim, as their relationship may be more associative than for the Study or Expert types. For each evidence type, the authors manually compiled a lexicon of words characterizing this type. Using held-out data, these lexicons were automatically expanded. Other features are named entity types, regular expressions for finding quotations and verb/named entity patterns, and subjectivity.

---

[6]This violates our definition of 'argument', but note that these researchers treat claim and evidence detection as distinct research tasks.

The **context-dependent** component aims to detect whether the candidate indeed supports the provided claim in the context of the topic. Hence, it is trained on [topic / claim / evidence] triplets. Four types of features are computed:

- semantic relatedness between the candidate and the claim;

- semantic relatedness between text related to the candidate and the claim;

- relative location of the candidate with respect to the claim; and

- sentiment agreement between the candidate and the claim.

Here, semantic relatedness is computed by several methods, including the cosine similarity between TF-IDF vectors representing each text (augmented with related words from WordNet) and by cosine similarity between word embedding representations of all pairs of words from the two texts.

Finally, the **claim selection** component aims to rank all input claims, according to the probability that evidence can indeed be found amongst top-ranking candidates for the claim. It uses a lexicon of 'claim words' (*lead, result, development, significant,* etc.) as well as a more specific lexicon that differentiates words used in factual claims (*increase, important, relate,* etc.) from those in non–factual claims (*natural, freedom, right,* etc.). The lists were derived from manually-annotated claims.

All components employ a logistic regression classifier. The evaluation of this multi-component pipeline, done by the authors via mean reciprocal ranks, is complex and we do not reproduce it here. The authors conclude that assessing both the coherence and the evidence characteristics of candidates is of great importance. For the context-dependent stage, semantic relatedness turned out as the most valuable feature.

6.1.3 COMBINED CLAIM/SUPPORT DETECTION

In Section 5.3, we described a few approaches that tackled the identification of claim and support simultaneously. In order to complete our survey on finding support, we just list these approaches and the relevant results again.

- Palau and Moens [2009] used the same feature set for discriminating claim and support (premise) in legal text, reaching an F-score of 0.68 for the premises, which was 0.06 lower than that for claims.

- The sequence kernel method employed by Rooney et al. [2012] yields much better results for support than for claims; the accuracies are in the area of 0.6, depending on parameterization.

- The 4-way SVM classifier developed by Stab and Gurevych [2014b] had an F-score of 0.83 for support, as compared to 0.63 and 0.54 for major claims and claims.

- For the CRF model of Goudas et al. [2014] (IOB tagging for claims and support), no class-specific results were given.

- The CRF model of Habernal and Gurevych [2017] obtained slightly better results for support than for claims, but only when using different feature sets.

- Saint-Dizier's rule-based approach also fared somewhat better for support than for claims.

Thus, with the exception of the work of Palau and Moens [2009], in these 'joint' approaches, the identification of support was easier than that of claims.

6.2 FINDING OPPOSING STATEMENTS

For many application scenarios, it is important to find both *pro* and *contra* positions on a given claim, or in other words, the *arguments* and *counterarguments* (or *attacks*). This is the case, *inter alia*, for product evaluations—recall Example 6.1 shown at the beginning of the chapter. When the *contra* is present in the same text as the *pro*, we call this the 'opposing view'. It is not uncommon at all—and often advisable from a rhetorical perspective—for an author to anticipate potential counterarguments, mention them, and rebut them. (The step of identifying those will be taken up in the next chapter.)

For illustration, here is another example from the 'argumentative microtext' corpus [Peldszus and Stede, 2016b]; we mark (C)laim, (S)upporting, and (A)ttacking statements.

(6.5) *Should health insurance cover alternative medical therapy?*
[Health insurance companies should naturally cover alternative medical treatments.]$_C$
[Not all practices and approaches that are lumped together under this term may have been proven in clinical trials,]$_A$ [yet it's precisely their positive effect when accompanying conventional 'western' medical therapies that's been demonstrated as beneficial.]$_S$
[Besides many general practitioners offer such counselling and treatments in parallel anyway –]$_S$ [and who would want to question their broad expertise?]$_S$
(micro_b013)

The author states her position up front, and then continues with a concession: there are some legitimate objections to her position (or there is at least this one). However, she considers this objection as being outweighed by the supporting material she then adds to complete her argument. In student essays, including such considerations is typically regarded positively by evaluators (the issue of avoiding the *myside bias*). But we find the technique in many other genres too, such as in court decisions, where the judge might concede that the defendant is right on one particular count, but still deserves punishment on the grounds of other, more weighty, factors.

Using the terms 'objection' or 'attack' for these cases may be a bit misleading, because authors rarely intend to attack themselves or argue with themselves; instead, they 'imagine' an opponent and the confrontation. We thus follow Govier [2011] and henceforth use the cover term *counter-considerations* for these phenomena.

When the detection of counter-considerations is operationalized as in the annotations of Example 6.5 above, the computational task remains essentially the same as in the previous section and merely adds a new class (in our example: A) to a premise/conclusion classifier. Some annotation schemes, however, go a step further and distinguish between two forms of counter-consideration: the *rebuttal* and the *undercutter*.

Peldszus and Stede [2013], who described the scheme underlying the 'microtext' corpus, illustrate the distinction with these examples.

(6.6) [We should tear the building down.]$_C$ [It is full of asbestos.]$_S$ [On the other hand, many people liked the view from the roof.]$_R$

(6.7) [We should tear the building down.]$_C$ [It is full of asbestos.]$_S$ [The building might be cleaned up, though.]$_U$

In 6.6, the third statement 'rebuts' the conclusion by making a point that would invalidate the proposal of tearing the building down; it thus questions the validity of the conclusion. In contrast, the third statement of Example 6.7 is directed toward the second (supporting) statement. It does not question the validity of the statement "full of asbestos" (i.e., it does not rebut it), but it questions the *relevance* of the support for the conclusion: Yes, there is asbestos, but that can be removed, and therefore we do not need to demolish the building. This is called an 'undercut' on the relation between S and C.

Notice that in authentic text, a speaker should produce some sort of continuation to Example 6.6 or 6.7, so that a coherent and strong argument results. Specifically, the rebutter and undercutter need in turn to be countered. This leads to configurations of 'counterattack', which we do not elaborate on here; the reader is referred to Peldszus and Stede [2013, sct. 2.2.4] for a comparative analysis of various cases.

'Microtexts' and newspaper editorials   In his approach to parsing the argumentation structure of (the German version of) texts in the microtext corpus, Peldszus [2014] operationalized the task with a hierarchical tag set, where the first distinction is for an argumentative text segment to be stated from the 'proponent' or the 'opponent' role: either the author advances her own viewpoint, or temporarily adopts that of the imagined opponent and produces a counter-consideration. Using a common feature set, role identification turned out to be the subtask yielding the best results (micro-F of 0.85 using a MaxEnt classifier). As opponent-statements are obviously relatively rare (22% in this dataset) it is instructive to also consider the κ, which was 0.52. The most predictive features were lemma unigrams and discourse connectives. The latter is not too surprising, because switching the perspective to an imagined opponent (and then back again) needs to be clearly signaled at the text surface, and contrastive connectives like *but* or *even though* are one standard way of doing that. In the sample text shown above as Example 6.5, the switch signal is *yet* in the third segment.

After some feature improvements, slightly better results (κ=0.55, macro-F=0.77) were obtained in Peldszus and Stede [2015b]. The authors compare the results to those for a corpus of German newspaper editorials (124 texts), where the results are considerably lower: κ=0.32, macro-F=0.66; the F-score for opponent class was only 0.38. This low performance is attributed primarily to the presence of longer *sequences* of opponent-role segments in the editorials—where a signal of perspective switching is typically present only in the first segment of such a sequence. The microtexts, on the other hand, are simply too short for such sequences to play a role.

Student essays A proponent/opponent distinction is also made by Stab and Gurevych [2014a] in their corpus of student essays (see Section 5.3.3). The 429 segments annotated as claim have an additional attribute 'for' (365) or 'against' (64). The stance of the premises is not labeled correspondingly, but in principle it can be inferred from the relational structure of the annotations. In total, there are 1,473 relations annotated, of which 161 are of the attacking type. However, due to the relatively low proportion, the authors restricted their automatic classification to the 'for' claims and the 'support' relations.

In follow-up work, Stab and Gurevych [2016] addressed the question of *absence* of the opposing view in essays, as this is relevant for essay grading. They did not address segments individually but classified the complete essays as containing opposing material or not. In their corpus of 402 essays, the opposing view was present in 151 (38%) of all texts. Their SVM classifier obtained an accuracy of 0.77; lexical unigrams, syntactic productions, and adversative connectives turned out as the most predictive features, whereas sentiment and other discourse features did not help.

Web text The annotation scheme of Habernal and Gurevych [2017] (cf. Section 5.3.5), derived from the Toulmin model, contains 'rebuttal' for opposing material (they do not distinguish it from undercut), and 'refutation' for the counter-attack by the author. In their web text corpus, only 8% of the documents present a rebuttal (attacked by refutation in 4% of the documents). In their IOB tagging experiments, it turned out that their system performs very bad for the rebuttal and refutation categories (e.g., F-scores of 0.037 and 0.118 for rebuttal-B and rebuttal-I, respectively). The authors attribute this to a corresponding low human agreement on the one hand, and to the small amount of data on the other.

6.3 IDENTIFYING STANCE

Stance detection is an NLP task in its own right that has given rise to several shared tasks, including one for Chinese tweets [Xu et al., 2016] and one for English ones. The organizers of the latter defined the task as follows [Mohammad et al., 2016, p. 31].

> Given a tweet text and a target entity (person, organization, movement, policy, etc.), automatic natural language systems must determine whether the tweeter is in favor of the given target, against the given target, or whether neither inference is likely. For example, consider the target-tweet pair:
>
> • **Target:** Legalization of abortion.

- **Tweet**: The pregnant are more than walking incubators, and have rights!

We can infer from the tweet that the tweeter is likely in favor of the target.

A connection to argumentation mining is evident in the analysis of online debates. In the most systematic cases of debate, the *two-sided* ones, a statement or claim is presented, and debaters position themselves explicitly on the 'for' or 'against' side, and ideally state arguments supporting their stance. This setting provides convenient train/test data for automatic classification.

Another genre that has received some attention is news text; Ferreira and Vlachos [2016], for example, present a classifier for news headlines that tries to predict the stance toward the claim made in the article.

But systems performing for/against classification can be employed in less regulated settings, too. For instance, a system aiming at retrieving arguments on a particular topic ('target') from general web text needs to first identify texts that are on topic and are argumentative; then, in order to identify the argument components and their roles, it can be helpful to know the general orientation of the text—the author's stance. And recall the point made at the beginning of Section 5.3: very often an argumentative text does not explicitly state its central claim. Depending on the specific application, stance detection may then serve as a way of inducing the implicit claim in a reduced form, i.e., as a for/against label. For these reasons, in the following we briefly point to some relevant stance detection research.

Online debates   The early work of Somasundaran and Wiebe [2009] used Integer Linear Programming (ILP) to determine the stance of posts from the debate site Convinceme.net. The debates in their corpus are restricted to be two-sided as well as oriented to two targets: posts either favor one product or one specific competitor (*Blackberry* vs. *Iphone*, etc.). In this setting, concessions are relatively frequent: An author grants the 'opposing' product some advantage, but then gives more weighty arguments for the favored product. Therefore, discourse features centering on the Concession relation were exploited by Somasundaran and Wiebe, in addition to topic and subjectivity clues extracted from the training data.

Anand et al. [2011], working with the same data source, emphasized the role of rebuttals in the interactions, which according to the authors should be treated differently from agreeing responses. Figure 6.4 shows a sample exchange where the three follow-up posts all are rebutting their predecessors. With Naive Bayes and decision tree classifiers employing a range of linguistic features, the authors were able to identify rebuttals with 63% accuracy, and the stance with accuracies between 54% and 69%, depending on the topic. A general insight was that the rebuttal posts are harder to identify, both for human raters and for the classifiers.

Picking up the work of Anand et al., Hasan and Ng [2013] suggested moving beyond the language of the post, to also take aspects of the interaction into account. Their data is from a different website, createdebate.com, and comprises 'ideological' debates on four topics: abortion, gay rights, Obama, and marijuana. The authors propose two features.

Dialogic Capital Punishment
Studies have shown that using the death penalty saves 4 to 13 lives per execution. That alone makes killing murderers worthwhile.
What studies? I have never seen ANY evidence that capital punishment acts as a deterrant to crime. I have not seen any evidence that it is "just" either.
When Texas and Florida were executing people one after the other in the late 90's, the murder rates in both states plunged, like Rosie O'donnel off a diet.. .
That's your evidence? What happened to those studies? In the late 90s a LOT of things were different than the periods preceding and following the one you mention. We have no way to determine what of those contributed to a lower murder rate, if indeed there was one. You have to prove a cause and effect relationship and you have failed.

Figure 6.4: Discussion posts with rebut links from `Convinceme.net` [Anand et al., 2011, p. 1], used with permission.

- **Interaction patterns:** In the data, stance labels of the posts in a sequence are not independent of each other: 80% of the time, a post is followed by a reply with opposite polarity. The authors trained a CRF model on sequences and used it to predict such stance sequences on the test data.

- **Ideology patterns:** The opinion of an author on one topic is not independent of his or her opinion on another topic. Thus, for posts written by the same author, the information gathered from other posts can be used. Hasan and Ng modeled this as conditional probabilities reflecting that, for instance, a pro stance on gay rights correlates with being pro-marijuana.

Notice that both of these features might be less helpful with less heated debate topics. But nonetheless, Hasan and Ng show how the two types of constraints can be combined in an ILP inference problem, and they demonstrate that both constraints improve overall system performance, which altogether beats a reimplementation of the linguistic approach of Anand et al. [2011] by 8–14 percentage points, depending on the domain. Later on, Hasan and Ng [2014] used their stance identification results to better predict classes of reasons given for an argument (see Section 6.1.2).

Qiu and Jiang [2013] worked with English and Chinese debate data sets, and were also interested in utilizing user interaction patterns for determining stance. In their unsupervised

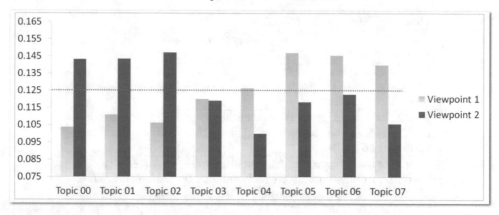

Figure 6.5: Topics mentioned in debate posts by 'for' (viewpoint 1) and 'against' users (viewpoint 2) [Qiu and Jiang, 2013, p. 1032], used with permission.

approach, they built a complete network representing the 'for'/'against' groups of users and the support/attack relations among them, as computed via their posts. Their main focus, however, was to also pay attention to the topics mentioned in the posts, following the intuition that given a contentious issue, the 'for' users tend to discuss different aspects of that issue than the 'against' users do. Figure 6.5 illustrates the idea by giving the distribution of seven topics addressed by users discussing whether to vote for or against Obama. The three factors—topic distribution, user identity, and user interaction—are combined in a latent variable model inspired by Latent Dirichlet Allocation [Blei et al., 2003]. The accuracies for stance identification range from 60–81% depending on the language and data set.

Finally, we mention the work by Sridhar et al. [2014], which combines linguistic and network structure features and proposes to jointly infer the stance labels by means of a probabilistic soft logic (PSL) model [Bach et al., 2013]. They used data from the Internet Argument Corpus (see Section 4.2.1), addressing topics similar to those mentioned above, and demonstrated—in line with the above-mentioned work—that accounting for both types of information outperforms a linguistics-only model. An interesting feature of the PSL approach is that weights of symbolic rules are learned, which can be inspected and exploited for error analysis (in contrast to the majority of 'black box' machine learning approaches).

Student essays   Besides online debate posts, another interesting genre for stance classification is argumentative student essays that were written in response to a prompt inviting a 'for' or 'against' opinion. Faulkner [2014] presented an approach to compute the essay-level stance automatically, which uses two key ingredients.

- Scoring essay words for being on-topic: Faulkner uses a Wikipedia link-based measure to compute the similarity between words in the essay and words in the essay's prompt.

- Parse trees for detecting stance expressions: With the help of a dependency parser and two lexical resources of stance words and attitudinal words (both taken from earlier research), Faulkner extracts parse subtrees that can be associated with a *stance-attitude profile*. This records a positive/negative evaluation of a for/against stance expressed in the sentence. Trees are generalized by means of their PoS labels.

The train/test data set consist of 1,135 stance-annotated essays from the International Corpus of Learner English (ICLE) [Granger, 2003]. Faulkner demonstrates that an SVM trained on the topic-word model easily outperforms two baselines: bag-of-words and an implementation of the best-performing linguistic features from the earlier work of Somasundaran and Wiebe (see page 88). Adding the subtree features yields another—if slight—improvement, resulting in an overall accuracy of 82%.

Topic-claim constellations   The team developing the *IBM argumentative structure dataset* [Aharoni et al., 2014] also added stance annotation to their data. As we explained in Section 5.3.4, their corpus was built by selecting debate topics from idebate.org and manually finding claim and evidence statements in Wikipedia articles. The version of this corpus used by Bar-Haim et al. [2017] encompasses 55 topics and 2,394 claims. (Examples were given in Figure 5.4 on page 72.) By definition, all claims in the dataset either support or contest the topic, and the new annotations make this explicit. Bar-Haim et al. decompose the automatic stance detection task into three subtasks.

1. Identify the *targets* of the given topic and claim. Targets (or 'aspects') are phrases that have been given a positive or negative evaluation by the author.

2. For each target, identify the polarity (sentiment) that is expressed toward it.

3. Determine whether targets are 'consistent' (have the same polarity orientation) or 'contrastive'; this can involve interpreting the targets and their relationship.

For labeling the data, each of the 55 topics received target and polarity annotation from the authors, and then annotators marked targets and sentiment in all the claims, and also added the consistent/contrastive relation. The claim stance is then derived automatically. A few examples of this annotation are shown in Figure 6.6, with the relation denoted by ⇔ and ⇎, and claim stance given in the rightmost column.

The various steps were then implemented as supervised classification tasks, and the authors claim that their decomposed approach beats monolithic stance classification.

#	Debate Topic (Motion)		Claim	
1	This house believes that **advertising** is harmful. ⊖	⇔	**Marketing** promotes consumerism and waste. ⊖	Pro
2	This house would ban **boxing**. ⊖	⇔	**Boxing** remains the 8th most deadly sport. ⊖	Pro
3	This house would embrace **multiculturalism**. ⊕	⇎	**Unity** is seen as an essential feature of the nation and the nation-state. ⊕	Con
4	This house supports **the one-child policy of the republic of China**. ⊕	⇎	**Children with many siblings** receive fewer resources. ⊖	Pro

Figure 6.6: Sample topic, claim, target, and stance annotations in the IBM dataset [Bar-Haim et al., 2017, p. 254], used with permission.

CHAPTER 7

Deriving the Structure of Argumentation

The tasks explained in the previous two chapters were to label the components of an argument and, along the way, to identify spans of text that are not part of the argument. We illustrate this with an extended version of Example 6.1, using the subscripts C, S, A for claim, support, attack:

(7.1) Last week I bought this new camera here. [You should also buy it,]$_C$ [because it has a brand-new excellent sensor.]$_S$ It's sold in the tech store around the corner. [OK, it is quite expensive.]$_A$ [But it's worth the money!]$_S$

For some purposes and for some texts, being able to do this is sufficient. Sometimes, however, it is not enough.

Assume that a text tries to persuade the reader not of one but of multiple different claims and provides the accompanying arguments. Now a flat labeling is insufficient because we need to know which argument components relate to each other: what supports what; what attacks what. Now we need to establish *explicit relations* between components, so that the correct mapping can be captured. Hence, in Section 7.1 we look at the task of identifying relations between argument components, which may be different kinds of support and attack.

Some approaches go a step further and aim at combining the various components of arguments and the relations between them into an overarching *structural representation*, which is the topic of Section 7.2. This is necessary for correctly capturing more complex arguments where, for instance, a statement supports the claim not directly but only indirectly via an additional statement; likewise, when several objections are being mentioned and refuted, the task is to appropriately record the attack and counterattack relationships and to show how they combine into a coherent argumentation structure.

7.1 ESTABLISHING RELATIONS BETWEEN ARGUMENT COMPONENTS

While in the previous chapters, we dealt with the task of identifying argumentative units and labeling them with their roles, we now turn to a *relation*-based perspective, which addresses this task:

Given two statements, determine the argumentative relation between them, such as:
Does one *support* or *attack* the other?

One practical motivation for taking this perspective stems from the analysis of multi-party interactions, where utterances by different speakers can be classified as being in agreement (corresponding to one utterance supporting the other) or in disagreement (one attacking the other).

But also when processing monologue text, relation identification can be important, as we argued in the introduction above. As soon as we cannot assume that the text in question contains just a single argument with no internal sub-structure (or when it is not relevant to account for that sub-structure), we need to explicitly mark the relations between argumentative units.

The dialogue and monologue settings obviously differ from each other: statements are taken from the utterances of different speakers, vs. from a single, coherent text. Thus, it can be assumed that the linguistic form is not the same, and that somewhat different approaches or feature sets are relevant. We will discuss the two settings in turn.

7.1.1   DISAGREEMENT IN ONLINE INTERACTIONS

Tracing the back and forth of argumentative exchanges in online interactions is a very attractive but at the same time quite ambitious goal. To date, no complete solutions have been proposed to our knowledge, but there has been work on the initial step of identifying relations between individual statements. Depending on the background (interaction analysis or argumentation mining), authors describe their aim either to classify agreement vs. disagreement, or support vs. attack (which amounts essentially to the same problem).

As analyzing online interactions is obviously of great practical relevance, several corpus annotation efforts have been undertaken. We listed some of the available resources in Section 4.2.1, including the information on download links. In the following, we look at work that involves those resources and uses different techniques to find an argumentative relation.

Textual entailment   Some researchers noted the similarity between the task of establishing a support relation and that of *Recognizing Textual Entailment* (RTE), which is commonly defined as follows: "A text T entails a hypothesis H if humans reading T would typically infer that H is most likely true" [Dagan et al., 2013, p. 3]. Notice the reliance on human judgment and the difference from strict logical entailment. TE is a fairly broad relation, covering also, for instance, physical causation, but it might be considered as subsuming argumentative support.

Cabrio and Villata [2012] tested how well an existing RTE tool (EDITS, Kouylekov and Negri [2010]), which applies an edit-distance measure, performs with pairs of argumentative statements gathered from Debatepedia and labeled with support/attack relations. EDITS was trained on 100 pairs and tested on 100 pairs. The authors reported a fairly promising accuracy of 0.67.

In the same spirit, Boltužić and Šnajder [2014] used the Excitement open RTE platform[1] [Padó et al., 2015] for classifying the relation between (manually created) argumentative statements and comments in the the ComArg corpus (see Section 4.2.1), expecting the comment text (which is usually longer) to entail the argument phrase. The classification is more difficult than in the other work reported here, as it uses five classes: explicit attack, implicit attack, explicit support, implicit support, and none. Excitement supplies seven different algorithms based on different types of information. Boltužić and Šnajder used the outputs (decisions and confidence values) of all seven algorithms as the features in their classifier, in addition to semantic similarity. The RTE approach was the more successful component, contributing an overall performance of 0.7 to a 0.82 micro-F in different problem settings (SVM classifier).

Recently, Bosc et al. [2016a] ran a similar experiment and applied Excitement to the DART corpus [Bosc et al., 2016b], which contains 4000 Tweets dealing with four different topics. They have been annotated pairwise with support/attack relations. Trying to predict the reations with the RTE platform leads to negative results, however.

Interactional structure   For threaded data, features of the structure of the interaction have been found to be useful. Rosenthal and McKeown [2015], for example, experimented successfully with meta-thread information in the IAC, ABCD, and AWTP data (see Section 4.2.1), such as the distance from the first post, the post coming from the same or a different author, and the length of the post.

When looking at longer stretches of conversation, it can make sense to differentiate the local stance in a single post from the *global* position a user has on an issue. Yin et al. [2012] showed that in their web forum thread data, aggregating the local positions over a user's posts leads to better performance than no-aggregation baselines. Mukherjee and Liu [2013] added another shift of perspective and modeled the dis/agreement behavior of individual user *pairs*, thus abstracting from the task of classifying individual Question-Response pairs to pairs of sets of user utterances. They use topic modeling and relevance-based ranking to derive phrases indicative of dis/agreement as their mean features.

Lexical and linguistic features   Various researchers showed that linguistically-motivated features can beat simple lexical n-gram models for dis/agreement classification. For instance, the feature analysis of Yin et al. [2012], who used a logistic regression model, suggested that sentiment, emotional and durational features can significantly improve classifier performance. In a similar vein, Abbott et al. [2011] worked with an early version of the Internet Argument Corpus (see Section 4.2.1) and measured the relative importance of a broad range of features for dis/agreement detection. They found that it is important to use local features (e.g., initial n-grams for approximating discourse markers such as *I don't know* and dependency triples) of both the quote and the response, rather than focusing on the response alone. In follow-up work, Misra

---

[1] https://hltfbk.github.io/Excitement-Open-Platform/ (accessed May 28, 2018).

and Walker [2013] emphasized the importance of finding topic-neutral features, in particular punctuation and cue words, for cross-domain performance of the models.

Ghosh et al. [2014] used a support vector machine to classify the agree/disagree relation on the callout/target annotation in technically-oriented blogs from technorati.com (see Section 4.2.1). A 'callout' is a statement that challenges another statement (by a different user), the 'target'. The authors achieved F-scores of 0.67 and 0.63 for the agree and disagree category, respectively, using a sentiment lexicon, initial unigrams in the callout, and lexical overlap between callout and target. Lexical overlap is one way to capture semantic similarity between statements, which has also been modeled by other researchers, including Boltužić and Šnajder [2014], as a domain-independent measurement.

Following an idea from Mukherjee and Liu [2013], Rosenthal and McKeown [2015] developed the notion of similarity further and worked with a theoretical motivation of 'accommodation', i.e., the phenomenon of interlocutors adopting the conversational characteristics of other participants as the conversation progresses. Thus, for dis/agreement detection in the IAC, ABCD and AWTP data (see Section 4.2.1), they used a sentence similarity tool measuring word/phrase overlap between Question and Response, and also computed the similarity of PoS n-gram overlap, the presence of social media-specific lexical material, and the distribution of LIWC[2] categories. Their results run up to an F-score of 0.78 for the ABCD corpus, and they provide interesting comparative analyses of the three datasets.

Neural networks   We mentioned above that Bosc et al. [2016a] sought to determine attack and support relations between tweets, and found that the task is very difficult when using an RTE platform. In addition, the authors implemented a neural approach running on tokens encoded as GloVe embeddings [Pennington et al., 2014]. With an encoder-decoder architecture and two LSTMs (the second LSTM initialized with the last hidden state of the first LSTM), they obtained results that also seem not promising (0.2 F-score for support and 0.16 for attack).

This work inspired Cocarascu and Toni [2017a] to try a similar approach on a set of 2,274 sentence pairs, which are taken apparently from newspaper text, but the source is not specified [Carstens and Toni, 2015]. While this data does not stem from online interaction, it is somewhat similar to the Twitter data above, in that it contains isolated sentence pairs. Examples are shown in Figure 7.1.[3] The architecture relies on two parallel LSTMs to model the two texts separately. The authors experimented with both unidirectional and bidirectional LSTMs and with (trained or non-trained) word embeddings (also via GloVe). The two output vectors are merged and the resulting vector fed to a Softmax classifier, which predicts the label for the relation. They achieved an accuracy of 89.5% by concatenating the output of the two separate LSTMs for the trained embeddings (which performed much better than untrained ones). Unexpectedly, results of the bidirectional LSTMs were lower than for the unidirectional ones.

---

[2]http://liwc.wpengine.com (accessed May 28, 2018).
[3]The data is available for research: https://www.doc.ic.ac.uk/~oc511/ACMToIT2017_dataset.xlsx (accessed December 9, 2018).

Parent	Child	Class
UKIP doesn't understand that young people are, by and large, progressive.	But UKIP claims to be winning support among younger voters and students.	a
It's a protest vote because (most) people know that UKIP will never net in power.	Emma Lewell-Buck made history becoming the constituency's first female MP.	n
It is because of UKIP that we are finally discussing the European question and about immigration and thank goodness for that.	I believe that what UKIP is doing is vital for this country.	s

Figure 7.1: Sample sentence pairs and attack/support/none annotations from Carstens and Toni [2015, p. 33], used with permission.

7.1.2   ARGUMENTATIVE RELATIONS IN MONOLOGUE

As we indicated at the beginning of the chapter, when mining arguments in monologue text, a flat labeling of argumentative roles is not sufficient if

- more than one claim is present, and support/attack material must be linked to the associated claim; or

- support and attack are directed not toward the claim but toward other argument components.

The second scenario holds for example in the case of 'serial support' (a transitive support constellation), as in the following example.

(7.2) [Vaccines are bad for kids!]$_1$ [They can cause all sorts of allergy problems.]$_2$ [A recent study reported a siginificant increase in allergic skin irritations.]$_3$

Here segment 1 represents the claim, which is supported by segment 2. Segment 3, however does not directly support the main claim, but provides evidence for segment 2, which thus plays both the roles of support (for 1) and a minor claim (for 3).

   Similarly, as we indicated in the previous chapter, once counter-considerations are admitted to the argument analysis, it is very likely that 'counter-attack' enters the picture, since a speaker probably is not going to let a possible objection just stand as is. Then, the counter-attack is obviously directed to the counter-consideration.

(7.3) [Vaccines are bad for kids!]$_1$ [I've seen some reports claiming tremendous infection reduction rates,]$_2$ [but those must have been sponsored by the pharmaceutical industry.]$_3$

Here, segment 2 is a counter-consideration to claim 1, yet it is immediately rejected by 3. In similar ways, it is possible for a speaker to give a counter-consideration and then to add potential evidence to it, before dismissing the entire move by means of a counter-attack.

Generally, we are here moving toward *recursion* in argumentative structure. We will discuss this in more detail in the next section on identifying full structures, but for now, establishing individual relations between components is a central intermediate step. The task is essentially the same as that described above for dialogue: given a pair of argumentative units, classify their relationship as support, attack, or none (or some more fine-grained subclasses of support and attack, but in practice that is only rarely done).

Note that the extraction of semantic/pragmatic relations is well known in other branches of NLP, too. Most often, the focus is on relations between entities, but sometimes, relations between events are also being considered (for example, causal relations in biomedical text, as in the BioCause corpus.[4]) Furthermore, as we mentioned in Section 2.6 and elsewhere, the automatic identification of discourse relations, for instance along the lines of the Penn Discourse Treebank [Prasad et al., 2008] is a well-known task. In the following, however, we only report work that has been explicitly geared toward argumentation.

Rule-based identification   In the early work of Palau and Moens [2009] on legal documents, classifiers were used for finding argumentative sentences and determining their role, as we reported above. Connections between the components are then established by means of a context-free grammar that checks for predefined cue words and punctuation symbols, identifies the non-terminal constituents as premises or conclusions, and joins them in a recursive tree structure. The evaluation yielded an accuracy of 60%. However, it is very difficult to adapt the approach to other domains, especially if the role of conventionalized, formulaic expressions is limited.

Feature-based classification   Working with texts from the argumentative microtext corpus (see Section 4.2.2), Peldszus [2014] operationalized relation detection as a combination of classifying the argumentative function of an ADU in isolation (thesis, support, attack) and the distance to the target unit, i.e., the unit being supported or attacked. Since the texts are short (on average, roughly 5 units), this usually ranges between -4 (four units to the left of the classified one) and +4 (four units to the right). Peldszus used lexical, morphosyntactic, positional, and cue (connectives, negation) features and experimented with a variety of classifiers. He found that a Naive Bayes approach worked best for the support/attack/thesis distinction (F-measure 0.74) as well as for a more fine-grained version that distinguishes 'normal' from 'example' support and 'undercut' from 'rebut' (F-measure 0.67). Connectives, lemma n-grams, and dependencies turned out to be the most helpful features. Finding the right target, however, proved to be very difficult, and thus in follow-up work, Peldszus and Stede [2015a] instead used an out-of-the-box discourse parser [Baldridge et al., 2007] for predicting segment attachment, reaching a macro-F measure of 0.73, with F being 0.56 for positive attachment.

A similar result was obtained by Stab and Gurevych [2014b] for the more complex texts in the corpus of persuasive student essays (see Section 4.2.2). For illustration, here is an excerpt

[4]http://www.nactem.ac.uk/biocause/ (accessed May 28, 2018).

from such a text. Subscripts show the unit number, the relation type and target (if any), and the argumentative function.

(7.4) [People who are addicted to games, especially online games, can eventually bear dangerous consequences.]$_{1;Claim}$ [Although it is undeniable that computer is a crucial part of human life,]$_{2>3;Premise}$ [it still has its bad side.]$_{3;MajorClaim}$

The approach disregarded the attack relation and thus solved the binary task of classifying pairs of segments as to whether one is in support relation with the other or not.[5] Using similar features as Peldszus [2014], but adding also word pairs of the two segments, and the results of an argumentative-function classifier (which assigned the labels Claim, Major Claim, Premise), this led to a macro F-score of 0.72, and 0.52 for positive attachment.

Topic modeling   On the same essay corpus, Nguyen and Litman [2016] also addressed the support detection task, using the same corpus setup as Stab and Gurevych. For non-/support, they re-implemented and slightly expanded the feature set, obtaining roughly the same results, which served as a baseline. Then, Nguyen and Litman showed that their technique of LDA-based differentiation between 'argument words' and 'domain words', which we described above in Section 5.3.3, can lead to superior results. They used the presence of argument words as binary features, and several features measuring the domain word overlap between the two segments. Here is an example, with argument words in bold face and domain words in italics [Nguyen and Litman, 2016, p. 1131].

(7.5) Essay 54. Topic: museum and art gallery will disappear soon?
Source/premise: **more** and **more people can** *watch exhibitions* through *television* **or** *internet* at *home* **due to** *modern technology*
Target/claim: **some people think** *museums* and *art galleries* **will** *disappear soon*

While adding topic features does not beat the baseline, significantly better results (macro-F: 0.75) are achieved when also adding the output of two discourse parsers (one for PDTB relations, one for RST structure, both of which have been introduced in Section 2.6).

In addition, Nguyen and Litman classified the relation type (support/attack), assuming that a relation between two segments has also been established. The best results were achieved with the same combination of features as in the first task, with a macro-F of 0.7. Note, though, the huge difference between the F-score for support (0.94) and for attack (0.4).

Some other researchers experimented with topic modeling features, too. Lawrence et al. [2014], for example, measured topical distance between argumentative units in philosophical papers, thus targeting a much harder type of text. However, the method was only evaluated on a very small data set and thus cannot be compared with the other research.

---

[5]Hence, 'no support' subsumes both the cases of attack and zero relation.

7.2   IDENTIFYING COMPLETE ARGUMENT STRUCTURES

Having considered all the prerequisite subtasks, we are now well prepared to study approaches that are interested in identifying the complete structures of arguments. Notice, however, that we restrict the discussion here to individual arguments—or, in the terminology of Bentahar et al. [2010], to the *micro-level* of argumentation. In contrast, the *macro-level*, which would represent relationships between different arguments (possibly across different documents), is out of our scope.

Given the variety of approaches to the subtasks we surveyed thus far, it does not come as a surprise that—in this young research field—there is no general consensus on what exactly *is* an appropriate description of an argument's structure. But we can identify a few general lines of research. First of all, it is important to distinguish between these.

- **Hierarchical structure:** Text segments are identified as argumentative units, these are being related to one another and ultimately to the single *claim*, yielding a graph structure; and

- **Sequential structure:** Any argument in text is presented in a certain linear order of the units, which influences rhetorical (and possibly even logical) felicity.

Hierarchical structure, by design, abstracts linear order away, and provides an extract that serves to represent the 'logos' dimension[6] of argumentation, i.e., the inferential relations of statements supporting (or attacking) another. In contrast, linear order is closely related to 'pathos', the persuasive effects intended by the speaker. So far, most work in structure derivation has concentrated on hierarchy. We will discuss these approaches first, and then come back to the sequential structure at the end of the section.

7.2.1   COMPUTING HIERARCHICAL STRUCTURE

As stated in Section 4.1, the prevalent conception for representing (and annotating) argument structure is that of a tree rooted in the central claim of the text. Besides purely theoretical considerations, evidence for this stems from data analysis and from experiences with annotation practice. For instance, Lawrence et al. [2014, p. 81] point out that "in many cases an argument can be represented as a tree. This assumption is supported by around 95% of the argument analyses contained in AIFdb [Lawrence et al., 2012] as well as the fact that many manual analysis tools (...) limit the user to a tree format." A sample tree from the argumentative microtext corpus (see Section 4.2.2) is shown below in Figure 7.2.

In contrast, the annotation of eRulemaking comments by Niculae et al. [2017] regards trees as unsuitable for capturing the argumentation structure in less well-organized texts. In the

---

[6]Recall the logos/pathos/ethos dimensions described on page 5.

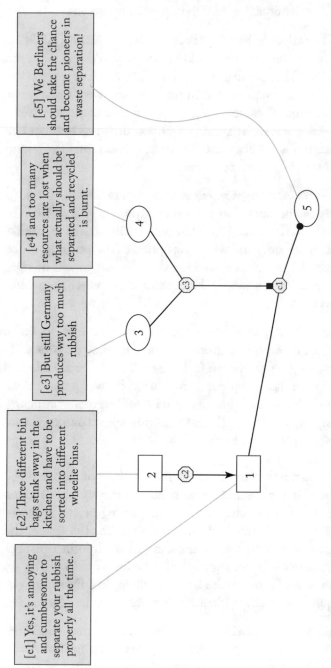

Figure 7.2: Argumentation structure graph from 'microtext corpus' (Peldszus and Stede [2016b]): 1 attacks claim 5 and is supported by 2; 3 and 4 jointly undercut the attack relation.

following, we first look at different ways that have been proposed for computing trees, and in the end briefly describe Niculae et al.'s approach to predicting graphs.

Rule-based parsing   The early rule-based work by Palau and Moens [2009] (cf. Section 5.3.1) computed premise-conclusion trees, with an additional unit type 'decision', by means of a context free grammar (CFG) model. The resulting trees can include serial support as well as convergent structures. Relation types are not represented in the tree, however. The other grammar-driven approach that we have mentioned before (Section 5.3.2) is that of Saint-Dizier [2012]: Using a logic- and constraint-based grammar language, which was designed to extend linguistic analysis from the level of sentence to that of discourse, his system determines the boundaries of various types of spans and produces embedded structures.

Template slot filling   When the target representation is a predefined set of (possibly related) components, the analysis can be framed as a slot-filling process. Recall the Modified Toulmin Scheme used by Habernal and Gurevych [2017], which was illustrated on page 49. When defining which components are obligatory and which are optional (and possibly, which ones can occur multiple times), these expectations can be used to guide the assignment of argumentative units to component types (or 'slots' in the schema). Habernal and Gurevych, however, used a different paradigm, to be descibed next.

Segment-wise classification   A classification-based approach can be applied to a pre-defined sequence of segments, or it can combine segmentation and labeling decisions. The latter was implemented in the IOB tagging approaches of Goudas et al. [2014] and Habernal and Gurevych [2017] (see Section 5.3.5). Of these, Habernal and Gurevych used a much richer type set (that of the Modified Toulmin Scheme) and thus produced a 'full' argument structure in the sense of a pre-defined set of components. Notice that recursion is not accounted for in such a tagging regime; there is no serial support, for instance. It is, however, possible to assign the same type more than once.

A pre-segmented short text is the input to the classifier of Peldszus [2014]. Using the annotation scheme encoded in the argumentative microtext corpus (see Sections 4.1 and 4.2.2), the system can produce recursive structures, where supporting or attacking statements can in turn be supported, etc. An example tree is shown in Figure 7.2. The system therefore needs to account explicitly for relations and does so by encoding all the information about a segment in a complex label. This includes the target segment of the relation, denoted by $-n \ldots + n$ with n being the distance to the target (either to the left or to the right). Even though the 'microtexts' used by Peldszus were quite short, target identification proved to be very hard in this approach.

Minimum-spanning tree (MST) algorithm   Having observed that an off-the-shelf discourse parser performs quite well on detecting the target segment of a relation, Peldszus and Stede [2015a] proposed a parsing technique for predicting the tree structure of argumentation in the 'microtext' corpus. The first stage of the system employs an improved version of the segment classifier introduced by Peldszus [2014], which for a segment determines probabilities for being central claim, proponent or opponent's voice, and support or attack function; and for a pair of segments, whether they are connected. The information gathered about the segments was then mapped to a fully connected weighted graph, where the weights represent the predictions made by the local classifiers. Then, an implementation of the standard MST algorithm [Chu and Liu, 1965, Edmonds, 1967] decoded the optimal structure. A central step in this approach is the specific way of 'translating' the numerical results of segment classification into the appropriate edge weights in the graph. The system achieved an F-score of 0.72 for identifying argumentative relations and 0.87 for recognizing claims.

Integer linear programming (ILP)   Besides MST, another candidate for optimizing the global structure is ILP. The key is to specify a suitable objective function to be maximized, as well as constraints on the target structure to be built, which then guide the search. Afantenos et al. [2018] suggest various groups of such constraints, including the following.

- **Tree constraints**: All nodes have one or no outgoing edge; the root node has no outgoing edge; cycles are ruled out.

- **Relation labeling**: Every node has exactly one function (support or attack).

- **Interactions**: The root node (central claim) must be in proponent's voice; a support relation can hold only between nodes in the same voice, etc.

Implementations of tree prediction in an ILP framework have been proposed by Persing and Ng [2016], Stab and Gurevych [2017b], and Afantenos et al. [2018], using either the persuasive essay corpus of Stab and Gurevych [2014a] (Persing/Ng) or the microtext corpus (Afantenos et al.), or both (Stab/Gurevych). Results are not directly comparable due to different versions of the essay corpus being used, and somewhat different feature sets. All authors, however, report improvements over previous pipeline-based approaches. Afantenos et al. also replicated the other two approaches as well as the MST approach of Peldszus and Stede [2015a] and provide a comparative analysis.

Neural networks   One of the first NN experiments on the persuasive essay and microtext corpora was done by Potash et al. [2017]. The authors solved the tasks of predicting argument components (claim, major claim, premise) and link detection (i.e., unlabeled relations), and they arrive at a tree structure. They propose that sequence-to-sequence attention modeling, specifically a Pointer Network [Vinyals et al., 2015] is well suited for this problem, as it can capture the sequential information of argument components, partly enforce the tree structure, and jointly predict multiple subtasks with the hidden representations. For representing components, the system uses bag-of-words, GloVe embeddings, and positional features. Despite the relatively small amount of training data in the two corpora, the authors report results that outperform those of the ILP approaches by Peldszus and Stede [2015a] and Stab and Gurevych [2017b] for the subtasks that are being addressed here. They also confirm the earlier insight that joint optimization (here for segment type and linking) is clearly better than combining individual solutions.

Eger et al. [2017] also ran a number of NN experiments on the persuasive essay corpus. As a potential advantage of neural sequence tagging models, they point out that (at least in this corpus) related ADUs need not be adjacent but, on the contrary, can be at a fairly long distance from each other; this is a well-known problem for CRF-like models. For ADU identification, Eger et al. obtained best results from a BiLSTM tagger. Identifying support and attack relations was a harder task, but still they achieved better results with an LSTM than the ILP approach of Stab and Gurevych [2017b] did.

Predicting graphs   In Section 4.1, we described the Cornell eRulemaking annotation scheme, which uses general graphs rather than trees for representing argmentation, and employs a set of role and relation labels that is more domain-specific than those used in the work described above. For building such graphs over pre-segmented input, Nicolae et al. use structured learning. They cast the problem in a *factor graph* approach [Kschischang et al., 2001], which can fully learn the correlations between role assignment and linking, and does not rely on handcrafted scoring, as via the objective function in ILP. Inference is done by the Alternating Directions Dual Decomposition (AD^3) algorithm. For parameterization, the authors experimented with two approaches: a linear structured SVM using the features proposed by Stab and Gurevych [2014b] for role identification and linking, and a bidirectional LSTM that encodes context for a segment represented as the average of the LSTM outputs of the words therein. Niculae et al. evaluated the approach on their own eRulemaking corpus as well as the persuasive essay corpus from Stab and Gurevych. For the latter, they obtained competitive results on the link prediction task. Generally, the feature engineering SVM approach outperforms the RNN, which, however, yields very good results on unit type classification in the persuasive essays.

7.2.2   SEQUENTIAL STRUCTURE

A tree or graph structure represents the logical gist of an argument, which for many purposes is useful and may constitute the final result of argumentation mining. But it should be noted that information about the *linear order* of the argument components found in the text is essentially neglected by the approaches shown in the previous subsection. So far, aspects of the linearization of texts have received only little attention in argumentation mining. To some extent, the step of constructing a graph may exploit locality constraints by preferring adjacent units when predicting argumentative relations; but beyond this consideration, aspects of linear order tend to be ignored.

On the other hand, the fact that linear order does matter has received quite a bit of attention in rhetoric (cf. Section 2.6). A simple example of its relevance is the *A, but B* pattern, which is known to express not just a symmetrical contrast but to assign different weights to *A* and *B*.

(7.6) The party has good ideas, but the leader is quite dumb. I won't vote for them.

(7.7) The leader is quite dumb, but the party has good ideas. I will vote for them.

Note that switching the order of *A* and *B* in either case (or, alternatively, switching the negation) produces odd results. This general insight can be extended to the text level; for instance, popular advice from rhetorics guidebooks suggests to place your 'best' argument maybe at the beginning of your text, or at the end, but definitely not in the middle. And plenty of more sophisticated recipes are being studied for their persuasive power.

Building upon ideas on assigning types to ADUs (recall, e.g., the work on 'argumentative zoning' mentioned in Section 2.6), Wachsmuth and Stein [2017] suggest to model an *argumentation strategy* as a sequence of rhetorical moves. They study different sets of move types, such as sentiment values (positive, negative, neutral), discourse relations (background, cause, circumstance, ...), or argumentative moves (claim, premise, none, ...). No matter what the type set is, the underlying computational problem is the same: given a segmented text and a classifier that assigns a move to each segment, the result is a sequence of labels, which Wachsmuth and Stein call a 'flow'. The idea is to explore attributes of these flows for predicting properties of the text, for example its persuasiveness. This presupposes, however, that flows of different texts can be individually compared, and subsequently analyzed for commonalities, e.g., by clustering algorithms. Comparing flows is not trivial, though, because texts (and thus flows) are of different lengths. Wachsmuth and Stein experiment with various techniques for normalizing flows to a unit length, so that follow-up computations are possible. Figure 7.3 illustrates the overall idea.

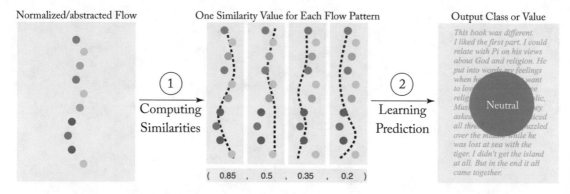

Figure 7.3: Illustration of the 'flow' comparison/clustering approach to predicting text features. A dot represents a text segment, and its color represents its type based on [Wachsmuth and Stein, 2017, p. A:7].

One more instantiation of this approach was presented by Al-Khatib et al. [2017], who apply it to newspaper editorials. The three moves of interest are types of evidence given for a claim: *statistics, testimony,* and *anecdote*. Since a flow must capture the text completely, every other segment receives the label *other*. These moves have been manually annotated on the 300 texts of the Webis Editorials corpus (see Section 4.2.2), and this data was used to build a classifier.

The features were different kinds of n-grams (including token, character, chunk, PoS), sentence length and position, NE type distribution, and sentiment. With an SVM, all groups of features were found to be useful, and the resulting F1-scores for the three important categories range between 0.5 and 0.59, while that for 'other' is 0.87.

This classifier was then used to label a corpus of 29,000 editorials from the *New York Times* corpus, which in addition have all been assigned to a broad topic class (such as economics, arts, health, etc.) by a Naive Bayes classifier. Al-Khatib et al. then applied the flow normalization algorithm and were able to correlate flow patterns with the topics: Significant differences emerged, from which the authors concluded that the topic of an editorial influences the flow pattern selected by the author (and, in addition, the proportional distribution of evidence types, as shown in a separate experiment).

Finally, we mention the work of Wachsmuth et al. [2017a], who demonstrate that for three downstream tasks (computing argumentative text genre, myside bias in arguments, and stance), the prediction benefits from considering *both* the explicit linear order of an argumentative text, and its implicit hierarchical structure. The authors propose a positional tree kernel model that is able to combine the sequence and hierarchy information.

CHAPTER 8

Assessing Argumentation

While finding argument components and possibly arranging them in a tree or graph structure constitute the core tasks of argumentation mining, there is a small body of research aiming at going further and computing 'deeper' information about arguments. The first to be considered here is the problem of detecting *enthymemes*, which amounts to construing the (logically) missing premises for an argument to make sense. Similarly, one can try to identify the underlying reasoning pattern or *argumentation scheme* (cf. Section 3.3), which explains why (or not) a particular constellation of inferences works. Finally, we discuss work on the *quality* of arguments, which encompasses both measuring how 'good' an argument is, as well as a set of various other attributes that researchers have drawn attention to.

8.1 RECONSTRUCTING ENTHYMEMES

Enthymemes are arguments that can be understood by a hearer only if she considers the given claim and premise, and reconstructs a 'hidden' premise that provides the link between the two. In the argumentation literature, these are often called *minor* premise (stated) and *major* premise (unstated). A classical example is as follows.

(8.1) Minor (stated) premise: Socrates is human.
     Major (unstated) premise: All humans are mortal.
     Claim/Conclusion (stated): Therefore, Socrates is mortal.

More examples from real-life text will follow below. Enthymemes are a very natural phenomenon, as already pointed out by Aristotle: when a (logically necessary) premise represents a fact that can be assumed as known to the hearer, then the speaker can leave this premise implicit in an argument. The hearer then needs to activate her common knowledge to perform the reconstruction [Walton, 2008].

     Not surprisingly, this reconstruction task is very difficult to automate—so far, only very few preliminary studies have been done in the argumentation mining community. Wyner et al. [2010] provided a manual pilot study on major (implicit) premises in online discussions. They first annotated the premises in a variant of 'Controlled English' (i.e., a simplified and semi-formalized language) and then defined propositional logic axioms to explicate the stances of discussion participants. Overall, this serves as an illustration of the kind of knowledge required for an in-depth treatment of enthymemes. Focusing more on the problem of manually annotating enthymemes, Razuvayevskaya and Teufel [2017] explored several variants of operationalizing the task and provide suggestions on how to reach sufficient inter-annotator agreement.

In another pilot study, which makes a connection to opinion mining in product reviews, Rajendran et al. [2016] propose linking the handling of implicit opinions (those that on the surface look like factual statements but contain an implicit evaluation) to enthymeme reconstruction. Their idea is to classify an opinion statement as to whether it is implicit or explicit, and to regard an explicit statement together with the overall judgment on the product (as derived from the rating given with the review) as complete arguments: The reviewer likes product X because of Y. Implicit opinions, on the other hand, when combined with the conclusion can create an enthymeme. Then, common knowledge is necessary to complete the argument—which is the major unsolved problem.

The other research perspective on enthymemes is: what is actually computationally feasible in practice? From this angle, Boltužić and Šnajder [2016] saw an analogy between major/minor premise on the one hand and the claim/claim type pairs that were collected by Hasan and Ng [2014], mentioned on page 82. These authors had gathered the reasons that authors provide for their stance toward an issue of public debate, clustered those reasons, and formulated a meta-statement describing each cluster. Three examples are given on the left hand side of Figure 8.1: The 'user claim' is from the forum post, and the 'main claim' is the abstract meta-statement provided by Hasan and Ng.

Like Hasan and Ng, Boltužić and Šnajder tackled the problem of matching user claims to main claims (or in other words: given a user claim, find the appropriate main claim). But here the idea is to explore the 'gap' between the two types of claim, which Boltužić and Šnajder proposed to fill with additional premises. This step amounts to making implicit major premises explicit, i.e., to enthymeme reconstruction. Annotators added the major premises to the original Hasan/Ng dataset,[1] following the instruction to formulate statements that 'bridge the gap'. In Figure 8.1, the top claim pair has been annotated with two implicit major premises, while annotators identified the other two pairs as non-matching or not in need of any explication, respectively. The authors regard the number of major premises as a measure of the size of the inferential gap (in their corpus, the average is 2.7). To gather evidence for this hypothesis, Boltužić and Šnajder ran a crowdsourcing experiment to obtain judgments on the semantic similarity between the user claim and main claim, and they indeed found a statistically significant (though weak) negative correlation between semantic similarity and gap size.

Next, the authors turned to the question whether the annotated gold premises can support the task of matching user claims to the given set of main claims. They computed semantic similarity between claim sentences via cosine distance, where the vectors were produced by summing up the embedding vectors for each word of a sentence. Having tested various operationalizations for making use of the major premises, they found that combining the premises with the main claim, and then running the similarity computations, is the best approach.

---

[1]And the result is in turn made available: `http://takelab.fer.hr/data/argpremises/` (accessed December 9, 2018).

Claim pair	Annotation
User claim: *Obama supports the Bush tax cuts. He did not try to end them in any way.* **Main claim:** *Obama destroyed our economy.*	**P1:** *Obama continued with the Bush tax cuts.* **P2:** *The Bush tax cuts destroyed our economy.*
User claim: *What if the child is born and there is so many difficulties that the child will not be able to succeed in life?* **Main claim:** *A fetus is not a human yet, so it's okay to abort.*	Non-matching
User claim: *Technically speaking, a fetus is not a human yet.* **Main claim:** *A fetus is not a human yet, so it's okay to abort.*	Directly linked

Figure 8.1: Examples of claim pairs annotated with implicit premises [Boltužić and Šnajder, 2016, p. 127], used with permission.

The obvious next question is whether it is possible to infer the major premises automatically; Boltužić and Šnajder conducted some first experiments but these were not particularly successful.

8.2   IDENTIFYING ARGUMENTATION SCHEMES

In Section 3.3, we explained the notion of 'argumentation scheme' as put forward by Walton et al. [2008], Rigotti and Greco Morasso [2010], and others. The central idea is to specify *on what grounds* a support or attack relation is supposed to hold among two ADUs, or in other words, what the underlying inferential motif is. A central assumption of this line of research is that a reasonably small set of such inferential patters can adequately describe the range of possibilities. For illustration, from the scheme set proposed by Walton et al. [2008], we reproduce the *Argument from positive consequences* scheme (p. 332).

- Premise: If A is brought about, good consequences will plausibly occur.

- Therefore, A should be brought about.

- Critical questions:

  - How strong is the likelihood that the cited consequences will (may, must) occur?

  - What evidence supports the claim that the cited consequences will (may, must) occur, and is it sufficient to support the strength of the claim adequately?

  - Are there other opposite consequences (bad as opposed to good, for example) that should be taken into account?

The critical questions point to potential objections and thereby guide the speaker in backing up the argument where necessary. Schemes have received some, but not too much attention in argumentation mining research. When premises and conclusions have been identified in a text, it is generally very difficult to reliably identify the underlying scheme automatically.

An early corpus annotated with scheme information was Araucaria DB [Reed et al., 2008a]. Some more recent work that assesses the feasibility of human scheme annotation, and suggests to exploit such data for argumentation mining, will be described in the first subsection below. The actual automatic labeling of scheme information has been addressed only rarely so far; it is the topic of the second subsection.

8.2.1   HUMAN ANNOTATION STUDIES

Not surprisingly, deciding on the kind of inference underneath an argumentative move involves subjective judgment to a large extent, and accordingly, it is not easy to obtain good results in agreement studies. For example, Reisert et al. [2017] started from Walton's argument from consequences (one variant is shown just above) and aimed at operationalizing it for argumentation mining by mapping it to a pattern instantiation task, where slots are characterized by their positive or negative consequences for participants of the event described. The authors suggested 24 such patterns in total (covering both support and attack under this argumentation scheme) and applied it to 20 texts from the 'microtext' corpus [Peldszus and Stede, 2016b]. For two annotators, however, they reached a rather low kappa ranging from 0.19–0.43 depending on how strictly agreement is defined.

Musi et al. [2016] developed guidelines for annotating schemes according to the 'Argumentum model of topics' of Rigotti and Greco Morasso [2010]. The authors favor this approach over Walton's, because the 15 schemes are organized in a hierarchy that more explicitly aims at devising mutually exclusive categories. Also, the definitions refer to semantic properties of the participating entities rather than to the logical inference steps. They applied the approach to 30 texts from the persuasive essay corpus of Stab and Gurevych [2014a], and report a Fleiss κ of just 0.1, but this involves nine, only lightly trained annotators. An informative error analysis, including a follow-up experiment, is provided. The annotation guidelines and data are available for research.[2]

More often given by	Can be prob.	Argumentation Scheme	Full corpus 72 debates (novices & experts)	Subcorpus 28 debates (novices & experts)	Subcorpus 28 debates (novices only)	χ^2	Sig. level
		Argument from Evidence to Hypothesis	19.29%	20.65%	21.51%		
		Argument from Rules	16.90%	18.66%	12.90%		
Experts		**Note**	**13.69%**	**10.14%**	**0.00%**	$\chi^2=3.66$	p < .05
Novices	⚠	**Argumentation from Values**	**4.20%**	**4.17%**	**9.68%**	$\chi^2=5.13$	p < .05
		Argument from Need for Help	4.12%	3.62%	2.15%		
		Argument from Bias	3.87%	4.53%	6.45%		
		No reason given	3.22%	3.62%	5.38%		
		Argument from Position to Know	3.05%	2.36%	4.30%		
Experts		**Argument from Precedent**	**3.05%**	**3.80%**	**0.00%**	$\chi^2=3.66$	p < .1
	⚠	Argument from Ignorance	2.97%	3.08%	4.30%		
		Argument from Composition	2.56%	2.54%	2.15%		
Novices	⚠	**Argument from Cause to Effect**	**2.31%**	**2.72%**	**7.53%**	$\chi^2=5.59$	p < .02
Novices	⚠	**Argument from Analogy**	**2.23%**	**2.36%**	**8.60%**	$\chi^2=9.86$	p < .05
	⚠	Argument from Waste	2.23%	2.54%	1.08%		
	⚠	Practical Reasoning	2.23%	2.72%	3.23%		
		Arg. from Verbal Classification	2.06%	1.45%	2.15%		

Figure 8.2: Distribution of argumentation schemes in Wikipedia page deletion discussion corpus [Schneider et al., 2013b, p. 28].

A larger study, which uses the scheme catalogue of Walton et al. [2008], was performed by Schneider et al. [2013b]. In several rounds of annotation, 741 messages from 72 debates on Wikipedia Talk Pages (discussing whether a certain page should be deleted) were labeled. In the first phase, the authors found that 17 of the Walton-type schemes were applicable to the data. Then, two annotators labeled the arguments in each message with one of these schemes, and reached a κ of 0.48. In the final corpus of 1,213 arguments, the authors determined the most common schemes—see Figure 8.2. The distribution, according to the authors, reflects the focus on precedent and rules, which is typical for this genre, and furthermore a tendency to discuss Wikipedia articles in terms of values and community norms. The authors also determined differences in scheme usage of novices vs. experts participating in the debates; some results are also shown in the figure. Generally, the study found that the most prevalent patterns are the 'Rules' and 'Evidence to Hypothesis' schemes from the Walton scheme catalogue (36% of arguments), and that familiarity with community norms correlates with the novices' ability to craft persuasive arguments. Also, the study looked into the success of arguments in the course of a debate, and found that successful arguments tend to use a rhetoric that is in line with the

[2]https://github.com/musielena/argscheme_aclworkshop2016 (accessed Sep 28. 2017).

policies and values established in the community, while unsuccessful arguments are mostly based on personal preference or on inappropriate analogy to other cases.

Likewise in the tradition of Walton's approach, Song et al. [2014] exploited the role of the critical questions for purposes of writing support. As stated in the beginning, these questions can serve to guide a writer in building up a successful argument, and the hypothesis of Song et al. was that adherence to such conventionalized rules in fact distinguishes good from bad essay writers. The authors found that the original Walton scheme catalogue is occasionally difficult to work with (due to ambiguity), and hence they made modifications; eventually they used three schemes (policy, causal, sample), each associated with various sub-categories and critical questions, for their essay annotation study. Two prompts were selected, and for each, 4 trained annotators labeled 300 texts. Agreement was calculated for a subset of 40 essays: for common schemes and categories, the pairwise κ ranged between 0.55 and 0.85, while rare categories proved to be more difficult to agree on.

Finally, we mention the work of Green [2015], who works on scientific papers, which generally are not yet heavily studied in argumentation mining. Green found the schemes from the 'standard' approaches not directly applicable and devised 10 schemes on her own, which she found to represent the major forms of argumentation for scientific claims in 4 genetics papers. Only some of these schemes overlap with the catalogue of Walton et al. [2008]. To evaluate the approach in a pilot study, Green worked with about 30 subjects and determined to what extent schemes were recognized, by means of test questions that had to be answered [Green, 2015]. Subsequently, a second pilot study tested whether 6 subjects from biology and computer science research could consistently apply 5 common schemes, this time defined contextually with genetics-specific concepts [Green, 2017]. Green has begun to investigate applying these schemes in combination with semantic types such as genes, mutations, proteins, and phenotypes which can be detected by generic bioNLP tools [Green, 2018].

8.2.2 AUTOMATIC SCHEME LABELING

Experiments on automatically labeling texts with scheme information have been rare so far. One initial study was done by Song et al. [2014] on the above-mentioned essay annotations. They trained a logistic regression classifier to determine whether a sentence raises critical questions or not (which is relevant for essay scoring), using n-grams, positional and PoS features, as well as lexical overlap between sentence and prompt. The crucial question for this task is how well the model generalizes across prompts. When training and testing on data including both prompts, the system reached a performance of κ=0.44, but when training on one and testing on the other, the average is only 0.26.

Focusing on the core schemes rather than the critical questions, Feng and Hirst [2011] tackled the problem of automatically assigning one of the five most frequent schemes from Walton et al. [2008] to pairs of premise and conclusion (which are assumed as given already) taken from the Araucaria DB data [Reed et al., 2008a]. The schemes are: argument from example, from cause to effect, from consequences, from verbal classification, and practical reasoning. The authors used positional features (absolute and relative, for premise and conclusion), length of the two components, the number of premises, as well as some scheme-specific features (largely cue phrases). In a separate experiment, they measured the impact of additionally specifying the type of argumentation structure (linked versus convergent) to the classifier.

In one-against-others classification via a C4.5 decision tree, the system produced rather promising results: for two schemes, the best average accuracies were better than 90%, while for the other three schemes the results were between 63% and 70%. Adding the linked/convergent feature generally helped, and most dramatically for the Argument from example schema.

In an experiment on AIFdb data [Lawrence et al., 2012] (which includes the Araucaria DB used by Feng/Hirst), Lawrence and Reed [2016] also classified the presence of a scheme, and in addition studied the task of identifying the scheme components (premise, conclusion) by means of similar features as used by Feng and Hirst. Here, the F-score results vary widely between scheme component type, and between classifiers (Naive Bayes, SVM, Decision Tree), ranging from 0.57–0.91. One reason for the different performances on different schemes is their varying connection to linguistic marking: some co-occur with particular connectives (e.g., *for example*) or other expressions relatively often, while others do not.

8.3   DETERMINING ARGUMENT QUALITY

In some sense, the question about the quality of an argument is the 'ultimate' one for argumentation mining: being able to reconstruct argumentative structures from a text is the groundwork, but assessing the degree of strength of an argument, or comparing the quality of arguments to one another, is a goal that many practical future applications will envisage. For example, an automated debating chatbot that constantly produces lame arguments will not be successful—so it better be aware of the quality parameter.

We divide this section in three parts. The first follows up on Chapter 3 and looks at the problem from a logical perspective, where the *consistency* of a constellation of argument components is of interest. Then, our second part considers the quality of an argument in a more general sense: How good is it, and, for that matter, what exactly does 'good' mean? Finally, the third part focuses specifically on the role of emotion in argumentation, which in many practical scenarios can be a decisive factor for perceived quality.

8.3.1   CONSISTENCY CHECKING

The step from argumentation mining in text to automated reasoning is, as of today, a very difficult one, but as we pointed out earlier, we believe it to be crucial for making progress with analyzing arguments 'underneath the linguistic surface'. Hence, in this section, we briefly consider the paramount 'quality' question for logical reasoning: given a constellation of arguments, which arguments are consistent with each other? Argumentation solvers address this question for formal argumentation models. Systems such as Arg&Dec, ASPARTIX, ASPIC, and Carneades which can reason over these formal models have been applied, typically to manually constructed formalisms drawn from real online debates. The underlying models vary, and many are based on Dung's abstract argumentation frameworks, which we introduced in Section 3.4.1, and which can be solved for *acceptability* with numerous argumentation solvers. For instance, Dung's frameworks have been extended by bipolar argumentation frameworks [Cayrol and Lagasquie-Schiex, 2009], which use both attack and support relationships, represented as different edge types, and which have also been used for consistency checking, and by abstract dialectical frameworks.

Argumentation solvers   Several existing systems, which we refer to as argumentation solvers and computational argumentation systems, can reason over argument frameworks. Cerutti et al. [2018] provide a broad review of formal systems and their implementations. Thimm and Villata [2017] summarize best-in-class argumentation solvers from the first biennial competition of the research community, and provides background on the answer set programming and satisfiability (SAT) solver approaches that underlie argumentation solvers.

For instance, Carneades [Gordon, 2013],[3] an opensource reasoning system with an online demo[4] can evaluate argument graphs, and takes multiple input and output formats. It is motivated by legal reasoning and can calculate whether an argument meets one of several common legal evidence standards. It can also compute the 'calculus of opposition', grounded, complete, preferred, and stable extensions of an abstract argumentation framework.

Connecting natural language to argumentation solvers   NoDE (Natural language arguments in online DEbates) [Cabrio and Villata, 2014] is a manually annotated corpus of bipolar argumentation from three data sources: the Debatepedia[5] online debate platform, the script of the courtroom play "Twelve Angry Men", and Wikipedia revision histories. The corpus also contains images of bipolar argumentation frameworks, such as Figure 8.3, which was generated by analyzing Act 3 of Twelve Angry Men.

Cabrio and Villata [2016] use abstract dialectical frameworks, which generalize Dungian frameworks by specifying an acceptance condition for each argument node. This enables abstract dialectic frameworks (ADF) to express arbitrary relationships (rather than just attacks as in Dungian frameworks), and in particular positive and negative weights can be used, also encompassing bipolar argumentation. They generalize textual entailment to groups of text fragments in what they call a *bipolar entailment graph* which uses arguments as nodes and the textual entailment relations as edges. They give two examples of using their pipeline to generate coherent sets of arguments starting from Debatepedia data from NoDE.

Cerutti et al. [2016] create and solve three different formalisms based on manual analysis of an online debate from the `createdebate.com` forum. These are: a Dungian abstract argumentation framework (see Section 3.4.1), a Quantitative Argumentation Debate (QuAD) framework [Baroni et al., 2015] (modeled after IBIS, see Section 3.4.1, and evaluated with the

---

[3]`https://carneades.github.io/` (accessed May 20, 2018).
[4]`http://carneades.fokus.fraunhofer.de/carneades/` (accessed May 20, 2018).
[5]`http://www.debatepedia.org` (accessed May 20, 2018).

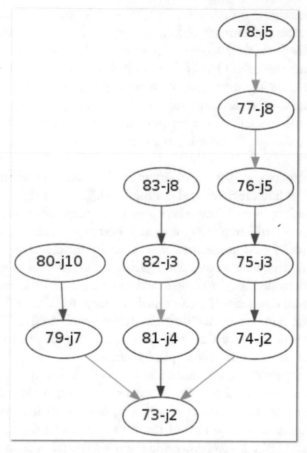

Figure 8.3: Bipolar argumentation framework resulting from Act 3 of Twelve Angry Men. Red edges represent attacks while green edges represent supports. Based on the NoDE data set [Cabrio and Villata, 2014].

Arg&Dec tool[6] [Aurisicchio et al., 2015]), and an Argumentation Framework with Recursive Attacks (AFRA) [Baroni et al., 2011] (evaluated with the ASPARTIX tool [Egly et al., 2010]). While none of the representations have complete fidelity to the fine-grained manual analysis they start with, they advocate for the AFRA. Unlike the Dungian abstract argumentation framework, it can represent attacks on the relationships. Unlike the QuAD framework, it allows cycles (such as two arguments that attack each other). Each computational argumentation

[6]http://www.arganddec.com (accessed May 20, 2018).

method has some advantages for their case. The Dungian approach can be used to identify acceptable arguments and sets of mutually defending arguments, which "allows participants in the dialogue to strategically focus their attention" [Cerutti et al., 2016, p. 70] on those arguments identified as as non-defeated. The QuAD framework represents both support and attack relationships (though the same argument cannot be represented as simultaneously supporting one argument and attacking another, leading them to duplicate certain arguments). QuAD can also numerically compare the strength of the arguments, given numerically assigned input on the intrinsic base strength, though the winning argument can change with small changes in these numerical assignments.

Similarly, Cocarascu and Toni [2017b] manually construct a bipolar argumentation framework from a set of hotel reviews, and use the DF-QuAD method [Rago et al., 2016] to quantify the strength of arguments. They also suggest using bipolar argumentation frameworks for summarization, since conflicting viewpoints and their support can be seen in the graph.

Wyner et al. [2016] modifies sentences from an online discussion hosted by the BBC Have Your Say[7] about who should pay tax on garbage. Rather than mining arguments, they envision leveraging controlled language input and enacting a series of transformations, using the automatic transformation from the controlled language ACE into first-order logic. Their use of a solver, however, is informative: ultimately, they use the ASPARTIX system to solve the argumentation framework. They consider *policy positions*, which are preferred extensions (in the Dungian sense), either for or against the original position.

Computational argumentation systems and solvers for a variety of formal argumentation frameworks are mature. There is clear potential for a pipeline from natural language argumentation to a 'solved' argument showing sets of coherent, non-contradictory positions. So far the most successful pipeline seems to be that of Cabrio and Villata [2016], using textual entailment and abstract dialectical frameworks, while there are several other promising approaches. An important open question is which formalisms are most appropriate, in the senses of being conducive for modeling natural language, cognitively intuitive, etc.

8.3.2   ASSESSING OR COMPARING QUALITY

Broadening the notion of quality from the logical perspective also to infomal treatments, the complexity of the question is attested by a body of literature in argumentation theory and rhetoric; a comprehensive overview is presented by Wachsmuth et al. [2017b]. For orientation, we mention here only the proposal of Blair [2012], who makes the term 'quality' more explicit by suggesting to decompose it into three dimensions.

- **Logical:** The argument is cogent. This in turn breaks down into three criteria that an argument should meet:

   - **Relevance:** All premises of the argument indeed provide support for the conclusion.

---

[7]http://www.bbc.com/news/have_your_say (accessed May 20, 2018).

- **Acceptability:** The premises are worth being believed.

- **Sufficiency:** The premises provide enough evidence for accepting the claim.

- **Rhetorical:** The persuasive effect or success of the argument.

- **Dialectical:** The argumentation is reasonable fur the purpose of resolving an issue.

It is obvious that this characterization does not straightforwardly lead to a computable task of determining quality, as it is rather abstract. One reason is that argumentation in text or dialogue can come with so many different purposes and in different forms, as pointed out by Wachsmuth et al. [2017b]: the goal may be to persuade an audience, to resolve a dispute, to achieve agreement, to recommend an action, and more. Depending on situation and context, the categories mentioned above are of different degrees of importance.

Still, some initial steps have been proposed, and three possible strategies can be identified: focus on one specific dimension; rephrase the problem as *comparing* two arguments in terms of (some aspect of) quality; and try to break the overall quality issue into a number of well-motivated dimensions that can be addressed individually. We discuss them in turn.

Focus on one dimension and genre   Exploiting the annotations in the corpus of 402 persuasive essays [Stab and Gurevych, 2014a], work by Stab and Gurevych [2017a] selected the *sufficiency* criterion (see above) and applied it to essays. The assumptions are that students have different abilities to actually support their arguments; and that trained annotators are able to perceive these differences; and that these judgments are not entirely subjective. Stab and Gurevych extracted 1,029 text portions corresponding to complete arguments (claims and premises) in a paragraph, with an average length of 4.5 sentences per argument. Three annotators answered the question whether an argument is 'sufficiently supported', and they agreed on 91.1% of 433 arguments (Fleiss κ=0.77).

Taking this result as indicative for the task to be solvable, the whole corpus was annotated, which lead to 681 sufficently supported arguments (66%) and 348 insufficiently supported ones (34%).[8] Turning to automatic classification, Stab and Gurevych compared a rich-feature SVM with a CNN using word embeddings [Mikolov et al., 2013]. The SVM with optimized features (including 4,000 most frequent unigrams, length, constituency parsing productions, frequency of named entities) achieved a macro-F1 score of 0.77, narrowly beating a SVM unigram baseline of 0.75. The main problem observed by the authors was a relatively low recall on the insufficiently-supported arguments. The CNN performed best, with a macro-F1 of 0.83.

Comparing arguments   When considering the quality question in general, it does not seem very practical to take an argument, outside any context of use, and ask a human being to score it on some scale of goodness. A more natural task is that of a choice between two (or more)

---

[8]Guidelines and corpus are available at https://www.ukp.tu-darmstadt.de/data/argumentation-mining (accessed September 29, 2017).

arguments: which one is more convincing? Labeled data for this scenario can be elicited from annotators, or derived from existing data. For example, Wei et al. [2016] worked with online debates. Their data comes from ChangeMyView, which is a subforum of reddit.com. Here, users initiate a discussion thread by posting their thoughts toward some topic, and others reply with opposing arguments, trying to change the initiator's mind. Also, users can vote which reply posts they consider more persuasive, so that each reply is associated with a 'success' score. Wei et al. selected 1,785 threads with 374,000 posts in total.

Given the post/score tuples, they trained a pair-wise ranker with three groups of features. In the experiments, the surface features (length, distribution of PoS tags, URLs, punctuation) turned out to be not very helpful. (Unigrams and named entities had also been tried but were eventually discarded.) The second group consisted of interaction features: the size of the reply tree generated by a post, and the level of the post in the overall tree (rooted in the initiating post). Finally, local argumentation features were computed with a binary classifier that labels sentences as non-/argumentative, using the features proposed by Stab and Gurevych [2014b]. The proportion of argumentative sentences was taken as a feature, in addition to the number of connectives and modal verbs. And the final feature was the cosine similarity between the post and its parents, meant to estimate relevance of the post.

Interestingly, the results differed depending on the stage of the discussion. In the initial phase, with only a small number of posts, the argumentation features, and in particular the semantic similarity, worked best. When threads are long, on the other hand, the relatively simple interaction features turned out to be more predictive.

The variant of gathering pairwise judgments from human raters was explored by Habernal and Gurevych [2016]. From two debate portals (createdebate.com and procon.org), they chose 32 discussion topics and randomly sampled about 30 arguments per topic. These were combined into 16,927 argument pairs (avoiding cross-topic pairs). Crowdsourcing was then employed to judge one argument as more convincing, or both as equally good. Habernal and Gurevych devised a method for performing quality assurance, which was based on constructing the transitive closure of all the pairwise rankings in order to detect problematic claim pairs. The final corpus contains the subset filtered in this way, but also the 'bad' pairs in a separate set.[9]

To automate the comparison, Habernal and Gurevych experimented with a feature-rich SVM and a bidirectional LSTM. The former obtained an accuracy of 78% and beat the LSTM (76%), but the authors point out that they did little optimization work on the NN, and that the feature engineering for the SVM was quite laborious, involving, among others, parsing features, sentiment analysis, and NER.

A follow-up experiment on the same dataset was reported by Chalaguine and Schulz [2017]. With a simple forward-feeding neural network (one hidden layer), they achieved an accuacy of 77%, essentially replicating the results of Habernal and Gurevych with much less

---

[9]The annotated data is available for research: https://github.com/UKPLab/acl2016-convincing-arguments (accessed September 28, 2017).

machinery. The authors attribute this success to their idea of doing a precomputation step on the feature values: instead of taking the values per argument 'as is', they computed for each value its relation to the *average* value for that feature in the entire dataset. In this way, they added some limited form of context knowledge to the feature space.

A taxonomy of quality dimensions   Another new dataset resulted from the work of Wachsmuth et al. [2017b]. The authors first provide a comprehensive survey of earlier work on argument quality, both from the argumentation theory and from the argumentation mining perspective. On the basis of that study, they propose a taxonomy of dimensions that together are taken to define 'quality'. It extends the three categories we cited at the beginning of this section.

- **Logic:** Cogency (Co)

  - Local acceptability (LA)

  - Local relevance (LR)

  - Local sufficiency (LS)

- **Rhetoric:** Effectiveness (Ef)

  - Clarity (Cl)

  - Credibility (Cr)

  - Appropriateness (Ap)

  - Emotional appeal (Em)

  - Arrangement (Ar)

- **Dialectic:** Resonableness (Re)

  - Global acceptability (GA)

  - Global relevance (GR)

  - Global sufficiency (GS)

The authors tested the taxonomy in an annotation experiment, using data from the above-mentioned corpus of Habernal and Gurevych [2016]. For every issue/stance pair, they took the five top-ranked texts and selected another five texts by stratified sampling, so that arguments of different degrees of quality are included. The resulting set of 320 arguments was annotated for all 15 dimensions by three annotators and, overall, the agreement was found to be promising. For illustration, we reproduce here (Figure 8.4) the scores given by the three annotators on two texts, which responded to the question whether plastic water bottles should be banned. Annotators had to assign 1 (low), 2 (medium), or 3 (high); the bottom line represents the majority vote for the three annotators.

Arguments

Pro Water bottles, good or bad? Many people believe plastic water bottles to be good. But the truth is water bottles are polluting land and unnecessary. Plastic water bottles should only be used in emergency purposes only. The water in those plastic are only filtered tap water. In an emergency situation like Katrina no one had access to tap water. In a situation like this water bottles are good because it provides the people in need. Other than that water bottles should not be legal because it pollutes the land and big companies get 1000% of the profit.

Con Americans spend billions on bottled water every year. Banning their sale would greatly hurt an already struggling economy. In addition to the actual sale of water bottles, the plastics that they are made out of, and the advertising on both the bottles and packaging are also big business. In addition to this, compostable waters bottle are also coming onto the market, these can be used instead of plastics to eliminate that detriment. Moreover, bottled water not only has a cleaner safety record than municipal water, but it easier to trace when a potential health risk does occur. (http://www.friendsjournal.org/bottled-water) (http://www.cdc.gov/healthywater/drinking/bottled/)

Pro scores:

Scores	Co	LA	LR	LS	Ef	Cr	Em	Cl	Ap	Ar	Re	GA	GR	GS	Ov
Annotator A	3	3	3	2	3	3	3	3	3	3	3	3	3	2	3
Annotator B	2	2	3	2	1	2	2	2	2	1	2	2	2	1	2
Annotator C	2	3	3	2	2	2	2	3	3	3	3	3	3	2	3
Majority score	2	3	3	2	2	2	2	3	3	3	3	3	3	2	3

Con scores:

	Co	LA	LR	LS	Ef	Cr	Em	Cl	Ap	Ar	Re	GA	GR	GS	Ov
Annotator A	3	3	3	3	3	3	2	3	3	3	3	3	3	3	3
Annotator B	2	3	3	2	2	3	2	3	3	2	3	3	2	2	3
Annotator C	3	3	3	3	3	2	1	3	3	3	3	3	3	3	3
Majority score	3	3	3	3	3	3	2	3	3	3	3	3	3	3	3

Figure 8.4: Annotations of scores on argument quality dimensions [Wachsmuth et al., 2017b, p. 184], used with permission.

8.3.3 ARGUMENT AND EMOTION

The role of emotion is often a contentious issue in argumentation: when a matter-of-fact, *logos*-oriented exchange is being aimed at, any appeal to emotion is seen as a flaw; while in some situation where the speaker intends to persuade the hearer, emotional involvement may be regarded as a legitimate rhetorical instrument, involving *pathos*. For a thorough discussion of these points, see the work of Govier [2010], who discusses the relation between logical reasoning and emotion in depth.

Besides being contentious, the role of emotion may be difficult to detect empirically. In the web corpus annotation project of Habernal and Gurevych [2017] (see Section 5.3.5), annotators were asked to also label arguments for the feature 'appeal to emotion', but the agreement obtained was not substantial. In contrast, Hidey et al. [2017] ran an Amazon Turk experiment to label premises (in claim-premise pairs of blog comments) for the logos, ethos, or pathos dimension. Comparing the majority view of the Turkers to the gold labels, agreement in terms of α was a solid 0.73. Notice that 'ethos'-type premises are very rare (3% of 1,068 premises in total), though.

Also, delegating the emotionality annotation task to Mechanical Turk, Oraby et al. [2015] were interested in the linguistic patterns that ditinguish factual from emotional arguments. To obtain data, they used quote-response pairs from the Internet Argument Corpus (see Section 4.2.1), and had them annotated by Turkers who were asked whether the respondent is attempting to make a fact-based argument or is appealing to feelings and emotions. This lead to a dataset of 3,466 'fact' and 2,382 'feeling' posts.

Then, using a syntactic-pattern learner [Riloff, 1996], Oraby et al. extracted characteristic constructions from both sets of posts, which they regarded as high-precision, and then used to accumulate more patterns by means of a bootstrapping approach on un-annotated data. In the

Patt ID#	Probability	Frequency	Pattern	Text Match
FACT Selected Patterns				
FC1	1.00	18	NP Prep <np>	SPECIES OF
FC2	1.00	21	<subj> PassVP	EXPLANATION OF
FC3	1.00	20	<subj> AuxVP Dobj	BE EVIDENCE
FC4	1.00	14	<subj> PassVP	OBSERVED
FC5	0.97	39	NP Prep <np>	RESULT OF
FC6	0.90	10	<subj> ActVP Dobj	MAKE POINT
FC7	0.84	32	Adj Noun	SCIENTIFIC THEORY
FC8	0.75	4	NP Prep <np>	MISUNDERSTANDING OF
FC9	0.67	3	Adj Noun	FUNDAMENTAL RIGHTS
FC10	0.50	2	NP Prep <np>	MEASURABLE AMOUNT
FEEL Selected Patterns				
FE1	1.00	14	Adj Noun	MY ARGUMENT
FE2	1.00	7	<subj> AuxVP Adjp	BE ABSURD
FE3	1.00	9	Adv Adj	MORALLY WRONG
FE4	0.91	11	<subj> AuxVP Adjp	BE SAD
FE5	0.89	9	<subj> AuxVP Adjp	BE DUMB
FE6	0.89	9	Adj Noun	NO BRAIN
FE7	0.81	37	Adj Noun	COMMON SENSE
FE8	0.75	8	InfVP Prep <np>	BELIEVE IN
FE9	0.87	3	Adj Noun	ANY CREDIBILITY
FE10	0.53	17	Adj Noun	YOUR OPINION

Figure 8.5: Examples of 'fact' and 'feel' argumentation style patterns [Oraby et al., 2015, p. 121], used with permission.

end, they tested the pattern sets and determined an accuracy of 80%. (Figure 8.5 shows some examples for extracted patterns.) However, while precision was good, the recall was significantly lower than that obtained by a supervised unigram baseline.

A study involving the same fact/emotion-annotated data, but aiming at quite ambitious research questions, was reported by Lukin et al. [2017]. Their goal is to quantify the extent to which readers' beliefs can change due to being confronted with different types of argument (factual vs. emotional, *inter alia*), and how this depends on personality traits. The experiments were all done via Amazon Turk. In a preparatory step, Lukin et al. assessed the personality of their Turkers by means of a survey that tries to measure standard traits: openness to experience, conscientiousness, extraversion, agreeableness, and neuroticism.

Next, for comparing the influence of factual vs. emotional arguments, the authors gathered examples from the above-mentioned IAC data, which were reliably annotated on the extreme ends of the fact—emotion scale. Examples are shown in Figure 8.6.

Factual: Climate Change	
Q4:	This is where the looney left gets lost. Their mantra is atmospheric CO2 levels are escalating and this is unquestionably causing earth's temperature rise. But ask yourself – if global temperatures are experiencing the biggest sustained drop in decades, while CO2 levels continue to rise – how can it be true?
R4:	Because internal variability from the likes of ENSO, which can cause short term swings of a full degree C, easily swamp the smaller increase we'd expect from CO2 forcing. Easy.
Emotional: Abortion	
Q5:	Undesired first pregnancy is an acute problem for many girls who choose to go under the surgical knife, even though that often ends up with infertility, broken life etc. Dry fasting is an alternative to first pregnancy abortion. If applied, up to 2-3 months old embryo gets dissolved after 15-16 days of the fast. Plus, there is no 'christian' sin.
R5:	No Christian sin??? Other then the intent to kill and then doing so:p

Figure 8.6: Examples of factual and emotional exchanges in the Internet Argument Corpus [Lukin et al., 2017, p. 745], used with permission.

In addition, for comparing the difference between dialogic and monologic argumentation, text for the latter was sampled from procon.org, which contains expert-curated summaries of arguments on contentious topics.

The core experiment then followed the before/after reading paradigm, involving three steps.

1. Turkers are being asked a stance question to determine their prior beliefs on a socio-political issue, such as "Should the death penalty be allowed?"

2. Turkers are being shown an argument from one of the three categories monological, emotional, factual.

3. Turkers are being retested with the original stance questions.

When measuring the stance differences, Lukin et al. found significant belief changes for all three argument types, but with certain nuances: As they had expected, the opinion change is greater for those Turkers who are initially more neutral about a topic, than for those who are entrenched in their beliefs. Regarding personality, a finding was that 'conscientious' Turkers are more convinced by dialogic emotional arguments, whereas 'agreeable' Turkers are more persuaded by dialogic factual arguments.

Then, Lukin et al. went a step further and looked into *predicting* belief change. Turkers now were asked to rate arguments for strength, and the authors then identified the combination of features that best predicted argument strength. The main finding was that, for all three types of arguments (neutral monologic / factual dialogic / emotional dialogic), feature sets containing all five personality traits perform significantly better than sets without those traits. The authors have made their argument+personality data set available for research.[10]

It seems clear that the relationship between argumentation and emotion will be an active area for future work. As a final example, we wish to point to another study that ventures to leave the core territory of NLP and argumentation mining. Benlamine et al. [2015] presented the first experiment that explicitly assesses the correspondence between the polarity of arguments in an exchange and the emotions felt by participants. Their emotional status was analyzed by webcams and face reading software on the one hand, and physiological sensors (EEG) on the other; both types of information were combined into scores reflecting the status of basic emotions (neutral, happy, sad, angry, surprised, scared and disgusted). The participants were engaged in debates on topics that were likely to stir people's temper, for instance 'Religion does more harm than good'. The debates were recorded and in a post-processing session mapped to an argument graph, so that support/attack relations could be anchored to points in time, and then correlated with the emotional states of the participants. The authors of the study indeed detected some correspondences between emotions and argumentative moves, e.g., when two opposite opinions were expressed, this was reflected in a negative way on the debaters' emotions.

---

[10]https://nlds.soe.ucsc.edu/persuasion_persona (accessed October 1, 2017).

CHAPTER 9

Generating Argumentative Text

Strictly speaking, the generation (or *synthesis*) of argumentative text is outside the scope of *mining*, but nonetheless we consider the topic here, as it is a part of the wider field of argumentation technology and will be increasingly relevant for many applications. However, in contrast to analysis, the generation of arguments has so far received much less attention. In the following, we discuss the topic along the lines of the two established techniques of text production: a system can generate from symbolic representations of knowledge or from data (Section 9.1), or it can map existing text to new (or revised) text (Section 9.2).

9.1 GENERATING TEXT FROM STRUCTURED DATA

Early work in automatic text generation was concerned with building systems that were able to produce short texts from a collection of structured data or from knowledge that was represented in a suitable formalism, such as Description Logic or Bayesian belief networks. The latter were employed by Zukerman et al. [2000], who showed how the logical structure of an argument can be systematically constructed by combining knowledge of a small set of argument schemes with a model of hearer beliefs, which the argument should try to influence. In complete generation systems, the path from plain data to a well-formed text is long, and it was commonly divided into three phases [Reiter and Dale, 2000].

1. **Text planning**: given a set of *communicative goals*, the system first selects the content units (data instances, knowledge chunks) that are to be expressed in the text, and then organizes them into a *text plan*, which specifies hierarchical relations between content units, and determines the linear order in which they will appear in the text. The text plan is totally agnostic of the target natural language that will eventually be produced.

2. **Micro-planning** or **sentence planning:** the text plan is traversed and mapped onto a sequence of *sentence plans*. This involves distributing the series of content units into a certain number of sentences. Furthermore, each sentence plan now gets linguistic (and language-specific) information, such as the intended embedding of complex sentences. An important task is *lexical choice*: deciding which words to use for expressing a content unit (or a part of it; or several content units).

3. **Realization:** each sentence plan is converted to a well-formed sentence in natural language, on the basis of grammatical knowledge: words are properly inflected, and appropriate function words (such as determiners or prepositions) are inserted in the right places.

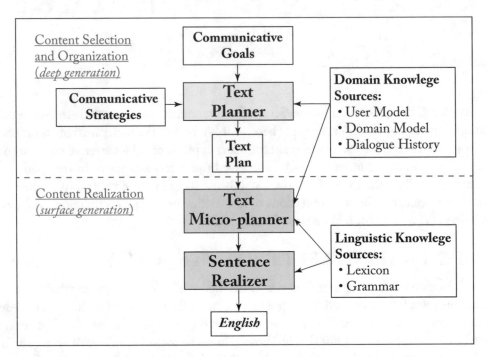

Figure 9.1: Pipeline architecture of typical text generation systems [Carenini, 2001, p. 2], used with permission.

A diagram outlining this architecture is shown in Figure 9.1. Notice that the knowledge sources include general domain knowledge (which entities occur, what their attributes are, how they are related), a history of the discourse produced so far (be it dialogue or monologue), and importantly a *user model*. Especially when part of a dialogue system, text generation has been conceived as a process whose output is geared toward a particular user, and the system normally has information about this user, so that the text can be specifically tailored to her or his needs. In the following, we will make this architecture more concrete by explaining three systems that instantiated the model for producing short monologue text of an argumentative nature, followed by one system aimed at conducting a dialogue with a user. Each one works in a particular domain, and in the absence of reusable or generic knowledge sources, the work of building such a generation system involved a lot of hand-crafting: designing domain knowledge representations, linking them to the lexical knowledge of the target language, etc.

ADVISOR II   This early text generator by Elhadad [1995] produced short texts simulating a student advisor, with the central issue being to recommend classes that are suitable for the student. Thus, the domain knowledge records all the courses offered along with a number of attributes such as content, prerequisites, difficulty level, and the like. The user model specifies what courses the student has already taken, what her interests are, etc. Three possible communicative goals can be posed as input to the system: *inform* the student about a course, *recommend* taking a certain course, or *recommend* not taking it. The latter two involve giving reasons, and hence a form of argumentation. Here is a sample output [Elhadad, 1995, p. 192].

> AI deals with many interesting topics, such as NLP, Vision and KR. But it has many assignments which consist of writing papers. You have little experience writing papers. So it could be difficult. I would not recommend it.

The content in the first sentence was selected by comparing the knowledge base (KB) and the user model (UM). The evaluation *interesting* is not a fact, i.e., an attribute of the course in the KB, but is produced by the system after determining that the topics covered by AI include many that the user enjoys. The comparison also reveals that the user has not produced many written assignments yet (according to the UM), while assignments are necessary to pass AI (KB). This leads ADVISOR to connect the descriptive second sentence to the first by the conjunction *but*: this signals a shift in argumentative orientation, which is appropriate here, since the first sentence amounts to a positive evaluation of the course (for the user), while the second is negative. Similarly, the predicate *difficult* is not an attribute of the course *per se*, but computed by the system on the grounds of comparing the weights of positive and negative evaluations of the course.[1]

The argumentation-theoretic underpinning of Elhadad's system is the notion of *topoi* as advanced by Anscombre and Ducrot [1983]. A topos is a gradual inference rule of the form "the more/less X is P, the more/less Y is Q", and one possible instantiation in the domain of ADVISOR is "the more difficult a class is, the less a student wants to take it". Topoi serve to connect the course knowledge base and user model on the one hand, and the linguistic decisions of the system on the other—they trigger the use of evaluative adjectives or of connectives (like *but* in our example above). But verbs, too, can be chosen on the basis of the argumentative orientation that is to be conveyed. One of Elhadad's examples is the following.

(9.1) You enjoyed AI.
       You took AI.
       You struggled with AI.

All three verbs express that the student has attended the AI class, but *enjoy* and *struggle* in addition convey evaluative connotations. The lexicon used by ADVISOR is aware of such differences and can choose among similar word on principled grounds.

---

[1] This overall setting has many parallels to contemporary *product recommender* systems.

GEA The idea of the Generator of Evaluative Arguments (GEA) [Carenini, 2001] is similar to that of ADVISOR. Again, the input to the system is a communicative goal to influence the user's attitude toward some entity. The sample domain implemented by Carenini was real estate, and thus the goal is to get a user to like or dislike a particular house. In analogy to ADVISOR, the KB holds the information about a set of houses, and the UM represents the user's preferences. Its format is quite elaborate, though: a tree structure that decomposes a domain concept (here: house) into its attributes, and associates importance values to them, which characterize the extent to which the user is keen on an attribute. A house thus is characterized by size, location, price, etc., which may in turn be decomposed further. The preference values indicate whether the user likes a quiet or a buzzlng location, whether a target size of five rooms is very important or only mildly important, and so forth.

On the basis of this information in the UM GEA computes how valuable a particular house is for the user, and how valuable the different attributes are. In this way, it also identifies which attributes can be used as evidence for parent attributes in producing an appropriate argument pro or contra a house.

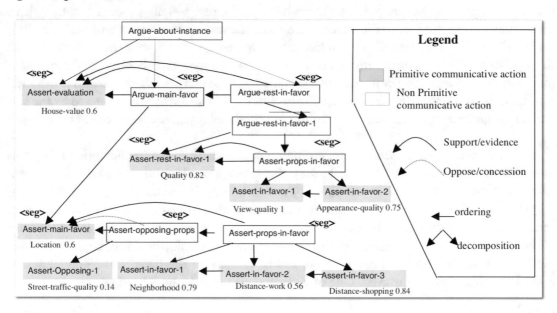

Figure 9.2: Sample text plan produced by the GEA system [Carenini, 2001, p. 8], used with permission.

GEA's text planner implements several argumentation strategies that specify how to order positive and negative points. Strategies are coded as operators that decompose abstract goals into simple, concrete ones. For illustration, Figure 9.2 shows a sample text plan. The chosen strategy (see the top of the tree) is to first assert the overall evaluation computed for the house—user match, then to provide the main argument in favor (decided via the preference values in the UM), and then the remaining positive observations. Decomposition stops at the grey boxes, which correspond to speech acts involving an attribute and its value.

Similar to ADVISOR, the microplanning module of GEA is then in charge of converting the speech act objects into linguistic predicate/argument structures; this mapping uses a lexicon, and the choices among near-synonyms are made on the basis of the values associated with attributes. Likewise, connectives are chosen to indicate a continuing or changing argumentative orientation. Here is a sample output produced by the system for a particular user (as represented by the UM) [Carenini, 2001, p. 8].

> House 2-33 is an interesting house. In fact, it has a reasonable location in the safe Eastend neighborhood. Even though the traffic is intense on 2nd street, house 2-33 is reasonably close to work. And also it offers an easy access to the shops. Furthermore, the quality of house 2-33 is good. House 2-33 offers an excellent view. And also it looks beautiful.

GenIE: The domain of the Genetics Information Expression Assistant [Green et al., 2011] is the production of genetic counseling letters, which explain the inheritance of recessive genetic disorders to patients. The system was designed after a phase of carefully analyzing authentic texts of this genre, discerning their structure and their use of argumentative moves.

In GenIE, the text plan is a tree structure along the lines of Rhetorical Structure Theory (RST) [Mann and Thompson, 1988], which we briefly introduced in Section 2.6.2. Many text planning modules developed in the 1990's and 2000's made this choice, because RST relations are defined in such a way that they can in principle also be operationalized used as planning operators.[2] In this use in text generation, an RST tree does not have natural language sentences at its leaf nodes, but semantic representations of content-to-be-verbalized. Hence, the text at the leafs in the sample text plan in Figure 9.3, while looking like English, is in fact a shorthand for a formal representation.

GenIE builds the text plan by means of hand-crafted discourse grammar, which encodes the structural regularities found in the corpus of counseling letters. Argumentation is added in a post-processing step: the RST plan is screened for material that needs more motivation for the patients, and a separate argument generation module then builds a small RST tree that is inserted into the overall text plan.

The argument generator uses argumentation schemes (as introduced in Section 3.3), for instance an effect-to-cause scheme and an increased-risk scheme. Green et al. started from the scheme catalogue of Walton et al. [2008] but found that for their specific purposes, they needed to formulate more specific versions of certain schemes.

---

[2]However, Reed and Long [1998] pointed out that in order to thoroughly distinguish common inference figures such as modus ponens and modus tollens, a more abstract layer of information—besides RST—is needed in text planning, and they suggest a possible formalization of corresponding planning operators.

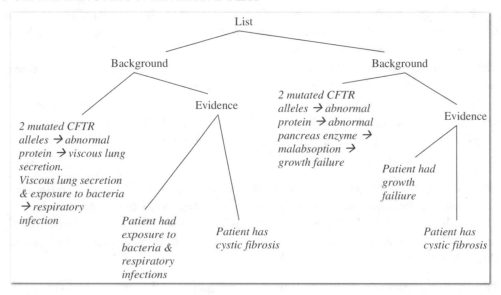

Figure 9.3: Sample text plan produced by the GenIE system [Green et al., 2011, p. 36], used with permission.

The GenIE system has been evaluated with an editing task: College students with genetics background were given either a human-authored letter or a computer-generated letter and asked to make it more understandable to non-specialist readers (i.e., the intended target audience of the letters). It turned out that while the computer-generated letter required more edits, fewer additions of extra material were needed.

Daphne   The Daphne system [Grasso et al., 2000] embeds the generation of arguments into the architecture of a dialogue system that aims to convince users to eat more healthy food. The underlying approach to argumentation is the schema-based 'New Rhetoric' theory of Perelman and Olbrechts-Tyteca [1969] (cf. Section 3.4.1). A knowledge base encodes information on what kinds of food have positive or negative effects on health, and a dynamic network models different perspectives and values associated with topics, as they can develop in a dialogue. Daphne has a component for reasoning about the user's beliefs, and the text and sentence planner (which are part of an entire dialogue management system) employ the results for trying to select and formulate arguments that will have a persuasive effect on the user. The system architecture is designed in such a way that domain-specific knowledge and argumentation-specific (strategic, rhetorical) knowledge are kept largely separate from one another, so that the latter could in fact be employed for other domains as well.

Toward presenting formal argumentation to users   Finally, we briefly turn toward formal argumentation. Cerutti et al. [2017] explored the idea of constructing a "natural language interface" to formal argumentation systems. Given a representation in an argument network or an abstract argumentation framework (cf. Section 3.4), the goal is to map it to English text, such that users can more easily grasp the contents of the representation. Hence, the authors consider four communicative goals.

- Present a single argument or an approximate argument.

- Present an entire argument network.

- Explain the acceptability status of a single argument or an approximate argument.

- Explain the extensions, given some semantics.

A user model is not accounted for, so presenting and explaining arguments here are not tailored to a particular user (or user group). The authors provide a blueprint for how the classical text generation pipeline model can be instantiated to produce such verbal descriptions, using a text planner based on RST relations that are relevant for this domain, in particular Evidence, Justify, and Antithesis.

9.2   GENERATING TEXT FROM TEXT

As we indicated in the previous section, the approaches to text generation mentioned there involve a lot of manual work, because (except for grammatical realization) up to now there are only very few re-usable or standardized components for the generation process. And even if representations of knowledge are designed carefully to avoid hard-wiring domain specific information, the actual knowledge acquisition process has to be re-started whenever a new domain is being tackled. The alternative to this laborious process is to combine argument mining with argument synthesis: find textual material that can be rewritten into new text. To make this feasible, the original text usually is taken not in its raw form, but annotated with linguistic information that supports the re-combining steps.

Legal arguments   An early proposal along these lines was made by Ashley and Walker [2013b], who describe a partial implementation with a vision of where the work could be taken. The approach occupies the middle ground between our two sections, as it involves quite 'deep' annotations. The idea is to generate legal arguments by re-combining parts of related arguments that have been made in similar cases. The underlying data is a corpus of 35 legal decisions on vaccine injuries, where each decision consists of 15–40 pages of text. These have been manually annotated with two types of information: (i) domain-specific semantic relations between entities, covering, *inter alia*, causal chains; and (ii) the complex propositional inference structure underlying the decision, using a default logic notation. The authors evisage this information being used in conjunction with more basic automatic annotations of syntactic dependencies and case-semantic relations, so that a retrieval engine could find components of arguments that are relevant to a new case and can be used to produce cogent arguments.

Wide-coverage paragraph generation   Less 'deep' in annotation but fully implemented is the text production system presented by Sato et al. [2015]. Here, the user can enter a topic in the form of a motion sentence (*This house should do X*) and a stance toward that motion, and the system generates three argumentative paragraphs, each relating to a particular aspect of the motion.

field	value	polarity	representative phrases	context phrases
economy	investment	+1	investment:27.8, development_aid:48.2	asset, bank, capital, fund, profit, stock, ...
finance	cost	−1	expense:35.9, expenditure:55.7	budget, dollar, fuel, lower, price, share, ...
finance	income	+1	revenue:35.4, wage:39.8	budget, company, earnings, higher, gain, ...
health	disease	−1	disease:36.6, complication:40.1	AIDS, Alzheimer, blood, cancer, death, ...
safety	crime	−1	crime:31.5, prostitution:56.2	arrest, gun, jail, kidnapping, victim, ...
...	...	...	...	...

Figure 9.4: Excerpt from the 'value dictionary' used in the argument generator by Sato et al. [2015, p. 113], used with permission.

The paragraphs are produced by selecting (and partly modifying) sentences from 10,000,000 news texts of the Gigaword corpus; hence, the system is not restricted to a few domains only. Manual work is restricted to creating various lexicons of epistemic verbs, evaluative modifiers, etc. The text corpus is stored in a database and annotated with automatic syntax parses plus instances of the lexical relations that are specified in the resources. The processing pipeline works as follows.

1. **Analyze the motion:** The sentence entered by the user—for example, *This house should ban gambling in the city*—is divided into a fixed number of components: a keyphrase capturing the motion topic, the predicate used in the topic, polarity, etc.

2. **Aspect selection:** For the generator, the potentially interesting aspects of the motion are those that trigger evaluative judgment in the audience; the authors hence call these aspects 'values'. The system retrieves sentences that contain lexical *affect*-relations between the motion keyphrase and a phrase found in the value dictionary (see the excerpt in Figure 9.4). The sentence "Gambling increases the number of crimes", for example, is a good candidate because *increase* is a verb of the semantic class *affect*, and *crime* is commonly evaluated as negative. The system tries to make sure that the polarity of the retrieved sentences matches that of the desired argumentation and selects sentence groups for five aspects/values.

3. **Sentence retrieval:** A full-text search is executed on the corpus, using a query that is being built from the motion and value phrases. Among the sentences retrieved, the system filters for the right polarity (so that an argumentatively-coherent text will result) and it prefers sentences that contain promote/suppress relationships.

4. **Sentence ordering, rephrasing:** To build a paragraph, sentences are arranged according to an ordering scheme suggesting that the text starts with a claim sentence and is followed by support sentences. To determine claims, a binary classifier is run on the sentences (this is the task we discussed in Chapter 5). The supporting statements are ordered by maximizing the connectivity between sentences, as suggested by Tan et al. [2013]. Finally, a certain amount of rephrasing is done: details such as dates or proper names are being eliminated from the sentences.

To evaluate the approach, texts were generated for 50 motions from `debatabase.org`. Human judges ranked the paragraphs (consisting of seven sentences each) on a scale from 0 (makes no sense) to 4 (sounds natural). Of the 150 sentences, 86 received label 0, indicating that—probably not surprsing—the overall problem is quite difficult. The three major problems identified in error analysis were polarity computation, analysis of difficult motion sentences entered by the user, and erroneous sentence retrieval due to lexical ambiguity etc.

Rhetorics in re-generation   Considering the difficulties in producing acceptable text by recombining sentences found 'in the wild', some researchers suggested to pay more attention to rhetorics when making selection and ordering decisions. Beyond the patterns of ordering that have been used in earlier work (and which were usually taken from guides to good writing), Aristotle's means of persuasion (*logos, ethos, pathos*; see Section 1.1.2) have already received some (if not much) attention in argument analysis; Duthie et al. [2016], for instance, presented a study on finding ethos in political debates. For the generation task, Wachsmuth et al. [2018] suggest that the three means also need to be accounted for when recombining sentences into a new text. They sketch a model for selecting and ordering sentences, which takes in particular the distinction between logos- and pathos-oriented argumentation into account. To gather evidence for the importance of this factor, they conducted an experiment with 26 human 'authors' who had to recombine ADUs from a subset of the argumentative microtext corpus (see Section 4.2.2). Ten topics were selected, each of which was addressed by 4-9 short texts from the corpus. Claims and other units (i.e., supporting and opposing statements) were put into topic-specific pools, where the authors could draw from. For this to work, the ADUs need to be as context-independent as possible, and the authors applied two operations: removing connectives, and replacing pronouns by their antecedents. Authors were instructed to build both logos- and pathos-oriented persuasive texts, using these instructions.

- **Logos-oriented:** Argue based on logical reasoning, which means to make rational and logical conclusions toward the intended stance on the given topic.

- **Pathos-oriented:** Argue based on emotional reasoning, which means to appeal to the emotions of the reader regarding the topic within your arguments.

The ADUs in the pool had no information on logos or pathos attached, so authors had to identify it themselves in the sentences. The study found that for *selecting* ADUs from the pool, the agreement between authors is significantly higher within the logos-oriented and the pathos-oriented texts, which indicates that authors (and hence also readers) can indeed sense the distinction. For *arranging* the ADUs in the text, three favorite ordering patterns emerged (the most popular one: claim - opp. - supp. - supp. - supp.), but no difference between logos and pathos texts clould be observed.

Open-domain claim generation An interesting step toward open-domain argument generation was reported by Bilu and Slonim [2016]. These authors sought to minimize the role of human intervention, and therefore reduced the problem to one subtask: claim generation. The basic idea is to produce new claims by "recycling" linguistic predicates found in the claims of other arguments, which Bilu and Slonim illustrate with the example: given the claim *banning violent video games is a violation of free speech* for the topic *banning violent video games*, one might transfer this to the topic *internet censorship* and generate the claim *internet censorship is a violation of free speech*. Thus, a key task for this approach is to learn the contexts allowing or disallowing a candidate re-combination. The proposed claim generation algorithm works in three steps.

1. **Preprocessing: build predicate lexicon (PL)** Given a set of manually detected claims from the work of Aharoni et al. [2014] (see Section 5.3.4), extract from each claim the verb and a concatenation of its right-modifiers, which together form the predicate p. It is added to the PL if it contains at least one sentiment word (to select predicates with a clear stance toward their topic). In this way, 1,203 PL entries are produced.

2. **Claim Generation:** given a topic t, the predicates p in the PL are sorted for their similarity with t, using a measure involving word embeddings. For the top k predicates, construct a claim candidate by setting the predicate to p and the subject to the topic t. (See the video-game example above.) This may require morphological adjustments (esp. for singular/plural matching), which are done with the 'SimpleNLG' sentence realization component [Gatt and Reiter, 2009].

3. **Claim Selection:** a logistic regression classifier ranks the candidate claims for their appropriateness. It uses three types of features for capturing:

   - predicates p that seem inherently amenable to generating claims: They state something fairly general about their subject, and they are not very specific to the topic of their original sentence (by computing similarity);

   - predicates p that seem relevant for the target topic; this is computed as similarity between p and the topic's *n-gram lexicon*. This resource in turn is built by measuring frequencies of occurrence in topic-related and unrelated Wikipedia articles. Identifying topic-related articles is a manual step in the overall procedure (and had been done in the earlier work reported in Section 5.3.4); and

   - claim sentences that seem to be linguistically acceptable and plausible, which is determined via frequencies of its words and n-grams in Wikipedia.

In an experiment for testing the system, it generated claims for 67 topics, which were extracted from motions on *debatabase* (at `idebate.org`). For all topics, previously annotated relevant Wikipedia articles were already available. The system produced 28 candidate claims per topic, and they were presented to crowdworkers via Amazon Turk. Given a *debatabase* motion and 10 candidate claims, an annotator had to decide which claims are appropriate for the motion. Evaluating this approach is not straightforward, but the authors report that the claim selection classifier achieved an accuracy of 0.75.

9.3   SUMMARY

The strength of the more traditional domain-specific, handcrafted work discussed in the first section was that it had to implement the complete process (text planning, microplanning, realization) as well as the required lexical and knowledge resources for systematically mapping an abstract specification of communicative goals to a short text in natural language. In doing so, it thoroughly attended to the influence of argumentative aims on the different stages of a text production process. The corresponding weakness, obviously, is that this type of work does not easily generalize to other domains, and that many of the fundamental questions on reusable linguistic and non-linguistic knowledge bases from the last century are still open. Therefore, as sketched in the second section, the turn to robust methods for re-producing argumentative text from pieces that have previously been found by automatic mining makes a lot of sense. For such approaches to work across several domains—or even in an open-domain setting—it seems that the robust automatic *annotation* of potential argument components is key: in order to build a good text from segments, we need to know something about the segments. Attributes exploited so far include topic aspects, stance/polarity, and means of persuasion (logos, ethos, pathos). As there is only early work along these lines so far, with very few running implementations, this list is likely to be revised and refined, on the way to producing readable and pragmatically appropriate argumentative text from segments that were found out there 'in the wild'.

CHAPTER 10

Summary and Perspectives

We conclude our survey of argumentation mining with four final steps. First, we provide a summary of the core tasks presented in Chapters 5, 6, and 7, formulated as a procedure for designing a task-specific annotation scheme of the desired level of complexity. Then, in Section 10.2 we observe that automatically finding arguments in text or dialogue is not an end in itself *per se*, and thus we briefly consider some follow-up tasks (e.g., visualization, summarization) that may be applied to the collected arguments in order to make use of them. Next, Section 10.3 turns to the applied side and summarizes a number of downstream applications—most of which have been mentioned already in previous chapters, but here they are collected. Notice that this is not intended as comprehensive survey; we merely provide some indicative pointers to the literature as food for thought. We close with a short outlook in Section 10.4.

10.1 ARGUMENTATION MINING: A COMMON KERNEL

Work on argumentation mining revolves around a fairly well-defined common target—the argument—but then quickly spreads into several different directions. This is because argumentation occurs in very different situations of language use, and with a variety of different purposes. Therefore, the common target does not easily translate into a common set of well-defined subtasks and methods for solving them. Instead, depending on the purpose, different sets of subtasks can become relevant.

Nonetheless, taking the gist of the exposition in Chapters 5–7, we now propose a common kernel of a procedure for defining the argumentation mining task, focusing here on monologue text. The procedure can serve as a guideline or orientation in developing some initial idea for an argumentation mining application into a more specific project outline or an algorithm.

How to design an argumentation mining algorithm.

1. We assume that we have a monologue text T that we know is argumentative (either because we have found out—see Section 5.1—or because we know beforehand, for example on the basis of its genre).

2. T includes a minimum of two argumentative discourse units (ADUs) of at least two different types (see step 3). Each ADU is a contiguous span of text: depending on task formulation, it may be restricted to be a sentence, or it can be a smaller or larger unit. ADUs do not overlap with each other. T may consist of just a sequence of ADUs, or of a mix

of ADUs and non-argumentative text spans. Note that defining what *content* is required for a text span to be an ADU is to some extent also task-dependent (we have suggested a fairly general definition on page 63).

3. The set of ADU *types* consists of `claim` and `evidence`, and possibly more, depending on the task.

4. **If** the task warrants the assumption that there is only one claim in the text, and if no further types of ADU are required, **then** the basic problem specification is complete: Find the `claim` ADU and all `evidence` ADUs in T. Implicitly, a `support` relation holds between each `evidence` ADU and the `claim` ADU. Go to step 8.
Otherwise, continue with step 5.

5. **If** the task suggests that there may be several claims, and associated evidence ADUs, **then** an explicit `support` relation needs to be established. `support` is a total and surjective mapping from `evidence` ADUs to `claim` ADUs. It may be decided that one item of evidence shall not support more than one claim; in this case, the mapping is injective.

6. **If** the task suggests that certain ADUs can function simultaneously as claim and evidence (i.e., they are supporting something else, and they receive support), **then** likewise the `support` relation needs to be established. In this case it is a transitive relation (allowing for 'serial support'; cf. Figure 3.1). One may also introduce a separate ADU type, but this is redundant, as the double-faced ADUs can be identified via outgoing and incoming relations.

7. **If** the task suggests that the 'opposing view' need not be accounted for in analyzing T, **then** go to step 8.
Otherwise, depending on the task, different levels of complexity are possible.

   - In the simplest case, when there is only a single `claim` and a number of `evidence` units (cf. step 4), it suffices to introduce an additional ADU type (e.g., `oppose`), because any `oppose` unit will implicitly attack the unique `claim`.

   - If the analysis allows for multiple claims in T, or if an `oppose` segment may be involved in a sub-structure (see below), a new relation type (typically: `attack`) needs to be added. Sub-structure arises when:

     - an `oppose` segment may be in `support` relation to another `oppose` segment, and/or

     - an `oppose` segment may be *countered* by the proponent, either by a single move, or recursively by a sub-structure. In this case, `attack` relations may hold between an `oppose` ADU and a `claim`/`evidence` unit, or vice versa. That is, it is necessary to make both the types and the relations explicit in the representation.

8. **If** the task suggests that sub-types of `claim`, `evidence`, or `oppose` should be introduced, **then** that can be done.
   Likewise, **if** sub-relations of `support`, `attack` are necessary, **then** they can be added. (For `attack`, a customary distinction is that between `rebut` and `undercut`.)

9. The result of establishing a set of relations on the set of ADUs in the text (either implicitly, as in step 4, or explicitly) is a representation of the argumentation structure of the text. Depending on the number of claims present and on the properties of the relations, it is either a tree, or a forest, or a (single-rooted or multi-rooted) graph, whose root node(s) are of type `claim`.

10.2   AFTER MINING: WHAT TO DO WITH ARGUMENTS

Visualization   In a way, visualization was at the very beginning of the computational work on argumentation: The mapping tools discussed in Section 3.6 help people to arrange their thoughts, or organize the web of contributions made in a dialogue involving two or more parties. Likewise, it seems natural to apply those techniques to arguments that have been gathered and analyzed by automatic mining techniques—both as a means of qualitative error analysis for the mining techniques, and to provide input to human analysts or debaters. Some current research is looking into building graphs from arguments or from stances (e.g., Toledo-Ronen et al. [2016]), which may also lead to visual presentation in one way or another. Also, Sanchan et al. [2017] suggest to build charts that show the flow of topics, and their intensity, in a debate. El-Assady et al. [2016] apply various visualization techniques to debate protocols, too, emphasizing the utility of such an approach for studying political deliberation processes.

Summarization   Another technique that may be needed once argumentation mining works in practice at a larger scale is textual summarization. Assuming that a set of arguments has been found for a topic, and it has been analyzed, the next step is to compute relations between those arguments, so as to identify identical, similar, and different arguments. For a good summary, the different aspects (or 'facets') raised by the variety of arguments would need to be identified. This is not yet an area of much active research, but as one initial step, a dataset from the Internet Argument Corpus (see Sections 4.2.1 and 7.1.1) has been extended with human-written summaries, and first results on argument facet similarity were reported by Misra et al. [2015, 2017].[1] Similarly, Boltužić and Šnajder [2016] explored the task of computing argument similarity by clustering techniques. Egan et al. [2016] outline an approach to summarizing the key issues brought up in political debates, and some researchers have applied standard text summarization techniques to online debates, extracting sentences that are topic-central and exhibit sentiment [Ranade et al., 2013]. Finally, Saint-Dizier [2018] proposes to use tools and techniques from lexical semantics (in particular, the 'Generative Lexicon' approach of Pustejovsky [1986]) for producing summaries of argumentation.

---

[1]The summary corpus is available for research: `https://nlds.soe.ucsc.edu/node/30` (accessed May 28, 2018).

Evaluation   Finally, argument mining also needs to address the important task of evaluation, which has been discussed in the discussion of argument quality assessments in Section 8.3. In particular, inconsistent lines of arguing can be determined through solving for acceptability in argumentation frameworks, implemented by a large number of argumentation solvers such as Arg&Dec, ASPARTIX, ASPIC, and Carneades. Whereas currently, consistency calculations assume manually-built arguments or controlled natural language (e.g., Wyner et al. [2016]), mined arguments can be directly evaluated, when mapped to a suitable representation. In the state-of-the art approach, Cabrio and Villata [2016] calculate argument acceptance conditions automatically from a Debatepedia debate using a weighted abstract dialectical framework, which has been automatically induced from textual entailment.

Besides logical consistency, we introduced in Section 8.3 some initial work on determining other dimensions of *quality* and the degree of *convincingness* of arguments. First sets of annotated data have been made available, and some results on automatic classification have already been obtained. Still, this line of research is certainly still in its infancy.

10.3 SOME APPLICATIONS OF ARGUMENTATION MINING

Supporting sensemaking   Sensemaking refers to making sense of larger or disparate amounts of information to construct narratives or explanations, as an individual or as a group. Tools for sensemaking support human reasoning, for instance by flagging inconsistencies or visualizing or summarizing information. For example, Dispute Finder highlights disputed claims on the web to support skeptical readers [Ennals et al., 2010]. Among numerous collaborative sensemaking platforms, Videolyzer provides a collaborative platform for assessing the veracity of claims in online political videos [Diakopoulos et al., 2009]; CommentSpace [Willett et al., 2011] helps teams gather evidence and organize comments on visualizations and websites. Schneider [2014] suggests argumentation mining could be used to support open source and open knowledge projects in sensemaking and decision-making. Group decision-making often depends on finding and comparing rationales for claims, and may start with a sensemaking process. For instance, visualization and representation of difficult conversations is key in dialogue mapping, an approach to meeting facilitation that uses argument mapping software [Conklin, 2006]. Argumentation mining could help extract and organize claims and arguments to support visualization, summarization, synthesis, or evaluation components in such applications.

Practical reasoning   Practical reasoning refers to deciding on a practical course of action. It has been extensively studied in the argumentation community; as just one pointer we mention Walton's book on the subject [Walton, 2015]. Argument maps are commonly used to help make a debate accessible. In a computer program called Virgil, for instance, Ball [1994] applied Toulmin's model to analyze public policy. More recently, Renton and Macintosh [2007] presented maps of the Scottish Parliament's debate and policymaking on banning smoking in public places that provide a 'policy memory'. Systems for supporting public discourse on topics of public concern, such as ConsiderIt[2] [Kriplean et al., 2012], have developed visualizations and analytics. Argumentation mining could reduce the manual work in creating support systems for practical reasoning.

Argument Retrieval   Retrieving arguments from text collections corresponds to the core tasks of finding claims and evidence, as discussed in Chapters 5 and 6. For many purposes, these steps also constitute a complete application. In the science domain, for instance, being able to find the main new points in collections of papers would be extremely helpful. This is the aim of Rastegar-Mojarad et al. [2016], who crawl PubMed abstracts and aim at detecting *evidence* statements, which are then mapped to a formal language ('Biological expression language'). Similarly, in the legal domain the retrieval of arguments made in support of a particular decision is of great interest. An overview is provided by Ashley and Walker [2013a].

Taking the retrieval task from specific domains and text collection out into the web presents a set of technical challenges for large-scale processing, as surveyed by Wachsmuth et al. [2017c]. One particular and very important subtask is to determine the appropriateness or relevance of a candidate argument for a specific search query. Wachsmuth et al. [2017d] suggest building a graph of arguments found in a document collection, and then applying a variant of the PageRank algorithm for ranking these arguments according to relevance. Those authors show that this approach outperforms various other candidate ranking methods. A benchmark dataset is made available.[3]

Supporting Web-Scale Discourse and Debate   The use of web data for argumentation mining has been mentioned many times in this book, and we have pointed to a number of corpora that have been drawn from online debate forums, as to provide training and test data for mining techniques. From a different viewpoint, the goal of actively *supporting* the exchange of arguments on the web constitutes another promising application of argumentation mining. This starts with providing technical frameworks for managing discussions, and including argument detection capabilities, as for instance suggested by Cabrio et al. [2013b]. A related task is that of providing active support to human debaters by suggesting suitable arguments to them. Rosenfeld and Kraus [2015] conducted large-scale empirical studies on what arguments people select under particular circumstance, and on this basis designed a *Predictive and Relevance-based Heuristic agent*. Taking this a step further to actual *debating* technology requires an interplay of many components (of which the core argumentation mining functionality is but one), as the overview by Lawrence et al. [2017a] explains.

Sentiment analysis   Connections between argumentation and sentiment analysis have been explored by many researchers, especially in the context of product reviews. For example, Wyner et al. [2012] studied the role of sentiment words and discourse relations for the analysis of cam-

---

[2]https://consider.it (accessed May 28, 2018).
[3]http://argumentation.bplaced.net/arguana/data (accessed May 28, 2018).

era reviews, and suggest an argumentation scheme for representing the underlying structure. Wachsmuth et al. [2015] predict the global sentiment of product reviews from the *flow* of sentiment, which is modeled as a sequence of sentence sentiment scores. The authors propose a method for comparing such sequences to each other and demonstrate its utility for three different review domains. They suggest thinking of sentiment flow as a key aspect of the argumentation structure underlying the review. Finally, we mention Liu et al. [2017], who found that manually-annotated argumentative moves (claim, premise, background, recommendation, etc.) can significantly improve the prediction of review *helpfulness* of hotel reviews.

Writing Support   Providing students with qualitative feedback on their writing starts with the word processor complaining about grammatical errors or stylistic infelicities. But it can go much further, and also include aspects of good argumentation. In the previous chapters, we have referred to work on student essays several times; recall the idea of checking whether arguments are sufficiently supported [Stab and Gurevych, 2017a], or whether critical questions of argument schemes are attended to by the writers [Song et al., 2014]. The latter approach is elaborated in more detail from the perspective of education research by Nussbaum and Edwards [2011]. For a broader survey of (pre-argumentation-mining) computational tools that can support teaching of argumentation, see Scheuer et al. [2010]. And an online demo of the *ArgRewrite PITT Revision Writing Assistant* shows how argumentative aspects are part of the feedback to the student.[4]

Essay Scoring   Closely related to writing support, automatic essay scoring is an application that in general needs to consider a wide range of linguistic parameters, but for the specific class of argumentative essays, techniques from argumentation mining have proven to be helpful. For instance, Ong et al. [2014] developed a rule-based approach to first label the sentences of an essay with a functional tag: Claim, Supports, Opposes, Citation, Hypothesis, and Current Study.[5] Then, another rule set maps the distribution of labels to a number of points corresponding to a grade. This relatively simple approach was found to yield acceptable results for comparative ranking (but not for grading). In contrast, a rich feature set for classification was employed by Persing and Ng [2015], which included semantic frames, coreference, predictions of agreement with the prompt, classified argument components, and more. On a corpus of 1,000 essays from the International Corpus of Learner English, Persing and Ng [2015] showed that their system, after feature optimization, significantly outperforms the results of Ong et al.

Song et al. [2014], who exploited the critical questions of argumentation schemes (see Section 8.2.2) concluded that their results can contribute "additional useful information about essay quality to a strong baseline essay scoring model", which is Educational Testing Service's E-Rater system. Argumentative features improved on another strong baseline, the open source Enhanced AI Scoring Engine, in Nguyen and Litman [2018]'s experiments, particularly when test and training sets responded to different writing prompts.

---

[4]http://argrewrite.cs.pitt.edu/ (accessed May 28, 2018).
[5]This resembles the 'argumentative zoning' of Teufel and Moens [2002], see p. 24.

Wachsmuth et al. [2016] provide a comparative analysis of a broad range of features (including assessments of linear order, as discussed in Section 7.2.2) in terms of four different aspects of essay scoring: organization, thesis clarity, prompt adherence, and argument strength. A strong feature is the distribution of argument components across the paragraphs of an essay. Similarly, Ghosh et al. [2016] manually annotated TOEFL essays and showed that knowledge about argument components and, more importantly, argumentative relations can contribute to predicting essay scores.

Dialogue systems   One long-term perspective is the automatic dialogue system, possibly built upon chatbot technology, that will be able to give advice (on how to act, on what to buy, and so on) and provide reasons for that advice. And ideally, it will be able to not only answer a user's question but also discern their arguments and respond to them intelligently. Such systems can be bootstrapped by first 'harvesting' arguments, counterarguments, and audience values from people, as Chalaguine et al. [2018] investigate for health-related behavior change. 'Persuasive dialogue' is a very active research area, which we have only touched upon in this book, when describing the Amazon Turk study by Lukin et al. [2017]. More connections between dialogue research and argumentation mining will most certainly be built, to textual dialogue but also to speech—a topic that we have excluded completely in this book. For a start, the work by Lippi and Torroni [2016b] can be considered, which reports on experiments on detecting claims in oral political debate, incorporating speech features. In terms of language resources, a new audio and textual dataset for debate research has recently been created by recording 60 speeches on controversial topics by professional debaters [Mirkin et al., 2018].[6]

10.4   OUTLOOK

Like any technology, argumentation mining has a potential to benefit society as well as to be turned to harmful uses. In sentiment analysis, for instance, work on analyzing and generating reviews has in recent years certainly increased the need for finding fake reviews. The potential impact of argumentation mining seems to us even larger, with its potential to integrate rationales as well as emotions. The ubiquity of argumentation makes it particularly powerful. Being able to quickly digest arguments in text, summarize them, and create a debating system would enable automated arguing systems to influence humans, whether in chatbots or in dialogue systems. Automated agents that can argue persuasively may be seen as beneficial when they convince us to exercise more, but harmful when used for marketing. Such agents might outreason humans, as chess systems do, yet interact in a home-like environment, such as current smartphone assistants and home automation systems do. When arguing with humans, there is little recourse against opponents who argue without conviction—playing devil's advocate—or who artificially strengthen a position (as the Greek sophists were criticized for making the weaker argument

---

[6]The recorded debating dataset is available for research: `https://www.research.ibm.com/haifa/dept/vst/debating_data.shtml` (accessed May 28, 2018).

appear the stronger argument). Researchers must be alert to such risks. Communities considering ethics[7] can provide guidance, and we encourage the reader to attend to comprehensive and thorough evaluations of computer systems and their impacts, including analysis of possible risks.[8]

While it may seem a little irritating that this new research field is not really quite settled yet, the positive side is that there are so many things still waiting to be done: argumentation occurs in everyday conversation between couples and in families, in the workplace, and of course everywhere in the media. There are the more regulated formats such as parliamentary debates, lawmaking and jurisprudence; the decidedly-informal claims made via Twitter or its cousins; and the intermediate form of the student's essay. All these—and more—invite digestion, sorting, and further availability for in-depth studies on how argumentation works, when it is successful or persuasive, and when it has flaws. The more reliable the automatic tools that support this, the bigger the picture that can be drawn.

As we remarked earlier, we believe that at some point, further progress will depend on the connection between language processing and automated reasoning (which in turn will require help from computational semantics). While there is little work on building bridges between these communities so far, supplementing an automatically constructed representation of the kind discussed in Chapters 5–7, with robust systems that can evaluate statements against background knowledge, and perform consistency checks, can open up a great many new doors.

---

[7]Such as the Ethics in NLP workshop series: http://www.ethicsinnlp.org (accessed May 28, 2018).
[8]See the ACM Code of Ethics and Professional Conduct https://www.acm.org/about-acm/acm-code-of-ethics-and-professional-conduct (accessed May 28, 2018).

Bibliography

Rob Abbott, Marilyn Walker, Pranav Anand, Jean E. Fox Tree, Robeson Bowmani, and Joseph King. How can you say such things?!?: Recognizing disagreement in informal political argument. In *Workshop on Language in Social Media*, pages 2–11, 2011. 95

Rob Abbott, Brian Ecker, Pranav Anand, and Marilyn Walker. Internet Argument Corpus 2.0: An SQL schema for dialogic social media and the corpora to go with it. In *Proc. Language Resources and Evaluation*, pages 4445–4452, 2016. 52

Stergos Afantenos, Andreas Peldszus, and Manfred Stede. Comparing decoding mechanisms for parsing argumentative structures. *Journal of Argumentation and Computation*, Pre-press, pages 1–16, 2018. DOI: 10.3233/aac-180033 103

Ehud Aharoni, Anatoly Polnarov, Tamar Lavee, Daniel Hershcovich, Ran Levy, Ruty Rinott, Dan Gutfreund, and Noam Slonim. A benchmark dataset for automatic detection of claims and evidence in the context of controversial topics. In *1st Workshop on Argumentation Mining*, pages 64–68, 2014. DOI: 10.3115/v1/w14-2109 64, 71, 78, 91, 134

Yamen Ajjour, Wei-Fan Chen, Johannes Kiesel, Henning Wachsmuth, and Benno Stein. Unit segmentation of argumentative texts. In *4th Workshop on Argumentation Mining*, pages 118–128, 2017. DOI: 10.18653/v1/w17-5115 63

Khalid Al-Khatib, Henning Wachsmuth, Matthias Hagen, Jonas Köhler, and Benno Stein. Cross-domain mining of argumentative text through distant supervision. In *Proc. North American Chapter of the Association for Computational Linguistics: Human Language Technologies*, pages 1395–1404, 2016a. DOI: 10.18653/v1/n16-1165 60

Khalid Al-Khatib, Henning Wachsmuth, Johannes Kiesel, Matthias Hagen, and Benno Stein. A news editorial corpus for mining argumentation strategies. In *Proc. International Conference on Computational Linguistics*, pages 3433–3443, 2016b. 54

Khalid Al-Khatib, Henning Wachsmuth, Matthias Hagen, and Benno Stein. Patterns of argumentation strategies across topics. In *Proc. Empirical Methods in Natural Language Processing*, pages 1351–1357, 2017. DOI: 10.18653/v1/d17-1141 105

Sergio Jose Alvarado. *Understanding Editorial Text: A Computer Model of Argument Comprehension*. Kluwer, Boston, 1990. DOI: 10.1007/978-1-4613-1561-2 36, 37

Pranav Anand, Marilyn Walker, Rob Abbott, Jean E. Fox Tree, Robeson Bowmani, and Michael Minor. Cats rule and dogs drool!: Classifying stance in online debate. In *2nd Workshop on Computational Approaches to Subjectivity and Sentiment Analysis*, pages 1–9, 2011. 88, 89

Jacob Andreas, Sara Rosenthal, and Kathleen McKeown. Annotating agreement and disagreement in threaded discussion. In *Proc. Language Resources and Evaluation*, pages 818–822, 2012. 52

Jean Claude Anscombre and Oswald Ducrot. *L'argumentation Darts la Langue*. Pierre Mardaga, Bruxelles, 1983. DOI: 10.3406/lgge.1976.2306 127

Nicholas Asher and Alex Lascarides. *Logics of Conversation*. Cambridge University Press, Cambridge, 2003. 50

Kevin D. Ashley and Vern Walker. From Information Retrieval (IR) to Argument Retrieval (AR) for legal cases: Report on a baseline study. In *Proc. Legal Knowledge and Information Systems*, pages 29–38, 2013a. 66, 141

Kevin D. Ashley and Vern Walker. Toward constructing evidence-based legal arguments using legal decision documents and machine learning. In *Proc. International Conference on Artificial Intelligence in Law*, pages 176–180, 2013b. DOI: 10.1145/2514601.2514622 131

Katrina Attwood, Paul Chinneck, Martyn Clarke, George Cleland, Mark Coates, Trevor Cockram, George Despotou, Luke Emmet, Jane Fenn, and Ben Gorry. GSN community standard version 1. *Technical Report*, Origin Consulting York, UK, Limited, 2011. 39

Marco Aurisicchio, Pietro Baroni, Dario Pellegrini, and Francesca Toni. Comparing and integrating argumentation-based with matrix-based decision support in Arg&Dec. In *Theory and Applications of Formal Argumentation*, pages 1–20, 2015. DOI: 10.1007/978-3-319-28460-6_1 35, 115

John L. Austin. *How to Do Things with Words*, second edition. Harvard University Press, Cambridge, MA, 1975. DOI: 10.1093/acprof:oso/9780198245537.001.0001 16

Stephen H. Bach, Bert Huang, Ben London, and Lise Getoor. Hinge-loss Markov random fields: Convex inference for structured prediction. In *Proc. Uncertainty in Artificial Intelligence*, pages 32–41, 2013. 90

Jason Baldridge, Nicholas Asher, and Julie Hunter. Annotation for and robust parsing of discourse structure on unrestricted texts. *Zeitschrift für Sprachwissenschaft*, 26(2), pages 213–239, 2007. DOI: 10.1515/zfs.2007.018 98

William J. Ball. Using Virgil to analyze public policy arguments: A system based on Toulmin's informal logic. *Social Science Computer Review*, 12(1), pages 26–37, 1994. DOI: 10.1177/089443939401200102 140

Roy Bar-Haim, Indrajit Bhattacharya, Francesco Dinuzzo, Amrita Saha, and Noam Slonim. Stance classification of context-dependent claims. In *Proc. European Chapter of the Association for Computational Linguistics (Volume 1, Long Papers)*, pages 251–261, 2017. DOI: 10.18653/v1/e17-1024 91, 92

Pietro Baroni, Federico Cerutti, Massimiliano Giacomin, and Giovanni Guida. AFRA: Argumentation framework with recursive attacks. *International Journal of Approximate Reasoning*, 52(1), pages 19–37, 2011. DOI: 10.1016/j.ijar.2010.05.004 115

Pietro Baroni, Marco Romano, Francesca Toni, Marco Aurisicchio, and Giorgio Bertanza. Automatic evaluation of design alternatives with quantitative argumentation. *Argument and Computation*, 6(1), pages 24–49, 2015. DOI: 10.1080/19462166.2014.1001791 35, 114

Pietro Baroni, Dov Gabbay, Massimiliano Giacomin, and Leendert van der Torre, Eds. *Handbook of Formal Argumentation*. College Publications, 2018. xiii

Maria Becker, Alexis Palmer, and Anette Frank. Argumentative texts and clause types. In *3rd Workshop on Argumentation Mining*, pages 21–30, 2016. DOI: 10.18653/v1/w16-2803 22

Sahbi Benlamine, Maher Chaouachi, Serena Villata, Elena Cabrio, and Claude Frassonand Fabien Gandon. Emotions in argumentation: An empirical evaluation. In *Proc. of IJCAI*, pages 156–163, 2015. 123

Jamal Bentahar, Bernard Moulin, and Micheline Bélanger. A taxonomy of argumentation models used for knowledge representation. *Artificial Intelligence Review*, 33(3), pages 211–259, 2010. DOI: 10.1007/s10462-010-9154-1 31, 33, 100

Gregor Betz and Sebastian Cacean. *Ethical Aspects of Climate Engineering*. KIT Scientific Publishing, Karlsruhe, 2012a. DOI: 10.1007/978-3-476-05333-6_48 37

Gregor Betz and Sebastian Cacean. *The moral controversy about Climate Engineering—an argument map*; Version 2012-02-13; Karlsruhe, KIT, 2012b. http://digbib.ubka.uni-karlsruhe.de/volltexte/1000026042 38

Floris Bex, John Lawrence, Mark Snaith, and Chris Reed. Implementing the Argument Web. *Communications of the Association for Computing Machinery*, 56(10), pages 66–73, 2013. DOI: 10.1145/2500891 39

Yonatan Bilu and Noam Slonim. Claim synthesis via predicate recycling. In *Proc. Association for Computational Linguistics (Volume 2: Short Papers)*, pages 525–530, 2016. DOI: 10.18653/v1/p16-2085 134

Or Biran and Owen Rambow. Identifying justifications in written dialogs by classifying text as argumentative. *International Journal of Semantic Computing*, 5(4), pages 363–381, 2011. DOI: 10.1142/s1793351x11001328 76, 78, 80, 81, 82

Peter Bishop and Robin Bloomfield. A methodology for safety case development. In *Proc. Safety-critical Systems Symposium*, pages 194–203, Springer, 1998. DOI: 10.1007/978-1-4471-1534-2_14 39

J. Anthony Blair. *Groundwork in the Theory of Argumentation*. Springer Netherlands, 2012. DOI: 10.1007/978-94-007-2363-4 116

David Blei, Andrew Ng, and Michael Jordan. Latent Dirichlet allocation. *Journal of Machine Learning Research*, 3, pages 993–1022, 2003. 70, 90

Tom Blount, David Millard, and Mark Weal. An ontology for argumentation on the social web: Rhetorical extensions to the AIF. In *Proc. Computational Models of Argument*, pages 119–126, 2016. 43

Filip Boltužić and Jan Šnajder. Back up your stance: Recognizing arguments in online discussions. In *1st Workshop on Argumentation Mining*, pages 49–58, 2014. DOI: 10.3115/v1/w14-2107 52, 53, 95, 96

Filip Boltužić and Jan Šnajder. Fill the gap! Analyzing implicit premises between claims from online debates. In *3rd Workshop on Argumentation Mining*, pages 124–133, 2016. DOI: 10.18653/v1/w16-2815 108, 109, 139

Tom Bosc, Elena Cabrio, and Serena Villata. Tweeties squabbling: Positive and negative results in applying argument mining on social media. In *Proc. Computational Models of Argument*, pages 21–32, 2016a. DOI: 10.3233/978-1-61499-686-6-21 60, 95, 96

Tom Bosc, Elena Cabrio, and Serena Villata. DART: A dataset of arguments and their relations on Twitter. In *Proc. Language Resources and Evaluation*, pages 1258–1263, 2016b. 95

Simon Buckingham Shum. Cohere: Towards Web 2.0 argumentation. In *Proc. Computational Models of Argument*, vol. 171, pages 97–108, 2008. 42

Katarzyna Budzyńska and Chris Reed. Speech acts of argumentation: Inference anchors and peripheral cues in dialogue. In *Proc. Computational Models of Natural Argument*, pages 3–10, 2011. 51

Jill Burstein and Daniel Marcu. A machine learning approach for identification of thesis and conclusion statements in student essays. *Computers and the Humanities*, 37(4), pages 455–467, 2003. DOI: 10.1023/A:1025746505971 67, 68, 69

Elena Cabrio and Serena Villata. Combining textual entailment and argumentation theory for supporting online debates interactions. In *Proc. Association for Computational Linguistics (Volume 2: Short Papers)*, pages 208–212, 2012. 94

Elena Cabrio and Serena Villata. NoDE: A benchmark of natural language arguments. In *Proc. Conference on Computational Models of Argument*, vol. 266, pages 449–450, 2014. DOI: 10.3233/978-1-61499-436-7-449 114, 115

Elena Cabrio and Serena Villata. Natural language argumentation for text exploration. In *Proc. Agents and Artificial Intelligence*, pages 133–150, 2016. DOI: 10.1007/978-3-319-53354-4_8 114, 116, 140

Elena Cabrio, Sara Tonelli, and Serena Villata. From discourse analysis to argumentation schemes and back: Relations and differences. In *Proc. Computational Logic in Multi-Agent Systems*, pages 1–17, 2013a. DOI: 10.1007/978-3-642-40624-9_1 80

Elena Cabrio, Serena Villata, and Fabien Gandon. A support framework for argumentative discussions management in the Web. In *Proc. Extended Semantic Web Conference*, pages 412–426, 2013b. DOI: 10.1007/978-3-642-38288-8_28 141

Giuseppe Carenini. Gea: A complete, modular system for generating evaluative arguments. In Vassil N. Alexandrov, Jack J. Dongarra, Benjoe A. Juliano, René S. Renner, and C. J. Kenneth Tan, Eds., *Computational Science, (ICCS)*, pages 959–968, Springer, Berlin, Heidelberg, 2001. DOI: 10.1007/3-540-45545-0_108 126, 128, 129

Lynn Carlson, Daniel Marcu, and Mary Ellen Okurowski. Building a discourse-tagged corpus in the framework of Rhetorical Structure Theory. In Jan van Kuppevelt and Ronnie Smith, Eds., *Current Directions in Discourse and Dialogue*, pages 85–112, Kluwer, Dordrecht, 2003. DOI: 10.1007/978-94-010-0019-2_5 25, 79

Jean-Claude Carron. Rhetoric: Overview. In Maryanne Cline Horowitz, Ed., *New Dictionary of the History of Ideas*, vol. 5, Charles Scribner's Sons, 2005. 23

Lucas Carstens and Francesca Toni. Towards relation based argumentation mining. In *2nd Workshop on Argumentation Mining*, pages 29–34, 2015. DOI: 10.3115/v1/w15-0504 96, 97

Claudette Cayrol and Marie-Christine Lagasquie-Schiex. On the acceptability of arguments in bipolar argumentation frameworks. In *ECSQARU*, pages 378–389, 2005. DOI: 10.1007/11518655_33 8

Claudette Cayrol and Marie-Christine Lagasquie-Schiex. Bipolar abstract argumentation systems. In Guillermo Ricardo Simari and Iyad Rahwan, Eds., *Argumentation in Artificial Intelligence*, pages 65–84, Springer, 2009. DOI: 10.1007/978-0-387-98197-0_4 114

Federico Cerutti, Alexis Palmer, Ariel Rosenfeld, Jan Šnajder, and Francesca Toni. A pilot study in using argumentation frameworks for online debates. In *1st International Workshop on Systems and Algorithms for Formal Argumentation*, pages 63–74, 2016. 114, 116

Federico Cerutti, Alice Toniolo, and Timothy J. Norman. On natural language generation of formal argumentation. *ArXiv Preprint ArXiv:1706.04033 [cs.AI]*, 2017. 131

Federico Cerutti, Sarah A. Gaggl, Matthias Thimm, and Johannes P. Wallner. Foundations of implementations for formal argumentation. In Pietro Baroni, Dov Gabbay, Massimiliano Giacomin, and Leendert van der Torre, Eds., *Handbook of Formal Argumentation*, pages 689–768, College Publications, 2018. 114

Lisa A. Chalaguine, Anthony Hunter, Henry W. W. Potts, and Fiona L. Hamilton. Argument harvesting using chatbots. *ArXiv Preprint ArXiv:1805.04253*, 2018. 143

Lisa Andreevna Chalaguine and Claudia Schulz. Assessing convincingness of arguments in online debates with limited number of features. In *Proc. Student Research Workshop at European Chapter of the Association for Computational Linguistics*, pages 75–83, 2017. DOI: 10.18653/v1/e17-4008 118

Nitesh V. Chawla, Kevin W. Bowyer, Lawrence O. Hall, and W. Philip Kegelmeyer. SMOTE: Synthetic minority over-sampling technique. *Journal of Artificial Intelligence Research*, 16(1), pages 321–357, 2002. DOI: 10.1613/jair.953 69

Carlos Chesñevar, Sanjay Modgil, Iyad Rahwan, Chris Reed, Guillermo Simari, Matthew South, Gerard Vreeswijk, and Steven Willmott. Towards an argument interchange format. *The Knowledge Engineering Review*, 21(4), pages 293–316, 2006. DOI: 10.1017/s0269888906001044 43

Yoeng-Jin Chu and Tseng-Hong Liu. On the shortest arborescence of a directed graph. *Science Sinica*, 14, pages 1396–1400, 1965. 103

Alexander Clark, Chris Fox, and Shalom Lappin. *The Handbook of Computational Linguistics and Natural Language Processing*. John Wiley & Sons, 2013. DOI: 10.1002/9781444324044 xiii

Oana Cocarascu and Francesca Toni. Identifying attack and support argumentative relations using deep learning. In *Proc. Empirical Methods in Natural Language Processing*, pages 1385–1390, 2017a. DOI: 10.18653/v1/d17-1144 96

Oana Cocarascu and Francesca Toni. Mining bipolar argumentation frameworks from natural language text. In *Proc. Computational Models of Natural Argument*, pages 65–70, 2017b. 116

Robin Cohen. A computational model for the analysis of arguments. *Technical Report CSRG-151*, Computer Systems Research Group, University of Toronto, Toronto, Canada, 1983. 35, 36

Robin Cohen. Analyzing the structure of argumentative discourse. *Computational Linguistics*, 13(1–2), pages 11–24, 1987. 36

Jeffery Conklin. *Dialogue Mapping: Building Shared Understanding of Wicked Problems*. Wiley, Chichester, UK, 2006. 39, 140

Ido Dagan, Dan Roth, Mark Sammons, and Fabio Massimo Zanzotto. *Recognizing Textual Entailment: Models and Applications*. Morgan & Claypool, 2013. DOI: 10.2200/s00509ed1v01y201305hlt023 94

Johannes Daxenberger, Steffen Eger, Ivan Habernal, Christian Stab, and Iryna Gurevych. What is the essence of a claim? Cross-domain claim identification. In *Proc. Empirical Methods in Natural Language Processing*, pages 2055–2066, 2017. DOI: 10.18653/v1/d17-1218 76

Nicholas Diakopoulos, Sergio Goldenberg, and Irfan Essa. Videolyzer: Quality analysis of online informational video for bloggers and journalists. In *Proc. Human Factors in Computing Systems*, pages 799–808, 2009. DOI: 10.1145/1518701.1518824 140

Phan Minh Dung. On the acceptability of arguments and its fundamental role in nonmonotonic reasoning, logic programming and n-person games. *Artificial Intelligence*, 77(2), pages 321–357, 1995. DOI: 10.1016/0004-3702(94)00041-x 34

Mihai Dusmanu, Elena Cabrio, and Serena Villata. Argument mining on Twitter: Arguments, facts and sources. In *Proc. Empirical Methods in Natural Language Processing*, pages 2307–2312, 2017. DOI: 10.18653/v1/d17-1245 60

Rory Duthie, Katarzyna Budzyńska, and Chris Reed. Mining ethos in political debate. In *Proc. Computational Models of Argument*, pages 21–32, 2016. 133

Judith Eckle-Kohler, Roland Kluge, and Iryna Gurevych. On the role of discourse markers for discriminating claims and premises in argumentative discourse. In *Proc. Empirical Methods in Natural Language Processing*, pages 2236–2242, 2015. DOI: 10.18653/v1/d15-1267 80

Jack Edmonds. Optimum branchings. *Journal of Research of the National Bureau of Standards*, 718, pages 233–240, 1967. DOI: 10.6028/jres.071b.032 103

Charlie Egan, Advaith Siddharthan, and Adam Z. Wyner. Summarising the points made in online political debates. In *3rd Workshop on Argument Mining*, pages 134–143, 2016. DOI: 10.18653/v1/w16-2816 139

Steffen Eger, Johannes Daxenberger, and Iryna Gurevych. Neural end-to-end learning for computational argumentation mining. In *Proc. Annual Meeting of the Association for Computational Linguistics (Volume 1: Long Papers)*, pages 11–22, 2017. DOI: 10.18653/v1/p17-1002 63, 104

Ekkehard Eggs. Vertextungsmuster argumentation: Logische grundlagen. In Klaus Brinker, Ed., *Text- und Gesprächslinguistik*, vol. 16 of *Handbücher zur Sprach- und Kommunikationswissenschaft*, pages 397–414. Walter de Gruyter, Berlin, 2000. DOI: 10.1515/9783110135596.1.6.397 3

Uwe Egly, Sarah Alice Gaggl, and Stefan Woltran. Answer-set programming encodings for argumentation frameworks. *Argument and Computation*, 1(2), pages 147–177, 2010. DOI: 10.1080/19462166.2010.486479 115

Mennatallah El-Assady, Valentin Gold, Annette Hautli-Janisz, Wolfgang Jentnerand Miriam Butt, Katharina Holzinger, and Daniel Keim. VisArgue—a visual text analytics framework for the study of deliberative communication. In *Proc. International Conference on the Advances in Computational Analysis of Political Text*, pages 31–36, 2016. 139

Michael Elhadad. Using argumentation in text generation. *Journal of Pragmatics*, 24, pages 189–220, 1995. DOI: 10.1016/0378-2166(94)00096-w 127

Luke Emmet and George Cleland. Graphical notations, narratives and persuasion: A pliant systems approach to hypertext tool design. In *Proc. Hypertext and Hypermedia*, pages 55–64, 2002. DOI: 10.1145/513352.513354 41

Rob Ennals, Beth Trushkowsky, and John Mark Agosta. Highlighting disputed claims on the Web. In *Proc. World Wide Web*, pages 341–350, 2010. DOI: 10.1145/1772690.1772726 140

Jeanne Fahnestock. *Rhetorical Style: The Uses of Language in Persuasion*. Oxford University Press, 2011. DOI: 10.1093/acprof:oso/9780199764129.001.0001 23

Mohammad Hassan Falakmasir, Kevin D. Ashley, Christian D. Schunn, and Diane J. Litman. Identifying thesis and conclusion statements in student essays to scaffold peer review. In *Proc. Intelligent Tutoring Systems*, pages 254–259, 2014. DOI: 10.1007/978-3-319-07221-0_31 67, 68

Richárd Farkas, Veronika Vincze, Görgy Móra, János Csirik, and Görgy Szarvas. The CoNLL 2010 shared task: Learning to detect hedges and their scope in natural language text. In *Proc. Conference on Computational Natural Language Learning: Shared Task*, pages 1–12, 2010. 12

Adam Robert Faulkner. Automated classification of argument stance in student essays: A linguistically motivated approach with an application for supporting argument summarization. Ph.D. thesis, City University of New York, 2014. 90

Vanessa Wei Feng and Graeme Hirst. Classifying arguments by scheme. In *Proc. Association for Computational Linguistics: Human Language Technologies*, pages 987–996, 2011. 112

William Ferreira and Andreas Vlachos. Emergent: A novel data-set for stance classification. In *Proc. North American Chapter of the Association for Computational Linguistics: Human Language Technologies*, pages 1163–1168, 2016. DOI: 10.18653/v1/n16-1138 88

Eirini Florou, Stasinos Konstantopoulos, Antonis Koukourikos, and Pythagoras Karampiperis. Argument extraction for supporting public policy formulation. In *7th Workshop on Language Technology for Cultural Heritage, Social Sciences, and Humanities*, pages 49–54, 2013. 60

James B. Freeman. *Dialectics and the Macrostructure of Argument*. Foris, Berlin, 1991. DOI: 10.1515/9783110875843 6, 45

James B. Freeman. *Argument Structure: Representation and Theory*. Argumentation Library (18), Springer, 2011. 45

Luanne Freund, Charles L. A. Clarke, and Elaine G. Toms. Towards genre classification for IR in the workplace. In *Proc. International Conference on Information Interaction in Context*, pages 30–36, 2006. DOI: 10.1145/1164820.1164829 58

Albert Gatt and Ehud Reiter. Simplenlg: A realisation engine for practical applications. In *Proc. European Workshop on Natural Language Generation*, 2009. DOI: 10.3115/1610195.1610208 134

Debanjan Ghosh, Smaranda Muresan, Nina Wacholder, Mark Aakhus, and Matthew Mitsui. Analyzing argumentative discourse units in online interactions. In *1st Workshop on Argumentation Mining*, pages 39–48, 2014. DOI: 10.3115/v1/w14-2106 52, 54, 96

Debanjan Ghosh, Aquila Khanam, Yubo Han, and Smaranda Muresan. Coarse-grained argumentation features for scoring persuasive essays. In *Proc. Association for Computational Linguistics (Volume 2: Short Papers)*, pages 549–554, 2016. DOI: 10.18653/v1/p16-2089 143

Thomas F. Gordon. Introducing the Carneades web application. In *Proc. International Conference on Artificial Intelligence and Law*, pages 243–244, 2013. DOI: 10.1145/2514601.2514637 114

Theodosis Goudas, Christos Louizos, Georgios Petasis, and Vangelis Karkaletsis. Argument extraction from news, blogs, and social media. In Aristidis Likas, Konstantinos Blekas, and Dimitris Kalles, Eds., *Proc. Hellenic Conference on Artificial Intelligence*, pages 287–299, 2014. DOI: 10.1007/978-3-319-07064-3_23 60, 74, 85, 102

Trudy Govier. *A Practical Study of Argument*. Wadsworth, Cengage Learning, Belmont, CA, 2010. 120

Trudy Govier. More on counter-considerations. In *Proc. Ontario Society for the Study of Argumentation*, pages 1–10, 2011. 85

Sylviane Granger. The international corpus of learner english: A new resource for foreign language learning and teaching and second language acquisition research. *TESOL Quarterly*, 37(3), pages 538–546, 2003. DOI: 10.2307/3588404 91

Floriana Grasso, Alison Cawsey, and Ray Jones. Dialectical argumentation to solve conflicts in advice giving: A case study in the promotion of healthy nutrition. *International Journal of the Human-Computer Studies*, 53, pages 1077–1115, 2000. DOI: 10.1006/ijhc.2000.0429 130

Nancy Green. Identifying argumentation schemes in genetics research articles. In *2nd Workshop on Argumentation Mining*, pages 12–21, 2015. DOI: 10.3115/v1/w15-0502 112

Nancy Green. Manual identification of arguments with implicit conclusions using semantic rules for argument mining. In *Proc. of the 4th Workshop on Argument Mining*, pages 73–78, 2017. DOI: 10.18653/v1/w17-5109 112

Nancy Green. Towards mining scientific discourse using argumentation schemes. *Argument and Computation*, 9(2), pages 121–135, 2018. DOI: 10.3233/aac-180038 112

Nancy Green, Rachael Dwight, Kanyamas Navoraphan, and Brian Stadler. Natural language generation of biomedical argumentation for lay audiences. *Argument and Computation*, 2(1), pages 23–50, 2011. 129, 130
DOI: 10.1080/19462166.2010.515037

Wayne Grennan. *Informal Logic: Issues and Techniques*. McGill-Queen's University Press, 1997. 28, 30

Jürgen Habermas. *Theorie des Kommunikativen Handelns*. Suhrkamp, Frankfurt, 1981. 4

Ivan Habernal and Iryna Gurevych. What makes a convincing argument? Empirical analysis and detecting attributes of convincingness in web argumentation. In *Proc. Empirical Methods in Natural Language Processing*, pages 1214–1223, 2016. DOI: 10.18653/v1/d16-1129 118, 119

Ivan Habernal and Iryna Gurevych. Argumentation mining in user-generated web discourse. *Computational Linguistics*, 43(1), pages 125–179, 2017. DOI: 10.1162/coli_a_00276 14, 33, 48, 49, 53, 59, 60, 62, 63, 64, 74, 75, 76, 85, 87, 102, 120

Ben Hachey and Claire Grover. Extractive summarisation of legal texts. *Artificial Intelligence and Law*, 14(4), pages 305–345, 2006. DOI: 10.1007/s10506-007-9039-z 66

Randy Allen Harris and Chrysanne Di Marco. Ontological representations of rhetorical figures for argument mining. *Argument and Computation*, 8(3), pages 267–287, 2017. DOI: 10.3233/AAC-170027 24

Randy Allen Harris, Chrysanne Di Marco, Sebastian Ruan, and Cliff O'Reilly. An annotation scheme for rhetorical figures. *Argument and Computation*, 9(2), pages 155–175, 2018. DOI: 10.3233/aac-180037 24

Kazi Saidul Hasan and Vincent Ng. Extra-linguistic constraints on stance recognition in ideological debates. In *Proc. Association for Computational Linguistics (Volume 2: Short Papers)*, pages 816–821, 2013. 88

Kazi Saidul Hasan and Vincent Ng. Why are you taking this stance? Identifying and classifying reasons in ideological debates. In *Proc. Empirical Methods in Natural Language Processing*, pages 751–762, 2014. DOI: 10.3115/v1/d14-1083 80, 82, 89, 108

A. Francisca Snoeck Henkemans. State-of-the-art: The structure of argumentation. *Argumentation*, 14(4), pages 447–473, 2000. DOI: 10.1023/A:1007800305762 28

Christopher Hidey, Elena Musi, Alyssa Hwang, Smaranda Muresan, and Kathy McKeown. Analyzing the semantic types of claims and premises in an online persuasive forum. In *4th Workshop on Argument Mining*, pages 11–21, 2017. DOI: 10.18653/v1/w17-5102 120

David Hitchcock and Jean Wagemans. The pragma-dialectical account of argument schemes. *Keeping in Touch with Pragma-dialectics*, pages 185–205, 2011. DOI: 10.1075/z.163.13hit 30

Michael H. G. Hoffmann. Analyzing framing processes in conflicts and communication by means of logical argument mapping. In William A. Donohue, Randall G. Rogan, and Sanda Kaufman, Eds., *Framing Matters: Perspectives on Negotiation Research and Practice in Communication*, pages 136–164, Peter Lang, 2011. 41

Robert E. Horn. Infrastructure for navigating interdisciplinary debates: Critical decisions for representing argumentation. In *Visualizing Argumentation: Software Tools for Collaborative and Educational Sense-making*, pages 165–184, Springer, 2003. DOI: 10.1007/978-1-4471-0037-9_8 36

Anthony Hunter and Matthew Williams. Aggregating evidence about the positive and negative effects of treatments. *Artificial Intelligence in Medicine*, 56(3), pages 173–90, 2012. DOI: 10.1016/j.artmed.2012.09.004 40

Anthony Hunter and Matthew Williams. Aggregation of clinical evidence using argumentation: A tutorial introduction. In Arjen Hommersom and Peter J. F. Lucas, Eds., *Foundations of Biomedical Knowledge Representation*, pages 317–337, Springer, 2015. DOI: 10.1007/978-3-319-28007-3_20 41

Fattaneh Jabbari, Mohammad Hassan Falakmasir, and Kevin D. Ashley. Identifying thesis statements in student essays: The class imbalance challenge and resolution. In *Proc. FLAIRS, Special Track on Applied Natural Language Processing*, pages 220–225, 2016. 69

Mathilde Janier, John Lawrence, and Chris Reed. OVA+: An argument analysis interface. In *Proc. Computational Models of Argument*, pages 463–464, 2014. 42

Dan Jurafsky and James H. Martin. *Speech and Language Processing: An Introduction to Natural Language Processing, Computational Linguistics, and Speech Recognition*, 2nd ed., Prentice Hall, Pearson Education International, 2009. xiii

Jussi Karlgren and Douglass Cutting. Recognizing text genres with simple metrics using discriminant analysis. In *Proc. International Conference on Computational Linguistics: Volume 2*, pages 1071–1075, 1994. DOI: 10.3115/991250.991324 58

Joel Katzav, Chris Reed, and Glenn Rowe. Argument research corpus. In *Communication in Multiagent Systems*, vol. 2650, pages 269–283, Springer, 2003. 43

Brett Kessler, Geoffrey Numberg, and Hinrich Schütze. Automatic detection of text genre. In *Proc. 35th Annual Meeting of the Association for Computational Linguistics and 8th Conference of the European Chapter of the Association for Computational Linguistics*, pages 32–38, 1997. DOI: 10.3115/976909.979622 58

Christian Kirschner, Judith Eckle-Kohler, and Iryna Gurevych. Linking the thoughts: Analysis of argumentation structures in scientific publications. In *Proc. North American Chapter of the Association for Computational Linguistics: Human Language Technologies*, pages 1–11, 2015. DOI: 10.3115/v1/w15-0501 46, 48

Josef Klein. *Die Konklusiven Sprechhandlungen*. Niemeyer, Tübingen, 1987. DOI: 10.1515/9783111371627 19

Martha Kolln. *Rhetorical Grammar: Grammatical Choices, Rhetorical Effects*. Longman, New York, 2003. 23

Robert Koons. Defeasible reasoning. In Edward N. Zalta, Ed., *The Stanford Encyclopedia of Philosophy*. Metaphysics Research Lab, Stanford University, summer edition, 2017. https://plato.stanford.edu/entries/reasoning-defeasible/ 29

Milen Kouylekov and Matteo Negri. An open-source package for recognizing textual entailment. In *Proc. Association for Computational Linguistics System Demonstrations*, pages 42–47, 2010. 94

Travis Kriplean, Jonathan Morgan, Deen Freelon, Alan Borning, and Lance Bennett. Supporting reflective public thought with ConsiderIt. In *Proc. Computer Supported Cooperative Work*, pages 265–274, 2012. DOI: 10.1145/2145204.2145249 141

Katarina Krüger, Anna Lukowiak, Jonathan Sonntag, and Manfred Stede. Classifying news vs. opinions in newspapers: Linguistic features for domain independence. *Natural Language Enginnering*, 23(5), pages 687–707, 2017. DOI: 10.1017/s1351324917000043 13, 59, 62

Frank R. Kschischang, Brendan J. Frey, and H. A. Loeliger. Factor graphs and the sum-product algorithm. *IEEE Transactions on Information Theory*, 47(2), pages 498–519, 2001. DOI: 10.1109/18.910572 104

Werner Kunz and Horst W. J. Rittel. Issues as elements of information systems. *Technical Report Working Paper No. 131*, Institute of Urban and Regional Development, University of California, Berkeley, 1970. 35, 42

Namhee Kwon, Liang Zhou, Eduard Hovy, and Stuart W. Shulman. Identifying and classifying subjective claims. In *Proc. International Conference on Digital Government Research: Bridging Disciplines and Domains*, pages 76–81, 2007. 73

Anirban Laha and Vikas Raykar. An empirical evaluation of various deep learning architectures for bi-sequence classification tasks. In *Proc. International Conference on Computational Linguistics: Technical Papers*, pages 2762–2773, 2016. 73

John Lawrence and Chris Reed. Argument mining using argumentation scheme structures. In *Proc. Computational Models of Argument*, pages 379–390, 2016. 113

John Lawrence, Floris Bex, Chris Reed, and Mark Snaith. AIFdb: Infrastructure for the Argument Web. In *Proc. Computational Models of Argument*, pages 515–516, 2012. 43, 100, 113

John Lawrence, Chris Reed, Colin Allen, Simon McAlister, Andrew Ravenscroft, and David Bourget. Mining arguments from 19th century philosophical texts using topic based modelling. In *1st Workshop on Argumentation Mining*, pages 79–87, 2014. DOI: 10.3115/v1/w14-2111 61, 99, 100

John Lawrence, Mark Snaith, Barbara Konat, Katarzyna Budzyńska, and Chris Reed. Debating technology for dialogical argument: Sensemaking, engagement, and analytics. *ACM Transactions on Internet Technology*, 17(3), pages 24:1–24:23, 2017a. Special issue on Argumentation in Social Media. DOI: 10.1145/3007210 141

John Lawrence, Jacky Visser, and Chris Reed. Harnessing rhetorical figures for argument mining. *Argument and Computation*, 8(3), pages 289–310, 2017b. DOI: 10.3233/aac-170026 24

Ran Levy, Yonatan Bilu, Daniel Hershcovich, Ehud Aharoni, and Noam Slonim. Context dependent claim detection. In *Proc. International Conference on Computational Linguistics: Technical Papers*, pages 1489–1500, 2014. 71, 72, 73, 82

Marco Lippi and Paolo Torroni. Context-independent claim detection for argument mining. In *Proc. of International Joint Conference on Artificial Intelligence*, pages 185–191, 2015. 72

Marco Lippi and Paolo Torroni. Argumentation mining: State of the art and emerging trends. *ACM Transactions on Internet Technology*, 16(2), pages 10:1–10:25, 2016a. Special issue on Argumentation in Social Media. DOI: 10.1145/2850417 57

Marco Lippi and Paolo Torroni. Argument mining from speech: Detecting claims in political debates. In *Proc. AAAI Conference on Artificial Intelligence*, pages 2979–2985, 2016b. 143

Bing Liu. *Sentiment Analysis and Opinion Mining.* Morgan & Claypool, 2012. DOI: 10.2200/S00416ED1V01Y201204HLT016 15

Haijing Liu, Yang Gao, Pin Lv, Mengxue Li, Shiqiang Geng, Minglan Li, and Hao Wang. Using argument-based features to predict and analyse review helpfulness. In *Proc. Empirical Methods in Natural Language Processing*, pages 1369–1374, 2017. DOI: 10.18653/v1/d17-1142 142

Stephanie Lukin, Pranav Anand, Marilyn Walker, and Steve Whittaker. Argument strength is in the eye of the beholder: Audience effects in persuasion. In *Proc. European Chapter of the Association for Computational Linguistics (Volume 1, Long Papers)*, pages 742–753, 2017. DOI: 10.18653/v1/e17-1070 121, 122, 143

William Mann and Sandra Thompson. Rhetorical structure theory: Towards a functional theory of text organization. *TEXT*, 8, pages 243–281, 1988. DOI: 10.1515/text.1.1988.8.3.243 25, 68, 78, 129

Daniel Marcu. *The Theory and Practice of Discourse Parsing and Summarization.* MIT Press, Cambridge, MA, 2000. 68

James R. Martin and Peter R. R. White. *The Language of Evaluation: Appraisal in English.* Palgrave Macmillan, London, 2005. DOI: 10.11606/issn.2236-4242.v0i21p133-137 12

Tomas Mikolov, Wen-tau Yih, and Geoffrey Zweig. Linguistic regularities in continuous space word representations. In *Proc. North American Chapter of the Association for Computational Linguistics: Human Language Technologies*, pages 746–751, 2013. 74, 117

Shachar Mirkin, Michal Jacovi, Tamar Lavee, Hong-Kwang Kuo, Samuel Thomas, Leslie Sager, Lili Kotlerman, Elad Venezian, and Noam Slonim. A recorded debating dataset. In *Proc. Language Resources and Evaluation*, pages 250–254, 2018. 143

Amita Misra and Marilyn Walker. Topic independent identification of agreement and disagreement in social media dialogue. In *Proc. SIGDIAL*, pages 41–50, 2013. 96

Amita Misra, Pranav Anand, Jean E. Fox Tree, and Marilyn Walker. Using summarization to discover argument facets in online idealogical dialog. In *Proc. North American Chapter of the Association for Computational Linguistics: Human Language Technologies*, pages 430–440, 2015. DOI: 10.3115/v1/n15-1046 139

Amita Misra, Shereen Oraby, Shubhangi Tandon, Sharath Ts, Pranav Anand, and Marilyn Walker. Summarizing dialogic arguments from social media. In *Proc. SEMDIAL*, pages 126–136, 2017. DOI: 10.21437/semdial.2017-14 139

Marie-Francine Moens, Erik Boiy, Raquel Mochales Palau, and Chris Reed. Automatic detection of arguments in legal texts. In *Proc. International Conference on Artificial Intelligence and Law*, pages 225–230, 2007. DOI: 10.1145/1276318.1276362 60

Saif Mohammad, Svetlana Kiritchenko, Parinaz Sobhani, Xiaodan Zhu, and Colin Cherry. Semeval-2016 task 6: Detecting stance in tweets. In *10th Workshop on Semantic Evaluation*, pages 31–41, 2016. DOI: 10.18653/v1/s16-1003 87

Arjun Mukherjee and Bing Liu. Discovering user interactions in ideological discussions. In *Proc. Association for Computational Linguistics (Volume 1: Long Papers)*, pages 671–681, 2013. 95, 96

Elena Musi, Debanjan Ghosh, and Smaranda Muresan. Towards feasible guidelines for the annotation of argument schemes. In *3rd Workshop on Argumentation Mining*, pages 82–93, 2016. DOI: 10.18653/v1/w16-2810 110

Huy Nguyen and Diane Litman. Extracting argument and domain words for identifying argument components in texts. In *2nd Workshop on Argumentation Mining*, pages 22–28, 2015. DOI: 10.3115/v1/w15-0503 70, 71

Huy Nguyen and Diane Litman. Context-aware argumentative relation mining. In *Proc. Association for Computational Linguistics (Volume 1: Long Papers)*, pages 1127–1137, 2016. DOI: 10.18653/v1/p16-1107 99

Huy V. Nguyen and Diane J. Litman. Argument mining for improving the automated scoring of persuasive essays. In *Proc. American Association for Artificial Intelligence*, pages 5892–5899, 2018. 142

Vlad Niculae, Joonsuk Park, and Claire Cardie. Argument mining with structured SVMs and RNNs. In *Proc. Association for Computational Linguistics (Volume 1: Long Papers)*, pages 985–995, 2017. DOI: 10.18653/v1/p17-1091 49, 50, 100

Kawsar Noor, Anthony Hunter, and Astrid Mayer. Analysis of medical arguments from patient experiences expressed on the social web. In *International Conference on Industrial Engineering and Other Applications of Applied Intelligent Systems*, pages 285–294, Springer, 2017. DOI: 10.1007/978-3-319-60045-1_31 41

E. Michael Nussbaum and Ordene V. Edwards. Critical questions and argument stratagems: A framework for enhancing and analyzing students' reasoning practices. *The Journal of the Learning Sciences*, pages 443–488, 2011. DOI: 10.1080/10508406.2011.564567 142

Eva Ogiermann. *On Apologizing in Negative and Positive Politeness Cultures*. John Benjamins, Amsterdam, 2009. DOI: 10.1075/pbns.191 18

Nathan Ong, Diane Litman, and Alexandra Brusilovsky. Ontology-based argument mining and automatic essay scoring. In *1st Workshop on Argumentation Mining*, pages 24–28, 2014. DOI: 10.3115/v1/w14-2104 142

Shereen Oraby, Lena Reed, Ryan Compton, Ellen Riloff, Marilyn Walker, and Steve Whittaker. And that's a fact: Distinguishing factual and emotional argumentation in online dialogue. In *2nd Workshop on Argumentation Mining*, pages 116–126, 2015. DOI: 10.3115/v1/w15-0515 120, 121

Sebastian Padó, Tae-Gil Noh, Asher Stern, Rui Wang, and Roberto Zanoli. Design and realization of a modular architecture for textual entailment. *Natural Language Engineering*, 21(2), pages 167–200, 2015. DOI: 10.1017/s1351324913000351 95

Raquel Mochales Palau and Marie-Francine Moens. Argumentation mining: The detection, classification and structuring of arguments in text. In *Proc. of International Conference on AI and Law*, pages 98–107, 2009. DOI: 10.1145/1568234.1568246 61, 63, 65, 66, 84, 85, 98, 102

Joonsuk Park and Claire Cardie. Identifying appropriate support for propositions in online user comments. In *1st Workshop on Argumentation Mining*, pages 29–38, 2014. DOI: 10.3115/v1/w14-2105 13, 19

Renate Pasch. Untersuchungen zu den gebrauchsbedingungen der deutschen kausalkonjunktionen da, denn und weil. *Linguistische Studien*, A(4), pages 41–243, 1982. 20

Andreas Peldszus. Towards segment-based recognition of argumentation structure in short texts. In *1st Workshop on Argumentation Mining*, pages 88–97, 2014. DOI: 10.3115/v1/w14-2112 46, 86, 98, 99, 102, 103

Andreas Peldszus and Manfred Stede. From argument diagrams to argumentation mining in texts: A survey. *International Journal of Cognitive Informatics and Natural Intelligence*, 7(1), pages 1–31, 2013. DOI: 10.4018/jcini.2013010101 6, 25, 45, 46, 47, 57, 62, 86

Andreas Peldszus and Manfred Stede. Joint prediction in MST-style discourse parsing for argumentation mining. In *Proc. Empirical Methods in Natural Language Processing*, pages 938–948, 2015a. DOI: 10.18653/v1/d15-1110 98, 102, 103

Andreas Peldszus and Manfred Stede. Towards detecting counter-considerations in text. In *2nd Workshop on Argumentation Mining*, pages 104–109, 2015b. DOI: 10.3115/v1/w15-0513 86

Andreas Peldszus and Manfred Stede. Rhetorical structure and argumentation structure in monologue text. In *3rd Workshop on Argumentation Mining*, pages 103–112, 2016a. DOI: 10.18653/v1/w16-2812 26, 80

Andreas Peldszus and Manfred Stede. An annotated corpus of argumentative microtexts. In *Argumentation and Reasoned Action: Proc. 1st European Conference on Argumentation, Lisbon 2015 / Vol. 2*, pages 801–816, College Publications, London, 2016b. 2, 22, 53, 76, 78, 85, 101, 110

Jeffrey Pennington, Richard Socher, and Christopher D. Manning. GloVe: Global vectors for word representation. In *Empirical Methods in Natural Language Processing*, pages 1532–1543, 2014. DOI: 10.3115/v1/d14-1162 96

Chaim Perelman and Lucie Olbrechts-Tyteca. *The New Rhetoric: A Treatise on Argumentation*. Notre Dame Press, University of Notre Dame, 1969. 34, 130

Isaac Persing and Vincent Ng. Modeling argument strength in student essays. In *Proc. 53rd Annual Meeting of the Association for Computational Linguistics and the 7th International Joint Conference on Natural Language Processing (Volume 1: Long Papers)*, pages 543–552, 2015. DOI: 10.3115/v1/p15-1053 142

Isaac Persing and Vincent Ng. End-to-end argumentation mining in student essays. In *Proc. North American Chapter of the Association for Computational Linguistics: Human Language Technologies*, pages 1384–1394, 2016. DOI: 10.18653/v1/n16-1164 63, 103

Philipp Petrenz and Bonnie Webber. Stable classification of text genres. *Computational Linguistics*, 37(2), pages 385–393, 2011. DOI: 10.1162/coli_a_00052 13, 58

Peter Potash, Alexey Romanov, and Anna Rumshisky. Here's my point: Joint pointer architecture for argument mining. In *Proc. Empirical Methods in Natural Language Processing*, pages 1375–1384, 2017. DOI: 10.18653/v1/d17-1143 103

Vinodkumar Prabhakaran, Owen Rambow, and Mona Diab. Automatic committed belief tagging. In *Proc. International Conference on Computational Linguistics: Posters*, pages 1014–1022, 2010. 74

Rashmi Prasad, Nikhil Dinesh, Alan Lee, Eleni Miltsakaki, Livio Robaldo, Aravind K. Joshi, and Bonnie L. Webber. The penn discourse treebank 2.0. In *Proc. Language Resources and Evaluation*, pages 2961–2968, 2008. 25, 70, 78, 98

Arthur N. Prior. *Logic, Traditional*, 2nd ed., vol. 5, pages 493–506. Macmillan Reference, 2006. 29

James Pustejovsky. *The Generative Lexicon*. MIT Press, Cambridge, MA, 1986. 139

Minghui Qiu and Jing Jiang. A latent variable model for viewpoint discovery from threaded forum posts. In *Proc. North American Chapter of the Association for Computational Linguistics: Human Language Technologies*, pages 1031–1040, 2013. 89, 90

Randolph Quirk, Sidney Greenbaum, Geoffrey Leech, and Jan Svartvik. *A Comprehensive Grammar of the English Language*. Longman, New York, 1985. 11

Antonio Rago, Francesca Toni, Marco Aurisicchio, and Pietro Baroni. Discontinuity-free decision support with quantitative argumentation debates. In *Proc. Principles of Knowledge Representation and Reasoning*, pages 63–73, 2016. 116

Iyad Rahwan. Mass argumentation and the semantic web. *Web Semantics: Science, Services and Agents on the World Wide Web*, 6(1), pages 29–37, 2008. DOI: 10.2139/ssrn.3199381 28, 45

Iyad Rahwan, Fouad Zablith, and Chris Reed. Laying the foundations for a World Wide Argument Web. *Artificial Intelligence*, 171(10), pages 897–921, 2007. DOI: 10.1016/j.artint.2007.04.015 43

Pavithra Rajendran, Danushka Bollegala, and Simon Parsons. Contextual stance classification of opinions: A step towards enthymeme reconstruction in online reviews. In *3rd Workshop on Argumentation Mining*, pages 31–39, 2016. DOI: 10.18653/v1/w16-2804 15, 108

Sarvesh Ranade, Jayant Gupta, Vasudeva Varma, and Radhika Mamidi. Online debate summarization using topic directed sentiment analysis. In *Proc. 2nd International Workshop on Issues of Sentiment Discovery and Opinion Mining*, pages 7:1–7:6, 2013. DOI: 10.1145/2502069.2502076 139

Christof Rapp. Aristotle's rhetoric. In Edward N. Zalta, Ed., *The Stanford Encyclopedia of Philosophy*. Metaphysics Research Lab, Stanford University, spring edition, 2010. `https://plato.stanford.edu/entries/aristotle-rhetoric/` 31

Majid Rastegar-Mojarad, Ravikumar Komandur Elayavilli, and Hongfang Liu. BELTracker: Evidence sentence retrieval for BEL statements. *Database: The Journal of Biological Databases and Curation*, 2016. DOI: 10.1093/database/baw079 141

Olesya Razuvayevskaya and Simone Teufel. Finding enthymemes in real-world texts: A feasibility study. *Argument and Computation*, 8(2), pages 113–129, 2017. DOI: 10.3233/aac-170020 108

Chris Reed. Implicit speech acts are ubiquitous. Why? They join the dots. In *Proc. Ontario Society for the Study of Argumentation*, pages 1–15, 2011. 50

Chris Reed and Katarzyna Budzyńska. How dialogues create arguments. In *Proc. International Society for the Study of Argumentation*, 2011. 51

Chris Reed and Derek Long. Generating the structure of argument. In *Proc. International Conference on Computational Linguistics*, 1998. DOI: 10.3115/980432.980748 129

Chris Reed, Raquel Mochales-Palau, Glenn Rowe, and Marie-Francine Moens. Language resources for studying argument. In *Proc. Language Resources and Evaluation*, pages 2613–2618, 2008a. 53, 60, 66, 76, 110, 112

Chris Reed, Simon Wells, Joseph Devereux, and Glenn Rowe. AIF+: Dialogue in the Argument Interchange Format. In *Proc. Conference on Computational Models of Argument*, pages 311–323, 2008b. 43

Chris Reed, Katarzyna Budzyńska, Rory Duthie, Mathilde Janier, Barbara Konat, John Lawrence, Alison Pease, and Mark Snaith. The Argument Web: An online ecosystem of tools, systems and services for argumentation. *Philosophy and Technology*, 30(2), pages 137–160, 2017. DOI: 10.1007/s13347-017-0260-8 43

Paul Reisert, Naoya Inoue, Naoaki Okazaki, and Kentaro Inui. Deep argumentative structure analysis as an explanation to argumentative relations. In *Proc. Association for Natural Language Processing*, pages 38–41, 2017. 110

Ehud Reiter and Robert Dale. *Building Natural Language Generation Systems*. Cambridge University Press, Cambridge, 2000. DOI: 10.1017/cbo9780511519857 125

Alastair Renton and Ann Macintosh. Computer-supported argument maps as a policy memory. *The Information Society*, 23(2), pages 125–133, 2007. DOI: 10.1080/01972240701209300 140

Eddo Rigotti and Sara Greco Morasso. Comparing the argumentum model of topics to other contemporary approaches to argument schemes: The procedural and material components. *Argumentation*, 24(4), pages 489–512, 2010. DOI: 10.1007/s10503-010-9190-7 31, 32, 109, 110

Eileen Riloff. Automatically generating extraction patterns from untagged text. In *Proc. of American Association for Artificial Intelligence*, pages 1044–1049, 1996. 120

David J. Rinehart, John C. Knight, and Jonathan Rowanhill. Current practices in constructing and evaluating assurance cases with applications to aviation. *Technical Report NASA/CR–2015–218678*, NASA, 2015. 39

Ruty Rinott, Lena Dankin, Carlos Alzate Perez, Mitesh M. Khapra, Ehud Aharoni, and Noam Slonim. Show me your evidence—an automatic method for context dependent evidence detection. In *Proc. Empirical Methods in Natural Language Processing*, pages 440–450, 2015. DOI: 10.18653/v1/d15-1050 81, 82, 83

Haggai Roitman, Shay Hummel, Ella Rabinovich, Benjamin Sznajder, Noam Slonim, and Ehud Aharoni. On the retrieval of Wikipedia articles containing claims on controversial topics. In *Proc. World Wide Web Companion*, pages 991–996, 2016. DOI: 10.1145/2872518.2891115 59, 62

Niall Rooney, Hui Wang, and Fiona Browne. Applying kernel methods to argumentation mining. In *Proc. 25th FLAIRS Conference*, pages 272–275, 2012. 66, 84

Ariel Rosenfeld and Sarit Kraus. Providing arguments in discussions based on the prediction of human argumentative behavior. In *Proc. National Conference on Artificial Intelligence*, pages 1320–1327, 2015. DOI: 10.1145/2983925 141

Sara Rosenthal and Kathleen McKeown. Detecting opinionated claims in online discussions. In *Proc. IEEE International Conference on Semantic Computing*, pages 30–37, 2012. DOI: 10.1109/icsc.2012.59 73, 74, 76

Sara Rosenthal and Kathy McKeown. I couldn't agree more: The role of conversational structure in agreement and disagreement detection in online discussions. In *Proc. Special Interest Group on Discourse and Dialogue*, pages 168–177, 2015. DOI: 10.18653/v1/w15-4625 52, 95, 96

Jerrold Saddock. Speech acts. In Laurence Horn and Gregory Ward, Eds., *The Handbook of Pragmatics*. Wiley, New York, 2005. DOI: 10.1002/9780470756959.ch3 16, 19

Patrick Saint-Dizier. Processing natural language arguments with the <TextCoop>platform. *Journal of Argumentation and Computation*, 3(1), pages 49–82, 2012. DOI: 10.1080/19462166.2012.663539 66, 80, 102

Patrick Saint-Dizier. A two-level approach to generate synthetic argumentation reports. *Argument and Computation*, 9(2), pages 137–154, 2018. DOI: 10.3233/aac-180035 139

Nattapong Sanchan, Ahmet Aker, and Kalina Bontcheva. Automatic summarization of online debates. In *Proc. 1st Workshop on Natural Language Processing and Information Retrieval associated with RANLP*, pages 19–27, 2017. DOI: 10.26615/978-954-452-038-0_003 139

Ted Sanders and Wilbert Spooren. Causal categories in discourse—converging evidence from language use. In Ted Sanders and Eve Sweetser, Eds., *Causal Categories in Discourse and Cognition*, pages 205–246. Mouton De Gruyter, Berlin, 2009. DOI: 10.1515/9783110224429.205 20

Christos Sardianos, Ioannis Manousos Katakis, Georgios Petasis, and Vangelis Karkaletsis. Argument extraction from news. In *2nd Workshop on Argumentation Mining*, pages 56–66, 2015. DOI: 10.3115/v1/w15-0508 74

Misa Sato, Kohsuke Yanai, Toshinori Miyoshi, Toshihiko Yanase, Makoto Iwayama, Qinghua Sun, and Yoshiki Niwa. End-to-end argument generation system in debating. In *Proc. ACL-IJCNLP System Demonstrations*, 2015. DOI: 10.3115/v1/p15-4019 132

Oliver Scheuer, Frank Loll, Niels Pinkwart, and Bruce M. McLaren. Computer-supported argumentation: A review of the state of the art. *International Journal of Computer-supported Collaborative Learning*, 5(1), pages 43–102, 2010. DOI: 10.1007/s11412-009-9080-x 41, 142

David C. Schneider, Christian Voigt, and Gregor Betz. ArguNet: A software tool for collaborative argumentation analysis and research. In *Proc. Computational Models of Natural Argument*, pages 57–61, 2007. 41

Jodi Schneider. Automated argumentation mining to the rescue? Envisioning argumentation and decision-making support for debates in open online collaboration communities. In *1st Workshop on Argumentation Mining*, pages 59–63, 2014. DOI: 10.3115/v1/w14-2108 140

Jodi Schneider, Tudor Groza, and Alexandre Passant. A review of argumentation for the Social Semantic Web. *Semantic Web*, 4(2), pages 159–218, 2013a. 41

Jodi Schneider, Krystian Samp, Alexandre Passant, and Stefan Decker. Arguments about deletion: How experience improves the acceptability of arguments in ad hoc online task groups. In *Proc. Computer Supported Cooperative Work*, pages 1069–1080, 2013b. DOI: 10.1145/2441776.2441897 111

John R. Searle. *Speech Acts: An Essay in the Philosophy of Language*. Cambridge University Press, Cambridge, 1969. DOI: 10.1017/cbo9781139173438 17, 18

John R. Searle. A classification of illocutionary acts. *Language in Society*, 5, pages 1–23, 1976. DOI: 10.1017/s0047404500006837 17, 18

Serge Sharoff, Zhili Wu, and Katja Markert. The Web Library of Babel: evaluating genre collections. In *Proc. Language Resources and Evaluation*, pages 3063–3070, 2010. 58

Eyal Shnarch, Ran Levy, Vikas Raykar, and Noam Slonim. Grasp: Rich patterns for argumentation mining. In *Proc. Empirical Methods in Natural Language Processing*, pages 1356–1361, 2017. DOI: 10.18653/v1/d17-1140 72

Simon Buckingham Shum, Albert M. Selvin, Maarten Sierhuis, Jeffrey Conklin, Charles B. Haley, and Bashar Nuseibeh. Hypermedia support for argumentation-based rationale: 15 years on from gIBIS and QOC. In Allen H. Dutoit, Raymond McCall, Ivan Mistrík, and Barbara Paech, Eds., *Rationale Management in Software Engineering*, vol. 4, pages 111–132, Springer, 2006. DOI: 10.1007/3-5403-0998-5_5 42

Carlota Smith. *Modes of Discourse. The Local Structure of Texts*. Cambridge University Press, Cambridge, 2003. DOI: 10.1017/cbo9780511615108 21

Mark Snaith, John Lawrence, and Chris Reed. Mixed initiative argument in public deliberation. *Online Deliberation*, pages 2–13, 2010. 42

Swapna Somasundaran and Janyce Wiebe. Recognizing stances in online debates. In *Proc. Joint Conference of the 47th Annual Meeting of the ACL and the 4th International Joint Conference on Natural Language Processing of the AFNLP*, pages 226–234, 2009. DOI: 10.3115/1687878.1687912 88

Wei Song, Dong Wang, Ruiji Fu, Lizhen Liu, Ting Liu, and Guoping Hu. Discourse mode identification in essays. In *Proc. Association for Computational Linguistics (Volume 1: Long Papers)*, pages 112–122, 2017. DOI: 10.18653/v1/p17-1011 22

Yi Song, Michael Heilman, Beata Beigman Klebanov, and Paul Deane. Applying argumentation schemes for essay scoring. In *1st Workshop on Argumentation Mining*, pages 69–78, 2014. DOI: 10.3115/v1/w14-2110 61, 112, 142

John Spriggs. *GSN—The Goal Structuring Notation: A Structured Approach to Presenting Arguments*. Springer Science and Business Media, 2012. 39

Dhanya Sridhar, Lise Getoor, and Marilyn Walker. Collective stance classification of posts in online debate forums. In *Proc. Joint Workshop on Social Dynamics and Personal Attributes in Social Media*, pages 109–117, 2014. DOI: 10.3115/v1/w14-2715 90

Christian Stab and Iryna Gurevych. Annotating argument components and relations in persuasive essays. In Junichi Tsujii and Jan Hajic, Eds., *Proc. International Conference on Computational Linguistics*, pages 1501–1510, 2014a. 46, 54, 60, 63, 69, 73, 87, 103, 110, 117

Christian Stab and Iryna Gurevych. Identifying argumentative discourse structures in persuasive essays. In *Proc. Empirical Methods in Natural Language Processing*, pages 46–56, 2014b. DOI: 10.3115/v1/d14-1006 61, 70, 76, 84, 98, 104, 118

Christian Stab and Iryna Gurevych. Recognizing the absence of opposing arguments in persuasive essays. In *3rd Workshop on Argumentation Mining*, pages 113–118, 2016. DOI: 10.18653/v1/w16-2813 87

Christian Stab and Iryna Gurevych. Recognizing insufficiently supported arguments in argumentative essays. In *Proc. European Chapter of the Association for Computational Linguistics (Volume 1, Long Papers)*, pages 980–990, 2017a. DOI: 10.18653/v1/e17-1092 117, 142

Christian Stab and Iryna Gurevych. Parsing argumentation structures in persuasive essays. *Computational Linguistics*, 43(3), pages 619–660, 2017b. DOI: 10.1162/coli_a_00295 103, 104

Manfred Stede. *Discourse Processing*. Morgan & Claypool, 2011. DOI: 10.2200/s00354ed1v01y201111hlt015 21, 25, 26

Manfred Stede and Arne Neumann. Potsdam commentary corpus 2.0: Annotation for discourse research. In *Proc. Language Resources and Evaluation*, pages 925–929, 2014. 46

Manfred Stede and Antje Sauermann. Linearization of arguments in commentary text. In *Workshop on Multidisciplinary Approaches to Discourse*, pages 105–112, 2008. 45

John M. Swales. *Genre Analysis: English in Academic and Research Settings*. Cambridge University Press, 1990. DOI: 10.1075/z.184.513swa 24

Nouredine Tamani, Patricio Mosse, Madalina Croitoru, Patrice Buche, and Valérie Guillard. A food packaging use case for argumentation. In *Research Conference on Metadata and Semantics Research*, pages 344–358, 2014. DOI: 10.1007/978-3-319-13674-5_31 39

Jiwei Tan, Xiaojun Wan, and Jianguo Xiao. Learning to order natural language texts. In *Proc. 51st Annual Meeting of the Association for Computational Linguistics (Volume 2: Short Papers)*, 2013. 133

Simone Teufel and Marc Moens. Summarizing scientific articles—experiments with relevance and rhetorical status. *Computational Linguistics*, 28(4), pages 409–445, 2002. DOI: 10.1162/089120102762671936 24, 66, 142

Matthias Thimm and Serena Villata. The 1st international competition on computational models of argumentation: Results and analysis. *Artificial Intelligence*, 252, pages 267–294, 2017. DOI: 10.1016/j.artint.2017.08.006 114

Orith Toledo-Ronen, Roy Bar-Haim, and Noam Slonim. Expert stance graphs for computational argumentation. In *3rd Workshop on Argumentation Mining*, pages 119–123, 2016. DOI: 10.18653/v1/w16-2814 139

Stephen Toulmin. The layout of arguments. In Jonathan E. Adler and Lance J. Rips, Eds., *Reasoning: Studies of Human Inference and its Foundations*, pages 652–677, Cambridge University Press, 2008. DOI: 10.1017/cbo9780511840005.007 34

Frans H. van Eemeren and Rob Grootendorst. *A Systematic Theory of Argumentation: The Pragma-dialectical Approach*. Cambridge University Press, Cambridge, 2004. DOI: 10.1017/cbo9780511616389 1, 4

Frans H. Van Eemeren, Rob Grootendorst, Sally Jackson, and Scott Jacobs. *Reconstructing Argumentative Discourse*. University of Alabama Press, 1993. 53

Frans H. van Eemeren, Peter Houtlosser, and A. F. Snoeck Henkemans. *Argumentative Indicators in Discourse*. Springer, Dordrecht, 2007. DOI: 10.1007/978-1-4020-6244-5 4

Frans H. van Eemeren, Bart Garssen, Erik C. W. Krabbe, A. Francisca Snoeck Henkemans, Bart Verheij, and Jean H. M. Wagemans, Eds. *Handbook of Argumentation Theory*. Springer, 2014. DOI: 10.1007/978-94-007-6883-3 xiii

Tim Van Gelder. Enhancing deliberation through computer supported argument visualization. In Paul A. Kirschner, Simon J. Buckingham Shum, and Chad S. Carr, Eds., *Visualizing Argumentation: Software Tools for Collaborative and Educational Sense-making*, pages 97–115, Springer, 2003. DOI: 10.1007/978-1-4471-0037-9_5 39

Tim Van Gelder. The rationale for rationale. *Law, Probability and Risk*, 6(1–4), pages 23–42, 2007. DOI: 10.1093/lpr/mgm032 42

Maria Garcia Villalba and Patrick Saint-Dizier. Some facets of argument mining for opinion analysis. In *Proc. Computational Models of Argument*, 2012. 80

Oriol Vinyals, Meire Fortunato, and Navdeep Jaitly. Pointer networks. In *Proc. Neural Information Processing Systems*, pages 2692–2700, 2015. 103

Nina Wacholder, Smaranda Muresan, Debanjan Ghosh, and Mark Aakhus. Annotating multiparty discourse: Challenges for agreement metrics. In *Linguistic Annotation Workshop*, pages 120–128, 2014. DOI: 10.3115/v1/w14-4918 63

Henning Wachsmuth and Benno Stein. A universal model for discourse-level argumentation analysis. *ACM Transactions on Internet Technology*, 17(3), pages 28:1–28:24, 2017. Special issue on Argumentation in Social Media. DOI: 10.1145/2957757 105

Henning Wachsmuth, Johannes Kiesel, and Benno Stein. Sentiment flow—a general model of web review argumentation. In *Proc. Empirical Methods in Natural Language Processing*, pages 601–611, 2015. DOI: 10.18653/v1/d15-1072 142

Henning Wachsmuth, Khalid Al Khatib, and Benno Stein. Using argument mining to assess the argumentation quality of essays. In *Proc. International Conference on Computational Linguistics: Technical Papers*, pages 1680–1691, 2016. 142

Henning Wachsmuth, Giovanni Da San Martino, Dora Kiesel, and Benno Stein. The impact of modeling overall argumentation with tree kernels. In *Proc. Empirical Methods in Natural Language Processing*, pages 2379–2389, 2017a. DOI: 10.18653/v1/d17-1253 106

Henning Wachsmuth, Nona Naderi, Yufang Hou, Yonatan Bilu, Vinodkumar Prabhakaran, Tim Alberdingk Thijm, Graeme Hirst, and Benno Stein. Computational argumentation quality assessment in natural language. In *Proc. European Chapter of the Association for Computational Linguistics*, pages 176–187, 2017b. DOI: 10.18653/v1/e17-1017 116, 117, 119, 120

Henning Wachsmuth, Martin Potthast, Khalid Al-Khatib, Yamen Ajjour, Jana Puschmann, Jiani Qu, Jonas Dorsch, Viorel Morari, Janek Bevendorff, and Benno Stein. Building an argument search engine for the Web. In *4th Workshop on Argumentation Mining*, pages 49–59, 2017c. DOI: 10.18653/v1/w17-5106 141

Henning Wachsmuth, Benno Stein, and Yamen Ajjour. "PageRank" for argument relevance. In *Proc. European Chapter of the Association for Computational Linguistics (Volume 1, Long Papers)*, pages 1117–1127, 2017d. DOI: 10.18653/v1/e17-1105 141

Henning Wachsmuth, Manfred Stede, Roxanne El Baff, Khalid Al Khatib, Maria Skeppstedt, and Benno Stein. Argumentation synthesis following rhetorical strategies. In *Proc. International Conference on Computational Linguistics*, 2018. 133

Douglas Walton. *Goal-Based Reasoning for Argumentation*. Cambridge University Press, 2015. DOI: 10.1017/cbo9781316340554 140

Douglas Walton, Chris Reed, and Fabrizio Macagno. *Argumentation Schemes*. Cambridge University Press, Cambridge, 2008. DOI: 10.1017/cbo9780511802034 30, 109, 111, 112, 129

Douglas Walton, Chris Reed, and Fabrizio Macagno. Argumentation schemes. In Pietro Baroni, Dov Gabbay, Massimiliano Giacomin, and Leendert van der Torre, Eds., *Handbook of Formal Argumentation*, pages 519–576, College Publications, 2018. DOI: 10.1017/cbo9780511802034 30

Douglas N. Walton. *Argumentation Methods for Artificial Intelligence and Law*. Springer, Berlin, 2005. DOI: 10.1007/3-540-27881-8 36

Douglas N. Walton. The three bases for the enthymeme: A dialogical theory. *Journal of Applied Logic*, 6(3), pages 361–379, 2008. DOI: 10.1016/j.jal.2007.06.002 107

Bin Wei and Henry Prakken. Defining the structure of arguments with AI models of argumentation. In *Proc. Computational Models of Natural Argument*, pages 60–64, 2012. 28

Zhongyu Wei, Yang Liu, and Yi Li. Is this post persuasive? Ranking argumentative comments in online forum. In *Proc. Association for Computational Linguistics (Volume 2: Short Papers)*, pages 195–200, 2016. DOI: 10.18653/v1/p16-2032 118

Simon Wells, Colin Gourlay, and Chris Reed. Argument blogging. In *Proc. Computational Models of Natural Argument*, pages 1–5, 2009. 43

Egon Werlich. *Typologie der Texte*. Quelle und Meyer, Heidelberg, 1975. 21

Janyce Wiebe, Theresa Wilson, Rebecca Bruce, Matthew Bell, and Melanie Martin. Learning subjective language. *Computational Linguistics*, 30(3), pages 277–308, 2004. DOI: 10.1162/0891201041850885 13

Janyce Wiebe, Theresa Wilson, and Claire Cardie. Annotating expressions of opinions and emotions in language. *Language Resources and Evaluation*, 39(2–3), pages 165–210, 2005. DOI: 10.1007/s10579-005-7880-9 11

Wesley Willett, Jeffrey Heer, Joseph Hellerstein, and Maneesh Agrawala. CommentSpace: Structured support for collaborative visual analysis. In *SIGCHI Conference on Human Factors in Computing Systems*, pages 3131–3140, 2011. DOI: 10.1145/1978942.1979407 140

Adam Wyner, Tom van Engers, and Anthony Hunter. Working on the argument pipeline: Through flow issues between natural language argument, instantiated arguments, and argumentation frameworks. In *Proc. Computational Models of Natural Argument*, 2010. 107

Adam Wyner, Jodi Schneider, Katie Atkinson, and Trevor J. M. Bench-Capon. Semi-automated argumentative analysis of online product reviews. In *Proc. Computational Models of Argument*, pages 43–50, 2012. 141

Adam Wyner, Trevor Bench-Capon, Paul Dunne, and Federico Cerutti. Senses of "argument" in instantiated argumentation frameworks. *Argument and Computation*, 6(1), pages 50–72, 2015. DOI: 10.1080/19462166.2014.1002535 28

Adam Wyner, Tom van Engers, and Anthony Hunter. Working on the argument pipeline: Through flow issues between natural language argument, instantiated arguments, and argumentation frameworks. *Argument and Computation*, 7(1), pages 69–89, 2016. 116, 140

Ruifeng Xu, Yu Zhou, Dongyin Wu, Lin Gui, Jiachen D., and Yun Xue. Overview of NLPCC shared task 4: Stance detection in Chinese microblogs. In *Proc. Conference on Natural Language Processing and Chinese Computing, and 24th International Conference on Computer Processing of Oriental Languages*, pages 907–916, 2016. DOI: 10.1007/978-3-319-50496-4_85 87

Hiroaki Yamada, Simone Teufel, and Takenobu Tokunaga. Annotation of argument structure in Japanese legal documents. In *4th Workshop on Argument Mining*, pages 22–31, 2017. DOI: 10.18653/v1/w17-5103 25

Jie Yin, Nalin Narang, Paul Thomas, and Cecile Paris. Unifying local and global agreement and disagreement classification in online debates. In *3rd Workshop in Computational Approaches to Subjectivity and Sentiment Analysis*, pages 61–69, 2012. 95

Fouad Zablith. ArgDF: Arguments on the semantic web [Master's thesis]. *Technical Report*, The British University in Dubai jointly with The University of Edinburgh, 2007. 43

Dimitraand Flouris Zografistou, Giorgosand Plexousakis, and Dimitris. ArgQL: A declarative language for querying argumentative dialogues. In *International Joint Conference on Rules and Reasoning*, pages 230–237, 2017. DOI: 10.1007/978-3-319-61252-2_16 43

Ingrid Zukerman, Richard McConachy, and Kevin B. Korb. Using argumentation strategies in automated argument generation. In *Proc. of the 1st International Conference on Natural Language Generation (INLG)*, pages 55–62, 2000. DOI: 10.3115/1118253.1118262 125

Authors' Biographies

MANFRED STEDE

Manfred Stede is a professor of Applied Computational Linguistics at the University of Potsdam, Germany. He obtained his Ph.D. in Computer Science from the University of Toronto in 1996 with a thesis on language generation; in those years he studied discourse structure primarily for its role in text generation. After working for five years in a machine translation project at TU Berlin, he moved to Potsdam in 2001, where his interests shifted to text analysis. He conducted research projects on applications like information extraction and text summarization, and on more theoretical matters like the semantics and pragmatics of connectives. In conjunction with research on discourse parsing, he began to work on argumentation in the 2000s, focusing first on newspaper editorials. Following the design of an annotation scheme, he proceeded to work on approaches to deriving argumentation structure trees from short texts, and on various other aspects of argumentation mining.

JODI SCHNEIDER

Jodi Schneider is an assistant professor in the University of Illinois at Urbana-Champaign's School of Information Sciences. She has held research positions across the United States as well as in Ireland, England, France, and Chile. She earned her Ph.D. in informatics (National University of Ireland, Galway), two Master's degrees in library & information science (UIUC) and in mathematics (UT-Austin), and a Bachelor's degree (Great Books, St. John's College, Annapolis, MD). She has authored over 30 research publications on topics in argumentation, artificial intelligence, biomedical informatics, and computer-supported collaborative work. Her research uses arguments, evidence, and persuasion as a lens to study scholarly communication and social media. She also develops and evaluates tools to manage scientific evidence from the biomedical literature with an NIH-funded project, Text Mining Pipeline to Accelerate Systematic Reviews in Evidence-Based Medicine.

Index

Printed in the United States
by Baker & Taylor Publisher Services